THE AUTOBIOGRAPHY OF GERALD OF WALES

THE AUTOBIOGRAPHY OF GERALD OF WALES

Edited and translated by
H. E. Butler

With an introduction by
C. H. Williams

and

A guide to further reading by
John Gillingham

THE BOYDELL PRESS

Guide to further reading © John Gillingham 2005

All Rights Reserved. Except as permitted under current legislation no part of this work may be photocopied, stored in a retrieval system, published, performed in public, adapted, broadcast, transmitted, recorded or reproduced in any form or by any means, without the prior permission of the copyright owner

First published 1937 as
The Autobiography of Giraldus Cambrensis
Jonathan CapeLtd, London

New edition 2005
The Boydell Press, Woodbridge

Transferred to digital printing

ISBN 978 1 84383 148 8

The Boydell Press is an imprint of Boydell & Brewer Ltd
PO Box 9, Woodbridge, Suffolk IP12 3DF, UK
and of Boydell & Brewer Inc.
668 Mt Hope Avenue, Rochester, NY 14620, USA
website: www.boydellandbrewer.com

A CiP catalogue record for this book is available
from the British Library

Library of Congress Catalog Card Number 2005007729

This publication is printed on acid-free paper

CONTENTS

INTRODUCTION: GIRALDUS AND WALES	9
THE MAN AND HIS WORKS	22
PREFACE TO THE 'DE REBUS A SE GESTIS'	33
CHILDHOOD AND EDUCATION (1145–1173)	35
THE YOUNG ARCHDEACON (1174–1176)	39
FIRST CALL TO THE BISHOPRIC (1176)	59
THE UNIVERSITY OF PARIS (1177–1179)	65
UNHAPPY DAYS AT MYNYW (1180–1183)	74
HE TAKES SERVICE WITH THE CROWN (1184)	81
THE VISIT TO IRELAND (1185)	86
THE PREACHING OF THE CRUSADE (1187)	98
HE VISITS FRANCE WITH HENRY II (1189)	105
HIS SERVICE OF KING RICHARD (1189–1195)	111
HIS RETIREMENT TO LINCOLN (1196–1198)	127
SECOND CALL TO THE BISHOPRIC (1198)	129
HE IS ELECTED BY THE CHAPTER IN DEFIANCE OF KING AND ARCHBISHOP (June 29, 1199)	158
FIRST VISIT TO ROME (Nov. 30th, 1199)	163
RETURN TO ENGLAND (Autumn 1200)	200
SECOND VISIT TO ROME (March 1201)	203
RETURN TO ENGLAND (Dec, 1201)	220
THIRD VISIT TO ROME (Jan. 4th, 1203)	266
HE RETURNS BAFFLED TO ENGLAND (Aug. 1203)	326
FINAL DEFEAT AND RECONCILIATION WITH THE ARCHBISHOP (Nov. 10th, 1203)	347
THE CLOSING YEARS (1204–1223)	351
APPENDIX	361
INDEX	365
A GUIDE TO FURTHER READING	369

ILLUSTRATIONS

MANORBIER CASTLE	*facing*	36
ST. DAVID'S CATHEDRAL		124
INTERIOR OF ST. DAVID'S CATHEDRAL		254
MAP		33

PREFACE

IN this book Giraldus speaks for himself; and I have added nothing save a few connecting links and explanatory notes. Sins of omission are, I trust, few. For certain abridgments and for the excision of tautologous phrases and many of the quotations, with which his story is overloaded, I make no apology. A few passages from the *Itinerarium Cambriae*, which might seem to claim insertion, have been excluded on the ground that they were not sufficiently important to justify a break in the narrative. In the works on Ireland, while there are passages from which inferences may be drawn as to the author's travel, there is little that is specifically autobiographical, and they too have been excluded. They are moreover already available to English readers in the Bohn Series, while the Itinerary and Description of Wales may be found in 'Everyman's Library' (272). Finally there are a few letters which have been omitted on various grounds; some because they are mere rhetorical exercises, others as being too allusive to admit of satisfactory interpretation.

The bulk of the narrative has been drawn from Brewer's Text of the *De rebus a se gestis* and the *De iure et statu Meneuensis Ecclesiae* (Rolls Series, *Giraldus Cambrensis*, Vols. I and III); I have collated the MSS. of both these works and a few corrections of the printed text are given in the footnotes. A few passages are drawn from the *Symbolum Electorum* (op. cit. Vol. I) and the *Speculum Ecclesiae* (op. cit. Vol. III, ed. Brewer). For the *De Principis Instructione* I have used Warner's Text (op. cit. Vol. VIII), and for the *Inuectiones* have gone to Davies' Text in Y Cymmrodor, Vol. xxx, Brewer's Text in R.S., Vols. I and III being, through no fault of his, fragmentary and no longer of any value.

I am indebted to the kindness and help of many on

PREFACE

whom I have thrust my perplexities in and out of season. I must especially acknowledge my obligations to Sir John Lloyd, to whom I have never applied in vain, whether I turned to him in person or to the pages of his great *History of Wales*. Scarce less is my debt to Professor C. H. Williams, but for whose adroit blend of importunity and encouragement this book would never have come into being, while he has rewarded me by contributing a much needed introductory chapter. I must also thank Professor F. M. Stenton, Professor L. Brandin, and Professor Paul Vallette for their assistance in solving problems which perplexed me. To the Publicity Department of the Great Western Railway I must express my gratitude for the three excellent photographs which adorn this book. Manorbier Castle was the birthplace of Giraldus; there is some doubt whether he was born in the existing building, but there is little question that it was erected in his lifetime. Not all the noble Cathedral of St. David's, as we know it to-day, was seen by him; but the great Norman nave was built by his enemy Bishop Peter de Leia, and he must have known it well. The so-called portrait of Giraldus, published in the *Inventory of Ancient Monuments in Pembrokeshire* (R. Hist. Com.), is no more than a pencil sketch, made many years ago, of the now defaced figure on the tomb at St. David's which tradition asserts to be his; the monument being a work of the fourteenth century, it has no claim to authenticity and is not reproduced here.

I have found Giraldus a very good companion since the day when I first became acquainted with his works, and I feel that my final expression of gratitude should be to him.

H. E. B.

INTRODUCTION

GIRALDUS AND WALES

THE reader anxious to set Giraldus against the background of twelfth-century Wales is at a disadvantage, for in the main Giraldus himself must be his guide. Valuable and important as his writings thus become, they have to be approached with a caution that will be all the more marked the more attracted we are to the man. The amusing foibles, prejudices and weaknesses that make Giraldus a human, lovable figure are just the features most likely to rouse suspicions as to his impartiality. Before we can use him as an historical source, we have to come to an opinion about his qualifications as a writer, and to do him full justice it is to the historical works that we must go. The list of those works reveals deliberate planning, and an appreciation of his ideas and ambitions as an historical writer may well begin from that list. Apart from what he has to say of himself, his ecclesiastical writings, his lives of other men, and his survey of recent history given in the last two books of the *De Principis Instructione*, the historical writings of Giraldus are concerned with Ireland and Wales. In the *Topographia Hibernica*, the *Expugnatio Hiberniae*, the *Itinerarium Cambriae*, and the *Descriptio Cambriae*, we have segments of a deliberate ambitious enterprise. Taken together they show that he had definite opinions as to the nature of history, and that he worked them out along quite definite lines. He deserves praise for thinking out what he wanted to do, even though he did not quite succeed in achieving his aims. Nor was he lacking in originality in the plans which he devised.

He deserves in the first place high credit for his choice

INTRODUCTION

of subject. He broke new ground. He himself has told us of the quest he made before arriving at his decision.[1] Like many a writer since his day he found it hard to discover a subject which had not been attempted by writers in preceding generations. What indeed could his feeble and unexercised efforts add to the histories of the destruction of Thebes, Troy or Athens, or the conquest of the shores of Latium? What was the use of doing over again what others had already done so well? To address the eloquent in barren phrases or to set before the learned what everyone knows, is useless. What sort of sounds would the 'cackling goose utter among tuneful swans'?[2] So, after long reflection, Giraldus was led to the discovery that there was one corner of the earth which, from its situation on the farthest bounds of the globe, had been neglected by other writers — namely Ireland. And having settled on Irish History as his first venture, he went on to dream of a like work for his native country, 'hitherto almost wholly overlooked by strangers but interesting to my kinsmen and countrymen'. There are indications that he intended a similar work for Scotland.[3] In a word, Giraldus set out to become the historian of the Celtic fringes, and by so doing he earns a place of no small importance among pioneers of medieval historical writing.

He had, too, considered opinions about the public he intended to reach. His books were written for the layman, for princes with little learning, who wanted a story told in easy, simple style. He was a popularizer. That he was not so successful in reaching his public as he had hoped may be gathered from stray hints. Thus, for example, in dedicating his revised version of the *Expugnatio* to John,[4] he suggests that the King should employ some learned man, skilled in French, to translate it into that

---

[1] See his Prefaces to all four works.
[2] Preface to *Topographia*. Cp. *Virg. Ecl.* 9, 36.
[3] *Top. Hib.* I. 26; III, 16.
[4] *Rolls Series*, vol. v, pp. 405 ff.

language, so that Giraldus might reap the fruits of his toil, which hitherto, under illiterate princes, had been lost, because there were so few to read his books. Who can blame him if he sought material rewards? As he shrewdly remarks, 'poets and authors, indeed, crave after immortality, but do not reject any advantages that may offer'.

In his general conception of the nature of history Giraldus differed little from his contemporaries and immediate predecessors in England. For him, as for them, history was the most excellent of the sciences, because it instructs and is an inspiration and a guide for human effort. So he does not resist pointing the moral, and often goes out of the way to find it. It is usual to dismiss him as a credulous writer because, like others of his contemporaries, he fills his works with old wives' tales of marvels, monstrosities and miracles. Such a sweeping condemnation, however, is far from just. Not only ought we to make allowance for the standards of his time, we must also read him in the light of his views of the functions of the historian. He held that it was the duty of the historical writer to narrate what he discovered. In collecting his facts it was his duty to take reasonable care that what he was getting was the truth, but beyond that he had not far to go. He was not called upon to pass judgment on the facts; his responsibility ended when he had distinguished between what he knew at first hand and what he had heard from others. More than once he openly admits that his readers will find in his works many stories that will tax their credulity. He did not expect that everything he said would be accepted blindly as the truth, since he himself had doubts of the things he had heard.

When we look at Giraldus's historical method, we can detect an independence of approach and a clearly defined conception of his function that was novel in his day. His interpretation of the meaning of history was wide. It

INTRODUCTION

included many things; above all there was a special emphasis placed on topography, geography and folk-lore as well as the narration of political events. His ideas can be judged from an examination of his achievements. We have seen that the first subject with which he dealt on a large scale was Ireland. Ignoring the severe censures aroused by that work, we may give Giraldus credit for approaching his subject in a thoroughly logical and enlightened way. He began his treatise with a study of the physical features, topography and natural history of the country. Only when this was done did he feel that he had laid foundations for his second work, the *Expugnatio*, which is history in a narrower sense of the word, the narrative of events in Ireland in his own day and in the period immediately preceding. He seems to have planned similar enterprises for Scotland and Wales. The former, if ever completed, has been lost; the latter was not worked out on the same scale.

His work on Wales sprang from the accident of events. In 1187 the capture of Jerusalem by the Turks had its repercussions in the West, and Henry II prepared to go on Crusade. He knew from the experience of his own campaigns, the value of the Welsh as soldiers, and wanted recruits for his army. So in 1188 Baldwin, Archbishop of Canterbury, set out to preach the Crusade in Wales, accompanied by Giraldus. Out of this visit came Giraldus's first book on Wales. The *Itinerary* is in the form of a diary of their tour, interspersed in Giraldus's inimitable manner, with fables, gossip, personal reminiscences, observations, and historical data, which indeed far out-bulk the story of the preaching. The work is not in any way the equivalent of the first book on Ireland, and may perhaps be regarded as the jottings from which such a work might be compiled. Even as a description of the actual journey it is very uneven. The route described was a circular tour of North and South Wales, but more time was spent in the south, and the greater part of the narrative is concerned with the journey to St. David's. A work bearing much more resemblance to the *Topographia Hibernica* was written three years later. The *Descriptio Cambriae* is a more connected treatise with much topographical and geographical information, an account of the genealogy of the ruling Welsh princely houses, a brief sketch of government, and a description of the habits and characteristics of the people. But unlike the *Topographia*, it had no successor.

These, then, are the main materials which Giraldus offers the student of twelfth-century Wales. What is its value? There is every reason for accepting it as an illuminating contribution. Giraldus was writing of a country, part of which he knew very well. A shrewd observer, he had enough of the Norman in him to enable him to stand aloof from Wales and the Welsh, while at the same time there was a strong enough Celtic strain in his nature to give him sympathy with the native population. The language in which he speaks of Manorbier, his birthplace, rings true with an intense love for that region, and is itself a very beautiful piece of prose, while in many of his observations of Welsh character, on the native love of music, or on the simple tastes, the hospitable ways, the independent characters of the Welsh people — not to mention the shrewd hits revealing his sure eye for the foibles and worse of his countrymen — Giraldus speaks as one showing in his own person some of those marked racial characteristics. Yet this Celtic strain in him must not be emphasized unduly. To depict Giraldus as a Welsh patriot, or even as a typical Welsh cleric of the period, would be to take too seriously his protestation of his affinities with the native Welsh. It would mean that we should miss the essential problem of his personality and his career. For the truth seems to be that, despite his family associations and anything he himself says to the

INTRODUCTION

contrary, Giraldus was not really at home in Wales. He was a foreigner, the child of a new culture that was finding its way into Welsh society and stirring up its age-old civilization into new life. It is a significant fact that there is no indication that any one of the eloquent orations he delivered during the itinerary was spoken in Welsh. That he had some knowledge of the language may be readily admitted, but at best it was only a colloquial knowledge. He was in truth an alien in the country that was so closely bound up with his ambitions. Here perhaps may be found the secret of his strange career. He was, moreover, an 'original', if ever there was one. Henry II's firm refusal to have him as head of a Welsh See was the consequence of that shrewd king's judgment of men. He knew an impulsive man of ideas when he saw one. It was his fear of Giraldus's independence of spirit that stood in the way of his promotion quite as much as the anti-Welsh prejudices ascribed to him by Giraldus.

When all this has been said, it remains true that much is lacking in what Giraldus says of Wales, or, if not entirely lacking, is only to be read between the lines. For behind his vivid descriptions there lies at least one century and a quarter of very strenuous history. It is the clue to much that is otherwise inexplicable in the works of Giraldus. The state of Wales as he knew it was the result of forces at work over the whole of the period. Both the changes brought about and those that did not happen contributed to the making of twelfth-century Wales, and they must be briefly described. It will be best to begin with the changes that did not take place. Of these the most significant was the failure of the Normans and Angevins to alter materially the social structure and the economic life of the native Welsh. That they introduced some new elements is true, but fundamentally the Wales Giraldus knew remained very much what it had been before the coming of the Normans. Throughout the

GIRALDUS AND WALES

occupation the almost unintermittent efforts of Norman barons and English Kings had been directed towards the conquest and subjugation of the native race. Yet by the twelfth century the old conditions had not been radically altered. Marcher lords seeking to consolidate and increase their possessions in Wales, and strong Kings like Henry I or Henry II, had left their mark on the country, but they had not done that which was essential to complete conquest. They had not managed to break down the old tribal organization of Wales, nor had they fully reduced to submission the many Welsh chieftains and native princes. At the end of a long period of occupation the great tribal divisions of the country still remained. Gwynedd, Powys, Deheubarth, and Morgannwg (representing respectively what is now North Wales, Central Wales, South-West Wales, and the south-east corner between the rivers Tawe and Wye) existed as the main tribal divisions with their separate lines of princes, and the rivalries of their leaders provided the cross-currents of Welsh politics, and the incalculable elements with which the statecraft of English kings had to deal. For the student of Welsh history these territorial divisions provide the main clue to events; but these events are confusing, and the narrative of Welsh history as a whole is not easy to tell. Puzzling as are the politics of these main divisions, they are not the only ones which have to be considered. The longevity of Welsh institutions and the pertinacity with which they resisted the attack of the Norman invaders is further illustrated by the territorial subdivisions, the cantrefs and commotes, existing within the main tribal areas. The complex questions of the origins of these governmental units would be out of place in this sketch, but no reader of Giraldus can escape them any more than he would expect to read about twelfth-century England without coming into contact with the hundred and the shire. Even to list their names would be a lengthy task

INTRODUCTION

and far less profitable than a glance at the map of medieval Wales. For our purposes it will be sufficient if we recognize the cantref and the commote as distinct geographical areas representing the subdivision for governmental purposes of the old tribal areas. What is worth notice is that up to the twelfth century they had not been broken down by the Anglo-Norman inroads. Geographically, the changes due to the invasion affected those areas in the Marches and South Wales where Norman barons had settled, and those parts, especially in South Wales, which were dominated by royal castles. By the end of the twelfth century progress had been made, but nothing like domination had been achieved, and the Wales Giraldus knew was one in which native princes and Norman lords lived side by side in an uneasy peace under submission, often more nominal than real, to their overlord in England.

Another feature of the unchanged tribal organization also calls for notice. This was the fact that, as long as it lasted, it continued to provide the Welsh with able leaders. During the lifetime of Giraldus the most successful and sustained effort to conquer Wales was made by that great king, Henry II. He had matched against him two men worthy of his steel. The first, Owain Gwynedd, had served an apprenticeship in wars against Welshmen, Normans and Flemings before he became King of North Wales in 1137. The anarchy of Stephen's reign gave him the opportunity to extend his territory and power so that when Henry II faced the Welsh problem in the early years of his reign, he was right in beginning by an attack on Owain. In July 1157 he launched his first great expedition against North Wales. It was not successful, but Owain realized that he was dealing with a real force and came to terms. He did homage to Henry, and for a long time deemed it wisdom not to tempt Henry to make another attack upon him.

GIRALDUS AND WALES

Not even the activity of his nephew Rhys ap Gruffydd of South Wales roused him until 1164. Counting on Henry's difficulties at that time, Owain yielded to the schemes of the Lord Rhys and joined him in open resistance to Henry. It was a really dangerous movement, and Henry organized a very full expedition to meet it. Of Owain's pre-eminence in North Wales up to this time there can be no doubt. He figures in the pages of Giraldus as one of the great Welsh leaders, a prince to be admired for his wisdom, nobility and courage. In Welsh history his name stands high for the part he played in resisting the Norman advance, and his resistance did much to preserve the spirit of Welsh independence at a critical time.

When Owain died in 1176 the place of command in Welsh affairs fell to the Lord Rhys of South Wales. He had been steadily growing in importance from the beginning of Henry II's reign. By the time Giraldus was writing his *Itinerary*, Rhys was the dominating figure in Welsh politics and we catch glimpses of him in the course of the autobiography. There seems to have been something in him which attracted Henry II, for we find Henry far more anxious to win him for a dependant than to crush him out of existence. The links between them were forged slowly, and in the years between 1158 and 1177 Henry could never be certain of Rhys. After that date they came closer together, and in Giraldus's time their relations were good.

The reign of Henry II was an important landmark in Welsh history, and by the time of Giraldus the grip of the English king upon Wales was firmer than it had been earlier. All the same the Norman and the Angevin period had not materially altered the institutional framework of Wales. Nor — as Giraldus plainly shows — had it done much to alter the character of the native Welsh or change the social and economic background. That

INTRODUCTION

new elements had been introduced need not be denied. It was especially true in South Wales where geographical factors made penetration easier and more permanent. Yet even in those parts where contacts with England were most close, the invaders had as yet made little impression on the native population, who still retained their primitive characteristics, and were little disposed to the settled existence of the agriculturist. Giraldus and others show them as a simple folk, bred to the use of arms, great lovers of their own liberty, independent, ready to fight on the slightest provocation and quick to seize the chance of harrying the foreigner in their midst. They were noted also for their hospitality, their bravery and their devotion to their family and tribal leaders. If Giraldus is to be credited, they had likewise many of the defects that often accompany these qualities, and their love of plunder, their quarrelsomeness, their adherence to tribal feuds were some of the reasons he adduced to explain their failure to unite against the invader.

If in many ways the Norman invasion left Wales and its people almost unchanged, there were on the other hand some striking effects of the coming of Norman rule. Nowhere can the traces of Norman activity be seen more clearly than in the transformation that was accomplished within the Welsh Church, a fact which is of special concern to the reader of Giraldus, since the prime interest of his career lies in the gallant fight he made for what he regarded as the rights and privileges of the See of St. David's.

Our sketch of what took place may well begin with the years following the Norman conquest; for as in so many other ways, that movement profoundly influenced the organization and government of the Church in Wales. The break with pre-Conquest religious history was in Wales so definite, that for our present purposes, we need recall nothing from the earlier period save the framework of the organization existing when Norman influence began to be felt. Just as in political affairs the old tribal divisions of the country remained despite Norman attacks, so the territorial divisions of the Church were carried over into the new period. Corresponding to the tribal principalities of Gwynedd, Powys, Dyfed and Morgannwg there were the Bishoprics of Bangor, St. Asaph, St. David's, and Llandaff. So much is certain. What is less easy to discover is the exact relationship of the four Sees to each other, and more important, their place in relation to the English Church. On the whole, it appears safe to say that in relation to each other the four Sees were independent and autonomous, and that in the pre-Conquest period the question that was later to cause such controversy, namely, the primacy of St. David's over the other three, was non-existent. With regard to the even more important question of the relationship of those bishoprics to the See of Canterbury, it is less easy to dogmatize. Some historians have tried to make use of dubious and confused references to prove that, in the century prior to the Norman Conquest, Welsh Bishops were, in certain instances, consecrated by the Archbishop of Canterbury. But the best modern opinion declines to put much trust in such evidence and tends to the view that before the Norman Conquest the Welsh Bishops had not generally recognized the authority of Canterbury. These two questions were to be the main threads of ecclesiastical history after the Conquest.

In the new period there is a tightening of authority, and the policy of Normanization that was being attempted in politics was also applied in ecclesiastical affairs. To assist in the establishment of royal authority in Wales the Norman kings adopted a policy of granting the higher ecclesiastical offices in Wales to Norman clerics, while the new masters of Welsh territory did not scruple to appropriate lands belonging to the Church.

INTRODUCTION

Norman Bishops proved amenable to royal authority and in many cases undermined the previous independence of the Sees by recognition of the spiritual supremacy of Canterbury. To illustrate these tendencies a brief summary of what happened at St. David's between the conquest and 1176 may be given. It is a prelude to the vital problem in Giraldus's career.

Pre-Conquest conditions seem to have continued at St. Davids until 1115. Wilfred, Bishop from 1085-1115 was apparently consecrated without reference to Canterbury; but Anselm, who was firm in his dealings with the Welsh clergy seems to have suspended him temporarily because — it is said — of his alienation of Church property. Not much is known of Wilfred's rule, though the general impression is that it was a period of comparative quiet, due possibly to some agreement at which he arrived with Anselm.

Trouble began in 1115, when his successor had to be chosen. The Welsh clergy at St. David's would have liked to choose Daniel, son of an earlier and very famous Bishop (Julian — 1011-91); but Henry I had a definite policy for the appointment, and intended that the See should be governed by someone certain to be friendly to himself. Thus, then, he forced on the Welsh clergy a royal chaplain, Bernard, who held the See for thirty-three years (1115-48). Bernard was ordained priest at Southwark (September 18th, 1115) and next day was consecrated. He made complete obedience to Canterbury; but strange as it may seem, the royal favourite, courtier and diplomat ended by being the first Bishop of St. David's to make the claim that his See was the Metropolitan See of Wales, and that he as Archbishop was of equal rank and authority with the Archbishops of Canterbury and York. Whether the claims were put forward during the lifetime of Henry I has been doubted; but it seems clear that by the pontificate of Innocent II (1130-43) such claims were being formulated. According to some accounts Bernard seems to have won his point for a time, but in 1147 the whole question was fought out between Theobald Archbishop of Canterbury and Bernard, before Pope Eugenius III at Meaux. There were two questions at issue; firstly whether Bernard was independent of the authority of Canterbury, and secondly, whether the See itself was independent. The first question was decided against Bernard, since at his consecration he had sworn complete obedience. The second question was more difficult, and Eugenius gave permission for it to be argued in the ensuing year. But Bernard died before the appointed date, leaving the question still unsettled.

Archbishop Theobald took steps to prevent the recurrence of the controversy, by persuading the clergy of St. David's to elect as Bernard's successor one of themselves, David FitzGerald, Canon of St. David's and Archdeacon of Canterbury. The Archbishop's choice is the less surprising, when it is remembered that he was the son of the Norman castellan of Pembroke, Gerald of Windsor. From him it was easy to obtain not merely a profession of canonical obedience, but also an oath promising never to revive the claim of Metropolitan rank for the See. David was Bishop for twenty-seven years. During that time he had many quarrels with the cathedral clergy, was a shameless nepotist and so unscrupulous in his manipulation of the temporal possessions of his See that even his nephew, Giraldus, could not wholly whitewash him. All the same he did not break his oath. In 1175, however, during a quarrel with his clergy, the latter forced his hand, once more raising the question of the independence of St. David's. From that time forth the story is best told by Giraldus himself.

C. H. W.

INTRODUCTION

THE MAN AND HIS WORKS

I

GIRALDUS Cambrensis has bequeathed a treasure unique for medieval England — a full autobiography of his long eccentric and adventurous life. It is only by a lucky chance that it has survived, since the two works which contain the bulk of it (the *De rebus a se gestis* and the longer edition of the *De iure et statu Meneuensis Ecclesiae*) are each preserved in a single manuscript, which in the case of the *De rebus* breaks off abruptly half-way through.

Bred for the Church and from his childhood conscious of his vocation, passionately devoted to learning of all kinds, a devout Christian eager for the reform of the many abuses which he saw prevailing among the Welsh clergy, he yet had many characteristics of the warlike stock from which he sprang, and would have made as gallant a knight as any of his kinsmen — the Norman conquerors of South Wales and Ireland on the one side, and the rebellious Welsh princes on the other. Tall and handsome, he was endowed with vast powers of physical endurance and did not know the meaning of fear. Confident of his own great gifts and obstinately sure of the justice of any cause he undertook, he held his head high among scholars, prelates and kings, and the great Pope, Innocent III himself. And yet his life is the story of a great failure. For his whole career is dominated by the desire to secure the Bishopric of St. David's for himself, and to raise it to Metropolitan dignity — its ancient rank as he firmly believed, though in old age he more than half admitted that he could not prove it. Twice — or even thrice — the cup was dashed from his lips. His Welsh blood stood in his way; so did his unquestioned ability, his fiery temper and his desire for reform. He frightened his opponents, and as Bishop, still more as Archbishop, of St. David's he might well have proved a thorn in the side of the royal power. His allegiance was not actually divided: he never desired the political independence of Wales; he only demanded justice for the conquered and independence for their Church. But he was proud of his Welsh blood, and his vanity and impulsive temper might, on occasion, easily have thrown him into the arms of his Welsh kinsmen.

His motives in seeking the Episcopal throne of St. David's were on the whole pure. He had refused too many bishoprics in Ireland and elsewhere in Wales to allow us to have any doubt on that point. It is possible that the methods which he employed to gain his end were less above suspicion. We have no evidence on this point save his own; but reading between the lines it is possible to find hints at least of intrigue and wire pulling. His failure to fulfil his ambition was probably a blessing in disguise; for its achievement would have brought him strife and troubles innumerable. The Welsh clergy with their deep-rooted distaste for celibacy, the monks whom he so hated, the officers of the secular power, and even his kinsmen, Norman and Welsh, would have found many occasions for resenting his strong hand, his fiery temper, and his passion for excommunicating his opponents.

But despite the faults and frailties, which the frankness of his autobiography reveals, he wins the interest and even the affection of the reader. His struggle to secure the Bishopric of St. David's has something of an epic quality, and it is hard not to be moved by his defeat. For he was brave and warm-hearted; in the darkest hour his courage and resource never fail him; his interest in every aspect of life is inexhaustible; his gifts as narrator, rhetorician and humorist are overflowing. And however much we may doubt his practical wisdom, and deplore the vehemence of his temper, we can never doubt the sincerity of

INTRODUCTION

his religion. If he rarely walked humbly before man, he yet walked humbly before God. That he was a pluralist and that he was absent for long periods from his Archdeaconry cannot be made a serious reproach. Such pluralism and absenteeism were 'common form' in his day. Nor yet are we justified in regarding him as a liar — the charge which is most often brought against him. His invectives were doubtless inclined to be libellous, and his rhetoric, when pleading in the Curia, not seldom carried him beyond the bounds of accuracy — as they have carried many a fiery advocate both before and since his time. But there is no reason to suspect him of conscious inveracity in his calmer moments. His superstition and his credulity were great, but he does not go beyond the average of his contemporaries, and if historians are permitted to meet in the next world, Giraldus should have found a boon-companion in Herodotus. His delight in a good story and his sense of fun are infectious; and the whole scene, which his story unrolls before us, is richly coloured and richly peopled. He himself is always intensely alive; his sketches both of his friends and enemies are vivid enough, even if they are not always just; and his story has an individuality which makes it one of the most singular and remarkable of autobiographies.

An autobiography can never tell the full story of any man's life; it can never be impartial, and would lose much of its charm if it could. Giraldus found himself no less interesting than he found the world at large; but his self-revelation is so frank that we can form a very good guess as to the impression which he made on others. We can rarely check his story; for he is almost our sole authority. It must be read with caution, but apart from the judgments passed upon his enemies — notably on Archbishop Hubert — and a certain vagueness in its chronology, there is little reason to suppose that it falls markedly below the level of autobiographical veracity.

HIS WORKS

11

His autobiographical writings may be left to speak for themselves in the translation. A few further words are however required concerning the *De iure et statu Meneuensis Ecclesiae*, since only the purely narrative portion of that work has been quoted. The rest, however, is cast in the form of a bogus dialogue between *Soluens* and *Quaerens*. The latter asks a question, e.g.: 'Why would not the Chapter of St. David's accept such a good and great man as Giraldus to be their Bishop?' — and *Soluens* answers it. The answers are often interesting, but the form of the work is artificial and irritating. It may be added that the work exists in two editions — the complete edition containing the long narrative here translated, and a shorter edition omitting the narrative on the ground that its substance is contained in other works, more especially in the *De rebus a se gestis*.

There remain the historical works on Wales and Ireland, the *Gemma Ecclesiastica* and *Speculum Ecclesiae*, the *De Principis Instructione*, and sundry minor works, such as the 'Lives' of St. Hugh of Lincoln, of Geoffrey, Archbishop of York, and of sundry Saints, together with a collection of documents and *pièces justificatives* entitled the *Inuectiones* and the collection of letters, excerpts and poems, known as the *Symbolum Electorum*.

The historical works have already been discussed, but a few words may be added here. The *Expugnatio Hiberniae* tells the story of the conquest of Ireland, accomplished to a large extent by his own kinsmen, the Geraldines, from whom he must in the main have drawn his materials with the natural result that both this work and the *Topographia Hibernica* are of a markedly tendencious character. The Norman sources are, however, supplemented by stories, often highly-coloured or half-understood,

INTRODUCTION

which he must have derived from the Irish themselves — a race not wholly devoid of a lively and inventive imagination. While both works contain much that is of real interest and much that is picturesque, they are often libellous in the extreme, and more than one Irish patriot has been at pains to refute their slanders.

These works broke new ground and wakened no small interest in England, but they lack the charm and intimacy of the two books on Wales. The *Itinerarium Cambriae*, though it ostensibly describes the journey round Wales, when Archbishop Baldwin and Giraldus preached the Crusade, tells us much less concerning their mission than does the *De rebus a se gestis*, and is remembered rather as a delightful and entertaining collection of folk-tales and marvels connected with the different places through which they passed. One does not easily forget the demoniac of Caerleon, nor the magnanimous weasel of Pembroke, nor the stories of fairies and changelings with which the book abounds; and there are few queerer or more amusing works to be found in medieval literature. The *Descriptio Cambriae* is of a more sober character, but gives an extraordinarily interesting picture of Welsh life in the twelfth century, and is remarkable for the extreme impartiality with which it depicts the vices and the virtues of the people and sets forth the best means for the conquest of Wales side by side with the best methods for repelling the invaders.

The *Gemma Ecclesiastica* is a charge to the clergy of his Archdeaconry, illustrated with stories as racy as they are apposite. The whole range of clerical life is covered. The first book deals with the sacraments soberly and sanely enough, but is none the less diversified with curious stories of miracles and of the errors and weaknesses of the clergy, among the most curious being the legend of a Pope who would never take the Holy Sacrament, and the scandalous story of a priest of Worcester who, standing before the altar, broke out into an English love-song instead of saying *Dominus uobiscum*. The second book is, in the main, an exhortation to holy living, illustrated by curious, and sometimes even ribald stories of unholy living. He denounces intemperance in drink, the sin of avarice (especially in bishops), and the gross illiteracy of the clergy, depicted in a series of 'howlers' perpetrated by members of all degrees of the hierarchy.

The *Speculum Ecclesiae*, whose title might be paraphrased as 'Scenes from Clerical Life' or 'The Legend of Bad Clergymen', contains a series of scenes or stories, vivid, satirical and scurrilous, curious, diverting and at times engaging, all tumbled together without any definite arrangement. Some of them are excerpted from earlier works; for this is one of the very latest of his writings, published when he was over seventy. It can hardly be described as seriously designed for edification, though he does at intervals point the moral and deplore the sin. But it is one of the most interesting of all his works and, despite the fact that the sole manuscript on which it depends suffered cruelly from the disastrous fire that worked such havoc among the Cotton manuscripts, it still provides us with a rich gallery of pictures, a strange miscellany, vivid, humorous, grotesque, which leaves a wonderful impression, and if at times it disgusts the reader, more often makes him smile or laugh aloud.

The *De Principis Instructione*, begun in early life, was not completed till after the death of King John, and is therefore at least as late as the *Speculum*, if not later. The first book alone strictly conforms to the title, giving a churchman's view of the ideal prince, copiously supported by a farrago of quotations from the Bible, the Fathers and classical literature. It is the dullest thing that Giraldus ever wrote. The theme and quality of the rest of the work is very different, and the whole atmosphere is changed. For the last two books give a picture of the rise

INTRODUCTION

and decline of Henry II, framed in a general denunciation of Norman 'tyrants'. The Angevin kings are an accursed race, with the devil himself among their ancestors — the pedigree is given — and the 'young King' (Henry III, as Giraldus and other writers call him) alone escapes sweeping condemnation — from which probably his untimely death alone saved him. Henry's fall is a just reward for his treatment of the Church, the murder of Becket and the betrayal of Christ's cause by his refusal to join in the Crusade. The conception is dramatic, the execution poor; there is too much quotation from earlier works — among his own, the *Expugnatio Hiberniae*, among those of others, the *Itinerarium Regis Ricardi*. But the episodes are often very striking and sometimes of real historical value; for Giraldus was with Henry II in France during the last years of his life, and there are many scenes described with remarkable power — Henry's last meeting with Richard, his reception of the news that John had turned against him, his death, the shameful despoliation of his dead body, and his lying-in-state at Fontévraud, together with others which will be found in the translation.

Of the minor works little need here be said. There are some charming passages in the otherwise disappointing 'Life of St. Hugh of Lincoln'. The 'Life of Geoffrey, Archbishop of York' tells a curious story with vigour and skill, and is notable for its scurrilous and amusing attack on William Longchamp. The character of the *Invectiones* is sufficiently illustrated by the passages given in the translation, though it should be added that it contains among its many excerpts from the lost portion of the *De rebus a se gestis* a curious collection of dreams relating to the career of Giraldus, some seen by himself, some by others — a topic which he found enthralling. The *Symbolum Electorum* also contains excerpts from the lost portion of the *De rebus a se gestis*, together with some

HIS WORKS

letters of great interest, which will be found in the translation, while there are others which are little more than rhetorical exercises and have only a stylistic interest. His poems are also included; they are good of their kind, but it is a poor kind; for they are almost all written in classical metres and, like almost all of their class, are lacking both in genuine poetic feeling and real technical skill; only the accentual verse of this period has living force and genuine beauty, and Giraldus did not seriously attempt it.

The 'Lives' of St. Ethelbert, St. Remigius and St. David call for no comment here. There are, however, three brief writings which deserve more than a bare mention: The *Retractationes*, in which he concisely acknowledges that his denunciations of Archbishop Hubert were many of them based on common gossip, and that one or two of the poems included in the *Symbolum Electorum* were not really by himself; the 'Letter to the Chapter of Hereford' — written not earlier than 1219 — in which he gives some account of his works, as he does also in his *Catalogus Minor* and at the close of the *De iure et statu Meneuensis Ecclesiae*; and finally the 'Letter to Archbishop Stephen Langton', from which an excerpt is given in the translation.

Only four of his works seem to have been lost: *Duorum speculum* (apparently an invective), *Vita Sancti Karadoci*, *De fidei fructu fideique defectu*, and the *Cambriae Mappa*. The loss of the latter is distressing. Wharton and Bishop Tanner both testify to having seen it in the Library of Westminster Abbey; it presumably perished in the fire which did such damage there in January 1695.

As a writer Giraldus is far from being faultless; for he is often diffuse and careless in the arrangement of his material. But he was no mean scholar, and as a stylist he has wide range and power. Brilliant as a narrator, when he is at his simplest, he has the gift of genuine eloquence

INTRODUCTION

as well, though the gift is not always employed with discretion and control. The language which he writes is not one to be despised. It is Medieval Latin, employing idioms, vocabulary and constructions unknown to classical writers, but it is still a beautiful and living language, flexible, sonorous, vivid, forcible. To call it Dog Latin would be an outrage. It is University Latin, it is Church Latin, the tongue in which the Pope spoke *Vrbi et orbi;* and when the occasion calls for fine writing Giraldus can rise nobly to the occasion. His eloquence would certainly be recognized by rhetoricians of the second century A.D. as possessing qualities closely akin to their own. It is not always realized how deeply the triumph of full-blooded 'Asiatic' oratory in that century influenced the whole course of later developments in the style of Latin prose. It was transmitted through the Fathers, notably St. Augustine, and that still greater master of Latin, both florid and colloquial, St. Jerome, down the dawn of the Renaissance and beyond. The Prelude to Giraldus's first public lecture at Paris might easily be mistaken for a lost fragment of the *Florida* of Apuleius. Even the study of rhythm continued, though its basis was accentual and not qualitative, and Giraldus in his rhetorical passages conforms to the laws followed by the Roman Curia and perhaps first definitely formulated by Gregory VIII. How beautiful at their best his writings can be may be illustrated by an almost lyrical passage from the close of the *De iure et statu Meneuensis Ecclesiae*, where he describes the death of Henry of Blois, Bishop of Winchester, who goes robed all in white to meet St. Thomas of Canterbury arrayed in the martyr's crimson.

'Vitam hic terminans Cantuariensem, rubris indutum roseisque coronis, punicieis coccineisque decenter purpuratum, niue nitidior longeque lacte candidior, liliorum sertis undique saeptus, Wintoniensis feliciter est secutus.'

HIS WORKS

'Then he of Winchester closing his life on earth, brighter than snow and than milk far whiter, girded about on all sides with lilies, blissfully followed the Saint of Canterbury, crowned with red roses, in robes empurpled of scarlet and crimson, arrayed in seemliness.'

Further he has a width of classical reading rare among his contemporaries in England. Like them he adorns his works with copious quotations from the Classics and the Fathers. Like them he probably owed something to a *millefolium* or anthology of quotations. But he quotes less mechanically and with a greater knowledge of the context of his quotations, while his range is exceptional; for he cites almost every classical author available in his day. Of Lucretius and Plautus alone he knows nothing; such at least is a reasonable inference, seeing that his one quotation from Plautus is actually a quotation from Lucretius. In an age of accomplished writers of Latin he stands high among his countrymen. He lacks the classic dignity and orderliness of John of Salisbury, and the delicacy and polish of his friend Walter Map. But he has a robustness, a raciness and an individuality that are all his own.

H. E. B.

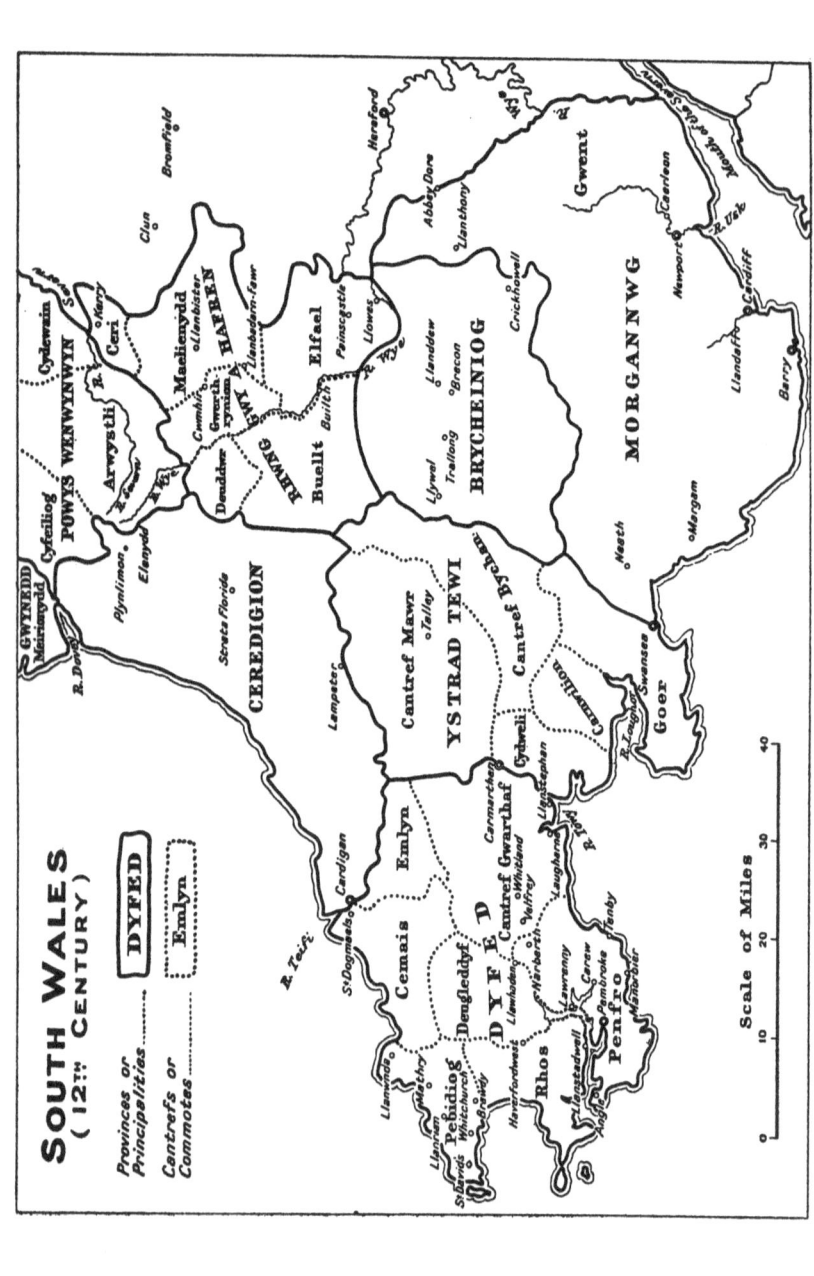

DE REBUS A SE GESTIS

PREFACE

IT was a custom of the ancient Greeks to commend the deeds of famous men to the memory of after-generations in such a manner as might cause them to be the better and the more clearly remembered. And this they did, firstly by portraits and secondly by writing, to the end that posterity might be inspired to the laudable imitation of the great virtues of days gone by. For no man is kindled to imitation by hearing or reading fabulous records of deeds that are extravagant or impossible. But when a man's true virtue flashes forth, then the virtuous mind is uplifted to imitate manly deeds and to take them to heart. Wherefore I have taken upon me to set forth in scholarly fashion, yet simply and without elaboration, the famous deeds of a man of our own time, which I either witnessed with my own eyes or took down from his own lips. And this I have done that men may be stirred thereby to praiseworthy achievement, in many ways, and may learn how easily two Churches, to wit, the Italian and the Welsh, were corrupted by the power of money, and further that the Church of Mynyw may be surely and faithfully advised of its own dignity and forewarned against like troubles in all time to come. And though from these documents it may be impossible to discover any remedy for what is past and gone, yet something of no small profit may be learned therefrom, namely, caution against evils yet to come. And as Giraldus built exceeding well on the foundations laid by Bernard[1], so too (if hereafter any honest man should ever arise in the Church of Mynyw[2] and find good faith among his

[1] See p. 20.   [2] Menevia = St. Davids.

brethren) may he, for the exaltation of his own Church and for the glory of all Cambria, so strive that he also in his own day may build upon that which Giraldus built before him, and open the Ark of safety[1] to such as shall come after him. For it is in truth a great thing and most worthy of praise faithfully to lay a sure foundation and to raise on high a stairway whereby others may climb aloft.

The first part of this work, therefore, tells of Giraldus's birth and of the deeds of his boyhood and youth; the second of the deeds of his manhood's prime; the third of the deeds of his later and riper years, being full of his labours and perils and persecutions.

---

[1] *arca materialis* 'the wooden ark', i.e. of Noah.

BOOK I

CHAPTER I

Concerning the birth of Giraldus and the deeds of his boyhood and youth

GIRALDUS was born[1] in South Wales on the sea-coast of Dyfed, not far from the chief town of Pembroke, in the Castle of Manorbier. He came of noble lineage; for his mother was Angharad, daughter of Nest, the famous child of Rhys ap Tewdwr, Prince of South Wales, and his father was her lawful husband, the noble William de Barri.[2] He was the youngest of four brothers, lawfully born of the same womb; and when the other three, preluding the pursuits of manhood in their childish play, were tracing or building, in sand or dust, now towns, now palaces, he himself, in like prophetic play, was ever busy with all his might in designing churches or building monasteries. And his father, who often saw him thus engaged, after much pondering, not unmixed with wonder, being moved by this omen, resolved with wise forethought to set him to study letters and the liberal arts, and would oft in approving jest call him 'his Bishop'.

Now it happened that one night, when the country was disturbed by a raid of the enemy, and all the young men of the castle sprang to arms, the boy on seeing this and hearing the tumult burst into tears and, seeking some place of safety, begged that he might be carried to the church, thus with marvellous foreknowledge proclaiming that the peace of the church and the sanctuary

[1] In August, 1165, at the birth of Philip Augustus he was *uicesimum annum adimplens* (*Princ. Instr. R.S.* viii p. 292), i.e. certainly over nineteen and possibly nearly twenty. In 1176 (June or July) he was not yet in his thirtieth year (*cum necdum tricesimum ageret annum*; see p. 59), though it is possible that he may mean 'when he was not yet thirty'. His birth therefore falls between 1145-7.
[2] See pedigree in Appendix 1.

DE REBUS A SE GESTIS

of God's house should be the strongest and most secure place of refuge; and in truth all that heard of this thing, as soon as the tumult was abated, when they pondered on this utterance of the child and spoke of it together, called to mind with wonder that he promised greater safety for himself in a lonely church exposed to all the winds and to the strokes of chance than in a town filled with men-at-arms and strongly fortified with walls and towers. Moreover, as often as he heard disputes concerning the law of the land and the law of the Church, the boy would put himself forward with all his might as the advocate and champion of the Church, God inspiring him with the same zeal and increasing His grace day by day and enduring with him all his life even to the end. For he desired naught so much on earth as the great glory of Christ's Church and its advancement and honour in all things, in every age and circumstance of his life.

CHAPTER II

Concerning his early failure in learning and his later progress

But in his childhood he was not a little impeded by the companionship of his brothers, who on holidays would play together and praise the knightly tasks of their chosen profession, and so his progress in learning was far slower than it should have been. But at length, being chidden and corrected by his uncle David, of blessed memory, then Bishop of Mynyw, and being greatly helped also by the mockery of two of the Bishop's clerks, one of whom rebuked him by rehearsing the degrees of comparison *durus, durior, durissimus*, while the other cried *stultus, stultior, stultissimus*, he began to make progress, spurred by conscience rather than the rod, from very shame rather than through any fear or because of the

MANORBIER CASTLE

EDUCATION

instruction received from any of his masters. For after this he took to his studies with such vehemence that in a brief space he far outstripped his schoolmates[1] and equals in age. But in course of time, desiring greater learning and profit, he thrice crossed the seas to France and spent three periods of several years at Paris in the study of the liberal arts and at last equalling the greatest teachers, taught the *Trivium*[2] there most excellently, winning especially fame in the art of rhetoric; and he was so wholly devoted to his studies, and so free from all levity and frivolity both in word and deed that, as often as the teachers of the Arts desired to produce a pattern of excellence from among their best scholars, with one accord they named Giraldus in preference to all the rest. And thus in the first years of his youth his merits made him worthy not merely to seek but also to set an example of excellence in the duties of a scholar.

The following incident (1165) *belongs to this period. It is recorded in* De Princ. Instr. III, 25 (R.S. VIII, p. 292).

Again, among other prognostications, I think I should not pass over a thing which befell the writer of these words. When in the years of his youth he was devoting himself most zealously to the study of the liberal arts at Paris, it came to pass that at the beginning of autumn, about the first sleep when the night was yet young, the said Philip was by the grace of God born of his mother's womb. And when the fame thereof was heard in the city and received with joy inexpressible by human speech through the whole of that great city there was such a sound and clanging of bells and such a multitude of tapers were kindled through all the open places of the town, that not knowing what such a sound and unwonted tumult might mean together with such a blaze of light by

---

[1] He was sent to study at the Abbey of St. Peter in Gloucester; see p. 79.
[2] Grammar, Logic and Rhetoric.

night, men deemed that the city was threatened by a great conflagration. Wherefore the author of this work, a stripling living in the city and then near the completion of his twentieth year, was awakened from the bed on which he had just fallen asleep and looking forth beheld in the place without, two women old and very poor, but none the less carrying tapers in their hands and showing great joy in their faces and in every movement of their bodies running with hasty steps to meet each other as though they would dash one against the other. And when he asked them for the cause of such commotion and rejoicing, one of them looked back at him and thus made answer:—'We have a King now given us by God, an heir to the Kingdom, who by God's grace shall be a man of great might, through whom loss and dishonour, punishment and great shame, full of confusion and woe, shall befall your King;' as though she had openly said, 'This night a boy is born to us, who by the blessing of God, shall assuredly be the hammer of your King and shall without doubt diminish the power and pastures of him and of his folk'. For the woman knew that he and his companions were from the realm of England, and it was therefore that the old woman thus sharply uttered these words against them and their King, words which uttered as it were under prophetic inspiration, were destined (all too truly) to be fulfilled in after time.

CHAPTER III

Of the zeal which he straightway showed for the good of the Church

WHEN he returned from his studies, he began forthwith to receive advancement and promotion in Churches and ecclesiastical benefices both in England and Wales; and feeling that he was 'born for his country not for himself

THE LEGATE'S LEGATE

alone',[1] and set on virtue for service of the common weal, he strove to employ his great gifts for the profit of the Church to make good its deficiencies.

Seeing, therefore, that throughout the diocese of Mynyw, and above all in Dyfed and Cardigan, no tithes of wool or cheese were paid owing to the carelessness of its rulers, he went to Canterbury, to which at that time the Church of Mynyw, like all Wales, was subject by provincial law, and there set forth these deficiencies to Archbishop Richard, who was then Primate of all England and Legate of the Roman Court[2]; by whom he was straightway sent back to Wales as the Legate's legate, that he might remedy these irregularities and such others as he should find there. Moreover the Archbishop in his letters warned all those who had not yet paid the aforesaid tithes, and enjoined upon them for the remission of their sins, that they should pay them forthwith. And further to such as, thus admonished, were ready to pay he relaxed a third of the penance which he had enjoined; but he commanded that those who were obstinate and refused to pay should be strictly forced to do so by the censure of the Church. And forthwith all the Welsh obeyed these salutary admonitions and consented to pay the tithes, as did all others in the land, except the Flemings of Rhos and their accomplices, who would have been placed under an interdict of long duration, but that at the instance of Henry II, King of the English, to whom they appealed, they obtained for the time being a remission of the Archbishop's sentence, to the condemnation both of those who so urgently sought and of him who so urgently insisted on this reprieve. Wherefore after no long time[3], when the King died and was taken with dishonour from the world, the Welsh, who in response to the admonitions of a righteous man readily

[1] An adaptation of *Lucan* ii, 383 and 390.
[2] Richard was consecrated and appointed Legate in 1174.
[3] Fourteen or fifteen years later in 1189!

paid their tithe of wool, proceeded to ravage the province of Rhos and carried off all the woolly sheep, not to speak of other booty, from those who had refused to pay their tithe of wool to God and to His Church. Wherein the words spoken by Augustine against withholders of tithes and the dues of the Church, seem on this occasion also to have been fulfilled; to wit, 'What Christ receiveth not, the Treasury taketh. That which thou wilt not give to the priest, thou shalt give to the ungodly soldier'.[1]

Now about the same time there came to pass a thing, which I have also thought worthy of note, namely that a certain man of those parts, one Roger, surnamed Bechet, owed ten stone of wool to his creditor at the time of shearing. Having no more than this amount, he sent the tenth stone, despite the protest of his wife, to his baptismal church of Caereu, and the remaining nine to his creditor at Pembroke, begging him to have patience, for he would soon make good the deficiency. Now his creditor, on receiving the wool, weighed it and found the weight to be ten stone; and though he weighed it again and again, he always found the full tale of ten stone; and so he made answer to his debtor that he had received satisfaction in full. Wherefore by this example, the wool having been miraculously multiplied like the oil of Elisha,[2] many persons in those parts were either converted to the payment of those tithes or confirmed in their readiness to pay. But, as Giraldus used to say, citing the verse,

> After forbidden things we strive alway,
> And that which is forbidden still desire,[3]

it is a wonder that the mind of man strives so obstinately after that which is unlawful. . . .

---

[1] *Dabis impio militi quod non uis dare sacerdoti* occurs in *Serm. Supposit*, 277, but is not preceded by *Hoc aufert fiscus quod non accipit Christus. Militi* would suggest 'knight' to the readers of Giraldus.
[2] 2 Kings iv. 2.   [3] *Ov. Am.* III, iv. 17.

THE UNGODLY SHERIFF

Now when he was performing his duty as legate, at the Priory of Pembroke which was not far off, no less a person than the Sheriff of the province, William Carquit by name, being jealous of his coming with such power, since 'no prophet is accepted in his own country',[1] and desiring to cover him with dishonour and confusion, at the very moment of his coming ordered his servants and officers to seize eight yoke of oxen belonging to the priory and to drive them away to the castle. But when after the third time of asking he utterly refused to restore them and even threatened worse things, Giraldus sent to him saying, that unless he returned the oxen, he would forthwith be placed under sentence of excommunication. And when he, being a haughty and abandoned fellow, replied that he would not dare to excommunicate the king's constable in his own castle, Giraldus made answer that as soon as he heard all the bells of the whole monastery rung at triple intervals, then he might know that without a doubt he was in process of excommunication. And as soon as the messengers had returned, in virtue of his authority as legate he solemnly and with candles lit pronounced sentence of excommunication, in the presence not only of the monks but of many priests of that country, and forthwith caused all the bells to be sounded, as is the custom, to confirm the sentence or rather to announce that it was done. But on the next day the robber came with all speed to the Castle of Lawhaden into the presence of David, Bishop of the diocese and likewise of Giraldus and Master Michael his colleague, whom the Archbishop had attached to him as his assistant; and after he had made restitution and satisfaction had been given, he was judged worthy to be beaten with rods, and then and not till then to receive absolution. But in the county of Pembroke round about, because the Sheriff and Constable complained in public that he had

[1] Luke iv. 24.

been excommunicated by Giraldus, others also complained that Giraldus had come with a strong hand and with men and armed forces to receive investiture of the Church of Talacharn (Laugharne). Now when Richard FitzTancred, who was then accounted a great man in those parts and had always hated Giraldus and all his family, heard of these things, he began to utter the most savage threats against Giraldus and those who had gone with him to Talacharn, saying that he would have put them to a most cruel death, had he known beforehand of their intentions. And after there had been much strife among the great men of those parts concerning these things, Odo of Caereu, the cousin of Giraldus, and Philip de Barri, his brother, both of them good and great men in those parts, although they were Richard's sons-in-law, yet spoke bitterly to him, telling him to be silent and to restrain his foolish tongue; for the vengeance that was taken for another Giraldus (to wit the eldest brother of Odo, for whose slaying aforetime by the men of Rhos, two hundred and more of them were killed in one day), was in no wise so great as the cruel and bloody vengeance that would be taken for this Giraldus, if he should fall by his hand or those of his men.

CHAPTER IV

How Giraldus performed his duties as legate and was promoted to be Archdeacon

THIS also I think should not be passed over in silence, how Giraldus, when he had entered the diocese of Mynyw at Brecknock, invested with the powers of legate, finding there an old Archdeacon of those parts,[1] who publicly

---

[1] His name was Jordan (See Lloyd, *Hist. Wales*, p. 557, n. 108).

THE OLD ARCHDEACON OF LLANDDUW
kept his concubine with him in his house, first diligently admonished him and then, when he paid no heed to his admonitions, commanded him in the name of the Archbishop, Primate and Legate, to cast her from him and to cease from giving an example of misconduct and shameful living to those in his charge, whom it was his duty rather to chide and to correct. But the Archdeacon not only refused to do this, but presumed in his excess of folly and recklessness to use foul and insulting words against no less a person than the Archbishop himself. When, therefore, he heard him speak thus, Giraldus suspended him from holding any ecclesiastical benefice and took his Archdeaconry and Prebend into the hands of the Archbishop, whose authority he had spurned and whom he had thus insulted. Wherefore when his duties as legate were completed and he had returned to the Archbishop, taking with him the Bishop of Mynyw, the latter at the instance of the Archbishop conferred the Archdeaconry and Prebend upon Giraldus, and assigned other revenues to that Archdeacon so full of days (and would they had also been blameless days!), that he might have the wherewithal to live in peace and quiet. Now, after performing these things, Giraldus perceived that owing to the remission for the time being, by order of the King and the Archbishop, of the sentence passed upon the men of Rhos, almost the whole country had been corrupted (for the Flemings, wherever they might be, without Rhos no less than within, wished to enjoy the same immunity); and considering that thus his labours had been impaired, he obtained letters from the Archbishop to the Bishop of St. David's, setting forth that he had released from the interdict none save those dwelling in the cantref[1] of Rhos and that he had only released them for the time being at the instance of the King and would strictly include under his former

[1] *sc.* Hundred.

DE REBUS A SE GESTIS

interdict all others who refused to pay tithes of wool and cheese. Whereupon the interdict was once more reimposed upon all those dwelling in the cantref of Deugleddyf and upon the men of Angle also who, though living in the province of Pembroke, nevertheless desired to enjoy the like privilege, because they were Flemings and like the men of Rhos and Deugleddyf had spent money to secure that immunity. The same was done to the men of Talacharn, who, being in part Flemings and far richer in sheep than their neighbours, were more rebellious and recalcitrant; and so it proved impossible fully to tame them and bring them to order, until at last a special mandate was issued by the Pope at the petition of Giraldus. There was therefore a great uproar in the country and great bitterness among the Flemings against Giraldus. The clergy on the other hand, over whose honour and welfare he watched, had great love and affection towards him. Moreover a beginning had long since been made and an example[1] set by Giraldus in the collecting of such tithes in Dyfed. For while he was a youth in the schools of Paris, his kinsmen, William FitzHay[2] and Odo of Caereu, and his own brother, Philip de Barri, knowing that he was of good character, had long ago, as if by agreement, given him their tithes of wool and flour. Wherefore afterwards when they heard of his proclamation and of the remission of penance granted by the Pope, they, as well as others moved by their example, were all the more ready to pay the tithes to their churches. Thus Giraldus, who himself had formerly made a beginning in this matter, contributed much thereto and by all his later labours carried this business to fuller completion.

Now it happened that the parishioners of Angle, whose

---

[1] *allectorium*, a word apparently found only here, presumably—'inducement' (from *allicio*).

[2] A son of Nest, perhaps by 'Hait', Sheriff of Pembroke in 1130 (See Lloyd, op. cit., p. 502, n. 64).

THE NEW ARCHDEACON'S ENERGY

Church belonged to Giraldus, being not only under interdict, but also excommunicate on account of their rebellion, on a certain day both sought and expected the coming of Giraldus to grant them the grace of absolution. But on the night before that day Giraldus lay at Caereu, together with the Bishop of St. David's, and when he was preparing for his journey in the morning and was intending to set forth, although a great storm and a strong wind had arisen with wind and hail blowing full in his face, the Bishop, whose bed was close to his, bade him on account of the violence of the storm to put off his business and stay quietly within doors. But he replied that delay under such circumstances was perilous, seeing that those who had been excommunicated were seeking absolution and promising amendment; and so, with the Bishop's leave and blessing, he set out upon his journey forthwith. And when on the same day the Bishop was sitting at breakfast, and the storm was growing more violent and belching forth fearful blasts of wind and rain, he looked round and (being a shrewd and prudent man) perceived that some were indulging in food and drink too greedily, while others were addressing girls and women with undue freedom and wantonness; wherefore he said to them, 'He that hastened forth to-day upon his journey and did not shrink from facing weather such as this, is one that does not leave his task undone for any gluttony or wantonness or sloth'. For Giraldus was wont to say that it was unmanly to watch for a breeze or calm before proceeding upon any business on dry land; for such watching of the weather was only tolerable in those who were crossing the sea.

DE REBUS A SE GESTIS

CHAPTER V

Concerning the things which he did immediately after his promotion

AMONG the very first deeds after his promotion to the Archdeaconry was the following. Finding that in the Church of Hay, the last church of the diocese of Mynyw towards England, a certain knight, the parson's brother, used to halve the offerings at the altar, the tithes from without and all other incomings with the parson, he at once put an end to this irregularity, though not without difficulty and only after he had fined and threatened the knight. And so having restored the church in its entirety to the parson, he deprived the knight of all share therein. And again when he went to visit certain remote parts on the borders of his Archdeaconry, between Wye and Severn[1], that is, in Elfael and Maeliennydd, there came to him two clerks who in the name of the Dean[2] and Chapter of those parts told him that he ought not to visit their Churches in person, but that he should take care to do whatever might be necessary in accordance with the custom of his predecessors, namely through his messengers and officers, and above all through the Dean, of whom they spoke among themselves as their Archdeacon. But when they received his reply, to the effect that he refused to imitate the sloth and cowardice of others, if any such there had been, and desired to make full use of his own powers and authority, they in the name of all the clergy and people and also of the chief men of the country forbade him to come to them, and after their custom held up the crucifix before him, that he might proceed no farther. But since he was not to be deterred thereby from the journey which he had

[1] A translation of Rhwng Gwy a Hafren. [2] Rural Dean.

begun, others of them met him at the entrance to a great wood, and told him that there had been of old a deadly feud between his family and certain nobles of those parts, which after long slumbering had now been recalled to memory by the rumour of his coming; wherefore brave men from among these his enemies had beyond all doubt set an ambush in the wood, fully armed, that they might slay him and his followers, if they proceeded further. But though this was frequently repeated to him and the rumour thereof increased, and though all his own folk dissuaded him, and his followers were in great fear, nevertheless, as though he heard not at all or despised utterly what he heard, he made no delay, but proceeded on his journey. For he at once perceived and asserted that the whole story had been devised by the cunning malice of those clerks who feared his coming; wherefore (he said), if he could thus at the outset be so easily dismayed by their threats, he would always thereafter have less authority and respect among them. So after crossing the Wye and passing through the shaggy forests of Elfael, when he drew nigh to Llanbadarn in Maeliennydd,[1] where he had resolved to hold a chapter and to lie that night, being still about a mile away, his household, which he had sent on before him with his drivers, cooks and pack-horses, as is the custom, to prepare his lodging, came flying towards him, full of fear, having been fiercely driven from the town with long lances and flights of sharp arrows. Whereat though all, both those that went with him and those that met him, exhorted him to return with all speed, and reproached him saying that it would have been more honourable and less unseemly to have done so before when his own folk counselled him, and that a prudent man ought

[1] Reading *ecclesiam Paterni* (W. S. Davies) for *ecclesiam patrum* (MS.); i.e. Llanbadarn Fawr a little north of Llandrindod. Brewer, reading *ecclesiam partium*, which is meaningless, takes the place to be Llanbister, which is too far north.

not to be so foolhardy as to expose himself and his people to such great and manifest dangers, he rejected all such advice and with heightened courage and quickened pace advanced towards the church and bade the others follow. Every door in the town was barred against him, and there being no other place for him he took up his abode in the church which he chanced to find open, and ordered his horses to be picketed in the churchyard. After these outrageous proceedings, he straightway sent two clerks with a message to the prince of that land, Cadwallon ap Madog, his kinsman, telling him of his coming and how his folk had been driven away, and how he himself was surrounded and besieged in the church. On hearing this the prince at once sent a sufficiency of victuals to the Archdeacon, with a message that he would come to him next morning and take sharp vengeance on his wrongs, as if they were his own. But on receipt of this news the siege was raised at once, and six or seven clerks, who after the Welsh fashion shared the church between them, came one after the other and bowed themselves humbly at the Archdeacon's feet, seeking pardon and receiving it, but only after they had given due satisfaction for their disobedience or rather for their insolence. On the morrow the prince came with his wife Eva, daughter of the Prince of Powys, and his two sons, Mailgwn and Howel, and placed at his disposal both himself and all that was his, his lands and towns, his goods and possessions, and attached his younger son to him that he might protect him while he was in his country; for his elder son had been brought up by those whom the clergy had incited against him.

CHAPTER VI

How he resisted the Bishop of Llanelwy at Kerry and manfully kept possession of the churches of that land

HAVING accomplished all that seemed necessary there, he turned rein towards Brecknock and returned to his house at Llandduw. And when he had been there for not more than three or four days there came to him in haste two clerks sent by the Dean and Chapter of those parts, with news that Adam, Bishop of Llanelwy,[1] would without doubt come on the next Sunday to the Church of Kerry, on the boundary between the two Sees, but none the less belonging from of old to the diocese of Mynyw, and would on that day dedicate the Church so that he might seize it and all that province;[2] they affirmed also that he could not be prevented from so doing, unless the Archdeacon came to meet him in person. For they asserted that, if he were thus permitted to seize that province, he designed to take and hold all the land up to the Wye, to wit, Maeliennydd and Elfael, as belonging to his Church of St. Asaph. Hearing this, the Archdeacon, though still weary from his former toils and though all his folk sought to dissuade him and, above all, those, who had been with him before, more out of fear than weariness refused to go with him, nevertheless on the morrow, to wit, Friday, he made no delay, but once more set forth with such as would follow him, and after fording the Wye and passing through the forest parts of Elfael, spent the night on the boundary of Maeliennydd. But on Saturday morning he rose and, having said matins and masses, sent forth messengers in different directions to gather clerks from all

[1] Adam de Paruo Ponte, appointed in 1175. This adventure took place in 1176 soon after the death of Bishop David.
[2] Not the 'commote' of Kerry, but the whole region described below.

quarters and cause them to come with him. Others too he sent to the princes and brothers, Einion Clut and Cadwallon, asking them to send after him good men from their own households with horses and arms, to help him at his need and with him to defend the rights of St. David, since it was said that the Bishop would come with a strong hand, accompanied by the men of Powys and Cydewain. And so hastening across Maeliennydd, he spent that night at the Church of Llanbister, not far from Kerry.

Now when on Sunday morning the Archdeacon came to the Church of Kerry, the two clerks, who shared the church, had gone to meet the Bishop, to whose coming they had actually given their assent, and had hidden the keys of the church. But after diligent search the keys were at length found, and the Archdeacon entered the church, where, the bells being rung forthwith as if in sign of investiture and possession, he caused mass to be celebrated. But meanwhile the messengers of the Bishop arrived with one of the parsons of the church, to give orders that it should forthwith be made ready for dedication, as though it were certain that everything would be done in accordance with his commands, resistance being impossible. But when the Archdeacon heard this, as soon as mass was ended, he sent certain discreet men of his clergy to meet the Bishop and tell him from Giraldus, that if he came in peace and as a friend and neighbour, he should be welcomed as a guest with gladness and all honour, but otherwise he should not come nigh. And when they had said this, the Bishop made diligent inquiry whether the Archdeacon was come in person, and was filled with wonder to hear of his presence, since it was but a little before that he had withdrawn from the province. But at length after taking counsel with his own folk, that he might not admit defeat (for he was very haughty and presumptuous),

CONFLICT AT KERRY

indulging his own arrogance he replied that he would come forthwith, not as a guest or neighbour, but as the Bishop of that place, to dedicate the church and perform his episcopal office. But the Dean and clergy, who had been sent to him, stoutly forbade him, as they had been instructed, telling him that he should not come thither after this fashion nor presume to perform the rite of dedication in another's parish, when he had neither been summoned nor invited for this purpose; and finally they appealed to the Pope. But since he was not to be deterred thus, they sent on some of the better mounted among them, as they had been forewarned to do, to carry the news with all speed to the Archdeacon. And when they came to him, the Archdeacon, leaving certain of his followers in the church to guard it from within and bar the doors, went forth at once to meet the Bishop as he came to the entrance of the churchyard. But the Bishop bade the Archdeacon to depart, himself and all his folk, without more ado and to leave him his church and churchyard that he might do that which he purposed; otherwise he would excommunicate him, though sore against his will, since they had been comrades and fellow-scholars at Paris. But the Archdeacon in answer begged the Bishop to depart in peace for the sake of their ancient comradeship and amity and to do naught to his injury or to the detriment of his jurisdiction. And when he utterly refused to withdraw, the Archdeacon in the name of God and the Lord Pope and the Archbishop and the King of England, in whose hand the guardianship of the Church of St. David then was, since it had lately been bereft of its shepherd, interposed his appeal and firmly forbade him to put his sickle into the harvest of another by performing the dedication or any other episcopal office. The Bishop, however, in answer produced letters of the Archbishop of Canterbury, by whom he had not long before been consecrated and caused them to be read aloud; in which letters he confirmed to him the Bishopric of Llanelwy with all its appurtenances, and excommunicated all who should unjustly take anything away from it. This done, the Bishop added that the Church of Kerry and all others between Wye and Severn belonged of parochial right to his Church of Llanelwy,[1] and in witness thereof he produced an ancient book, at the end of which he said this statement was to be found; and he caused it to be read, saying that, unless the Archdeacon desisted at once, he would excommunicate him and his folk forthwith. But the Archdeacon replied that the Church of Kerry and others between Wye and Severn, in Elfael and Maeliennydd and Gwerthrynion, in no wise appertained to the diocese of Llanelwy and did not come within the confirmation made by the Archbishop, it being well known that for three hundred years and more they had been part of the diocese of Mynyw; he might write in his book what he pleased; if, however, he had a charter or privilege to that effect with an authentic seal, let him show it; but if, not having this, he wished to excommunicate him for standing in defence of his own church, he himself with like audacity would launch his sentence upon the Bishop. The latter made answer that he was a Bishop and that an Archdeacon had no power to excommunicate a Bishop. Whereto the Archdeacon replied, 'If you are a Bishop, you are not my Bishop, nor have you power to pass sentence on me, any more than I have power to do the like by you. Wherefore let the sentence have such validity as it may, since on both sides it is uttered recklessly and without due right'.

But the Bishop, when he heard this, withdrew a little, and, suddenly slipping from his horse, caused the mitre to be placed upon his head and, thus mitred and bearing

---

[1] This region had once formed part of the Kingdom of Powys, it was probably on this fact that the Bishop based his claim.

MUTUAL EXCOMMUNICATION

his pastoral staff stripped of its covering, that his sentence might seem to have greater authority, he drew nigh on foot with his throng of followers. The Archdeacon, on the other hand, ordered a number of priests and clerks, clad in white stoles and surplices and other priestly raiment to go forth from the church and march to meet him after the manner of a procession with candles lighted and the cross carried at their head. For he knew the nature of the man, that he was headlong in his actions and presumptuous. And therefore while they were wrangling, because the Bishop was garrulous and verbose, the Archdeacon had taken care to see that preparations should be made to this end. And when the Bishop saw the clerks advancing, he asked what this might mean and wherefore they came thus. To which the Archdeacon made answer, 'For this — that, if you dare to pass sentence on us and them, then they with no less boldness may pass sentence in their turn on you and yours'. But the Bishop, when he heard this, replied, 'On account of the friendship that was once between us and because of our school-companionship, we will now spare your person and those who are with you, and will not pass sentence on any of you by name. But as the Archbishop said in his letters, we will in general terms place under sentence of excommunication all those who seek to usurp the rights of our patron St. Asaph'. To this the Archdeacon made answer, 'If you will pass such general sentence from yonder hills,' (and he pointed to certain hills not far distant in a parish of Llanelwy), 'aye and continue to do so from morn till eve, we shall not care a rap, since it will not touch us at all who are only defending our just rights. But on account of the by-standers who would not comprehend, but would think that your sentence, if passed here in any form whatever, was passed against us in person and to our prejudice, we will not have it done here in any way whatever'. And when the Bishop swore that he meant to excommunicate them on the spot in the manner of which he had spoken, the Archdeacon asserted that he would pass sentence on them in like form. And when the Bishop, that he might not seem to have done nothing at all, began in a loud voice to excommunicate in general terms all enemies and adversaries of St. Asaph, the Archdeacon in a still louder voice, together with his folk in the churchyard, excommunicated all those who presumed to appropriate or disturb the rights of St. David; and looking back at the bells, which hung above their heads hard by, he ordered that they should all be rung at triple intervals for the shaming of their adversaries and for confirmation of his sentence. And when this was done, since the Welsh greatly dread such ringing of bells when they are rung against themselves, the Bishop and his men straightway broke off their sentence of excommunication and mounting their horses made off as fast as they could. But the people who had gathered from every side to behold this spectacle, raised a great shout behind them, after their fashion, and pursued them as they fled with clods and sticks and stones. And when the Bishop was making his way to Cadwallon, in Maeliennydd (for he had his consent in this matter), he met a great throng of clerks on good horses with lances and arrows, who were following after the Archdeacon; and when they asked how things had gone at Kerry, the Bishop, since he did not feel himself safe, replied that he had no wish to do anything against the Archdeacon, who had of old been his good comrade and friend, and that he was going in peace to speak with Cadwallon.

But the Archdeacon, in the presence of the Dean and clergy who had just come, began sharply to accuse the parsons of the church for what they had done in bringing the Bishop thither. And they in answer swore that this had not come to pass with their good will and, asking his forgiveness, they promised that they would be staunch and faithful for the future. So he took their oath of allegiance to the Church of Mynyw, to himself and also to the Bishop that should be thereafter appointed. But when he heard from his own clerks who had met the Bishop of Llanelwy, that the latter had gone to Cadwallon within his own Archdeaconry, he straightway went thither and was given lodging in the church nearest to the place where Cadwallon had entertained the Bishop. And at the hour of supper, that is, in the evening (for such is the custom of the Welsh), he sent the Bishop some of his own bread and some choice wine which he had brought with him — a fair gift for the sake of courtesy — and he enhanced his gift with fair words, saying that he would show him all honour and reverence, having found him within his own jurisdiction and Archdeaconry and, above all, intent on peace, and further that if chance offered, he would most gladly welcome him in his own house and give him honourable entertainment. He asked him also that, as they had of old been good comrades in France when they were poorer and no more than private persons, so now that they were in place of power, they should be good and friendly neighbours. And the Bishop, though his own folk urged him not to receive Giraldus because of the shame that had been put upon him and the defeat that he had suffered, none the less followed wiser counsel and received him with thanks for his courtesy, saying that the Archdeacon was not less valued by him because of that which he had done, but would win the greater praise from all men hereafter, because he was quick to defend the rights of his Church to the best of his power, and that he did not on this account desire in any way to refuse him his love and neighbourliness.

But Cadwallon, together with his nobles and good men, was loud in praise of the courage and manhood shown by the Archdeacon, saying that such a man was most worthy of honour and power. On the morrow, however, when the Bishop was gone, the Archdeacon spoke to Cadwallon, chiding him because he had given the Bishop leave to come and had assented to the seizure of his parish. But Cadwallon swore that he had not done so (for he feared to incur the anger of the Archdeacon), and with a solemn oath he declared that he would henceforth be faithful to St. David and his Church. Now there were three things that had given the Bishop an occasion for making this attempt: first that the Church of Mynyw was shepherdless; secondly that he had heard for sure that the Archdeacon had left those parts because of the enmity he had awakened and that he would never return thither; and lastly that he had the secret assent of the prince, though he swore to the contrary; for Cadwallon feared to be divorced from his wife Eva on the ground of affinity and also of consanguinity, and the Bishop had arranged by way of security that he should be the judge appointed by the Archbishop to try the matter. But on the other side the Archdeacon took care to secure, both in peril and in toil, that the Church of Mynyw should not suffer any hurt within his jurisdiction, while it lacked a Bishop, and that neither the diocese should be robbed of any portion of its territory nor the Archdeaconry suffer any mutilation or diminution, while he had charge of it.

CHAPTER VII

How the news of these things reached the King

So, after accomplishing these things, the Archdeacon went with all speed to the King, by whom a day had been appointed for the election of a Bishop in the

HENRY II HEARS NEWS OF VICTORY

presence of himself and of his Church; and finding him at Northampton, he at once told him of the attack made by the Bishop of Llanelwy upon the diocese of Mynyw, and how he sought to seize a parish of the Church of St. David, which was in the King's own hand during the vacancy of the See. Wherefore he warned the King and asked him to restrain the Bishop from such presumption by royal letters and messengers. He also added to his story a sally[1] whereby he moved the bystanders to laughter, saying that as the laity and people of Wales were thieves and stealers of other things, so their Bishops were thieves and stealers of churches. Whereto the King replied, 'In truth that was what the Bishop sought to do, but you withstood him manfully and defended your Church right well'. And calling the magnates who were then present, he began to tell how the Bishop sought to seize a church of the Bishopric of St. David and to dedicate it, and how the Bishop excommunicated the Archdeacon when he withstood him, and how the Archdeacon with no less boldness forthwith excommunicated the Bishop, whereat all who were then at court and heard the tale laughed loud and long. For the King had been told that each had excommunicated the other by name. Wherefore the Archdeacon marvelled greatly that the King had already got knowledge of the affair, and also that any man should have reached the King sooner than himself, who had travelled at great speed, unless indeed it be that, since rumour does in truth fly on wings to kings and princes, from whom scarce anything may be hid, notable events are ever quick to reach them. But enough of this. Before, however, we speak either of the death of David, Bishop of Mynyw, or of the election or substitution of another, there are certain things which happened a little before which must not be passed over in silence.

[1] *uentam.* An unknown word; but the sense is clear from the context.

DE REBUS A SE GESTIS

CHAPTER VIII

How the Canons of Mynyw approached both the King and the Legate Hugo concerning the dignity of their Church

SINCE about the close of Easter Uguccione[1], Cardinal of Sant'Angelo, then Legate in England, had summoned a general council of the whole realm at London, the Archdeacons of Mynyw and the more discreet of the Canons came to London to protest and, if possible, to establish before the Cardinal the rightful claim of their Church to be of metropolitan rank. For since the Bishop had at his consecration sworn to have nothing to do with that dispute, he was unwilling to come in contravention of his solemn oath, even though it had been extorted from him. But first to try the King's mind in this matter and to discover whether he could be moved to consent, they offered both himself and his counsellors a great sum of money, and after they had spent much labour on the business, since the King was slow to reply, they at length received this answer, that the King would never suffer it in his time nor set up a head for rebellion against England by giving the Welsh an Archbishop. On hearing this, they did what they could and in public audience protested the rights of their Church and its former dignity in the presence of the Legate. But the Legate's council was brought to naught by the quarrel of the two Archbishops, Richard of Canterbury and Roger of York, concerning precedence and the Primacy.

[1] Ugo Pierleone.

NOMINATED FOR BISHOPRIC OF MYNYW

CHAPTER IX

Concerning Bishop David, who died soon after, and the nomination of Giraldus

But a little later, their Bishop having died about fifteen days before Pentecost[1], the Canons assembled at Mynyw, in order that they might discuss in common the election of a new Shepherd. Wherefore entering their Church and Chapter, and having closed and barred the doors, after a long sitting and an unusually protracted debate, they at last agreed unanimously to nominate their four Archdeacons, since their Church had no more than these four nor any greater dignitaries than these, that the King might choose whomsoever he desired, and that this man should afterwards be formally elected to the vacancy in preference to the rest. And forthwith, as though they had made a lawful choice of a single individual, they broke into a loud hymn of praise[2], prompted thereto by impulse rather than design. For although they nominated more than one in deference to the King's honour, yet they had the strongest hope and confidence that Giraldus would be chosen over the heads of the others, since they were all obscure men both in fame and fortune; this was the Canons' sole intent and this their sole expectation. And the people, who stood without and heard the hymn, began to cry out all together that Giraldus alone of all was chosen and alone was most worthy to be so chosen, though he had not yet entered on his thirtieth year[3]. But on the same night Giraldus pondered within his heart, and, thinking that in this matter they had proceeded with excessive haste and unwisdom, since in the realm of England it is not customary to nominate or elect without first approaching

[1] May 23rd, 1176. [2] *alta uoce* omitted by Brewer. [3] See p. 35.

the King or his Justiciar, announcing the death of the Bishop to him and securing his assent, he entered the Chapter in the morning and before them all he refused the nomination, though every man among them was filled with wonder and sought to dissuade him. But he declared that he did not desire in any wise to fail his Church nor to prevent its making its free and lawful choice, provided always that things were done in due order. And forthwith the rumour of this affair flew to the King, alleging that the election was made and that the choice had beyond all doubt fallen on Giraldus the Archdeacon. Now when the King heard this it seemed to him that the thing had been done contrary to the custom of the realm and to the great injury of himself, and he was very hot with anger and straightway ordered that all the Canons should be deprived of their lands and revenues. He swore also that as they had given him no part in their election or nomination, even so should they be deprived of any part or share in the promotion to the See. But he directed his anger and indignation more especially against Giraldus the Archdeacon, both because he was commonly asserted[1] to have been elected by them all, and also because he had no fear that any rebellion or protest would be raised in the Church of Mynyw save by him alone; for not only did he excel all the rest in clerkship and in courage, but he was also of high lineage, being the kinsman of all the princes and great men in Wales.

---

[1] *et uulgo dicebatur* omitted by Brewer.

HE IS REJECTED BY THE KING

CHAPTER X

Concerning the commendation of Giraldus before the King

BUT meanwhile Richard, Archbishop of Canterbury, and almost all his suffragans being assembled in the presence of the King, the latter consulted them concerning the appointment of a Bishop to the Church of Mynyw. Now when they inquired among themselves whether some suitable person could be found within that church (for the right procedure is that a man should be chosen from the church itself, if one worthy may be found therein), at length all the Bishops agreed upon Giraldus, Archdeacon of that same Church, because he was a man of great learning and born in lawful wedlock. And after others had been heard, the Archbishop likewise supported Giraldus and added that he was not only an excellent clerk but that he was also a man of boundless courage and energy. But the King who had listened patiently and attentively to all the others, when he heard the Archbishop say this, made answer to him thus, since he thought that his words carried greater weight and authority than those of the rest: 'It is neither necessary nor expedient for King or Archbishop that a man of great honesty or vigour should be Bishop in the Church of St. David, for fear lest the crown of England or the See of Canterbury should suffer loss thereby.' And so, dissolving the council, the King in greater privacy revealed his opinion to the Archbishop and others in whom he placed especial trust, namely that the Archdeacon was not a safe man to set over the See of Mynyw, because he was akin by blood to Rhys, Prince of South Wales, and almost all the other great men of Wales; nor was it expedient by the promotion of such a man, so honest and of such high birth, to give new strength to the Welsh

DE REBUS A SE GESTIS

and increase their pride. And when Roger, Bishop of Worcester, a man of virtuous and praiseworthy memory, secretly revealed these things to the Archdeacon, he said that he ought to value such a testimony to his merits before such an audience more than the best of Bishoprics, not to speak of such a poor See as that of Mynyw.

CHAPTER XI

Concerning the promotion of Peter to the Bishopric and how Giraldus dissuaded him from abjuring the just rights of the Church of Mynyw

THEREFORE, whereas all the Canons and Archdeacons, to recover their revenues and hold them in peace, bowed themselves wholly to the King's will and for their common support took pay from his treasury[1] that they might at the King's bidding be able to follow him from place to place for the election of a bishop, nonetheless Giraldus, as though 'fearing the Greeks even when gifts they bring'[2] alone of all of them would not accept anything for himself; but approaching now the Archbishop, and now the Legate, laboured for the liberty of his own Church that, even if they could not obtain one from the body[3] of their Church, they might at least succeed with the King's consent in obtaining from among its members an honest man, neither unknown nor ignorant of the language of their fathers. At length, however, the Legate, who had at first promised his help, failed him utterly, and his own Church

---

[1] The context seems to indicate that *fiscus* denotes the private treasury of the King, which he carried with him.
[2] Virgil, *Aen.* II, 49.
[3] i.e. from the Canons, the 'members' being priests from the diocese outside the Chapter.

BISHOP PETER DE LEIA

gave way, every man of them, out of cowardice; and when at last the Canons were assembled in the King's presence at Winchester, the King offered them a monk of the Cluniac order, namely the Prior of Wenlock, a man known not even to one of them either by face or fame. With a very quavering hymn of praise they elected him on the spot, even in the King's chamber before his bed, he himself being present with his guards and commanding them to do his bidding after the manner of the English tyrants. And when the Bishop Elect (and Elect in such a manner!) whose name was Peter[1], came to London on the appointed day to be consecrated, Giraldus, omitting naught that should be done, did what he could for the honour and security of his Church. Both by letters and by messengers he urged the Bishop Elect, whose face he had not yet seen, that he should not presume to make any profession or submission, save in general terms, that might be contrary to the dignity of the Church to which he had been assigned rather than called; and above all, on behalf of God and of St. David, he was at pains to prevent him from taking any oath carrying with it the abjuration of the rights of his Church. But the Bishop, being of the King's planting and creation, obeyed the King's will in all things, gave a solemn oath that he would not pursue the Church of Mynyw's claims to Metropolitan rank, and so received his consecration.

---

[1] Peter de Leia, consecrated Nov. 7th, 1176.

BOOK II

CHAPTER I

Concerning the deeds of his manhood and prime

AFTER these achievements Giraldus, 'thinking naught done, while aught remained to do'[1] nor ever looking back, but continually pressing forward and mounting higher with unfaltering step, that his knowledge might be increased and ripened, resolved, having collected his treasure-store of books, to cross the sea to France and once more to apply himself with all his heart and soul to the study of the liberal arts at Paris, that thus he might have power upon the foundation of arts and letters to raise high the walls of civil and canon law and above them to complete the sacred roof of theological learning, and finally to secure this triple edifice with bonds that time should not destroy. When therefore he had for many years applied his studious spirit first to the Imperial and then to the Pontifical Constitutions, and finally to the Holy Scriptures, he won such popularity by his exposition of the Decretals, which they were accustomed to discuss on Sundays, that on the day on which it was known in the city that he desired to discourse, the pleasure of listening to his voice drew such a gathering of almost all the teachers together with their scholars, that scarce even the largest hall could contain his audience. For he reasoned on civil and canon law in such lively fashion and so enhanced his exposition with all the persuasions of rhetoric and adorned it with figures and flowers of speech as well as with profound argument, and made such apt use of the sayings of the philosophers and other authors by the wondrous art with which he applied them to appropriate topics,

[1] *Lucan* II, 657.

GIRALDUS RETURNS TO PARIS

that the more learned and expert his audience, the more eagerly and attentively they applied their ears and minds to drink in his words and fix them in their memory. For they were so drawn and charmed by the sweetness of his words, that they hung upon his lips as he spoke, however long and protracted his discourse ... and were never weary nor could hear enough of his eloquence. Wherefore numbers of students used to take down his lectures word by word just as they fell from his lips, and strove with great eagerness to take them to heart. But on a certain day, when a great throng had come to hear him, so soon as he ceased to speak and a murmur of praise and applause arose from all the multitude, a famous doctor who had read at Paris in the arts and studied for a long time at Bologna in the laws, a certain Master Roger, a Norman who afterwards was Dean of the Church of Rouen, burst out suddenly as follows: 'There is no knowledge under the sun, which brought to Paris does not acquire incomparable strength, of an excellence that may not be found elsewhere in all the world.' And I have thought it not beside the mark here to set down the prelude of this discourse, which began as follows.

CHAPTER II

The beginning and prelude of Giraldus's first discourse

'I HAD proposed to hear before I was heard, to learn before I spoke, and to doubt before I argued. For to learned ears and to men of the highest eloquence the oration which I am about to deliver will seem poor in thought and in language lean and meagre, and it is no less useless and superfluous to utter that which is arid before an audience of orators than to produce that which

DE REBUS A SE GESTIS

is trite before an audience of philosophers and sages. Hence spring the sayings of the moral Seneca and after him Sidonius, who writes, "Until our nature has drunk in knowledge, there is no greater glory in saying what you know than in keeping silence concerning that which you do not know".[1] But since, as Augustine bears witness,[2] "Vile is the part that agrees not with the whole", that I may not seem an anomaly among you and by reason of my silence be found a disciple of Pythagoras beyond compare, I have chosen rather to make myself ridiculous by speaking than by keeping silence to appear a churl. What sound then shall the noisy goose utter among melodious swans?[3] Shall he set forth what is new or what is known to all? Things well-worn and trite awaken scorn, while novelties lack authority; for as Pliny[4] says, "It is a hard task to give novelty to that which is old, authority to that which is new, gloss to that which is well worn, grace to things contemptible, light to things obscure, truth to that which is doubtful, and naturalness to everything". The question which we have before us is old, but not yet too old; the controversy had often been ventilated, but is still undecided[5]'. For the question propounded was 'Whether a judge should give judgment according to what is alleged by witnesses or according to his own conscience'. And on the latter limb of this dilemma, which is by far the most difficult of proof, he brought to bear such cogent reasons drawn from the civil and canon law that all were filled with wonder and knew not whether greater praise should be given to the ornateness of his language, or to the force of his reflections and arguments. So great indeed was their wonder that a

---

[1] Giraldus seems to attribute the quotation both to Sidonius and to Seneca; the words however come from Sidonius (*Ep.* VII, ix. 5). The only passage in Seneca that seems to have any bearing here is in *Ep.* LII, 10, where he alludes to the five years' silence imposed by Pythagoras on his pupils; see below.
[2] *Conf.*, III. 8.   [3] Cp. *Virg. Ecl.* IX. 36.   [4] *Plin. Nat. Hist. Praef.* 15.
[5] Cp. *Hor. Ars. Poet.* 78.

HIS SUCCESS AS A LECTURER IN LAW

man of noble birth, a Canon of the Church of Paris and son of the castellan of Montmorency, who a little later was made Dean of the said Church, being a man quick to learn and eager in the pursuit of the knowledge of letters, spoke privately to Giraldus, as he left the hall, where he had been with many others, and asked him how many years he had given to the study of the laws and canons at Bologna. And on receiving the reply that he had never been at Bologna, he asked him again where he had studied law; and when he learned from him that he had given but three years to the study,[1] and that only at Paris, he departed, marvelling much. And the teacher of Giraldus in that faculty, whom he visited after breakfast, spoke to him as follows in his lecture room where there were many present, applauding and congratulating so distinguished a pupil on the glory that he had won: 'In truth I would not for an action of a hundred sous,' (he spoke after the fashion of those at Bologna) 'that you had failed to speak thus excellently to-day before such a vast assembly of scholars.' For, as Jerome says,[2] the success of their pupils is the greatest honour and glory that teachers may win. It also happened that Master Matthew of Anjou, whose discourses on the laws and decrees Giraldus used to attend, being summoned by Pope Alexander III to the Lateran Council that he might be made a cardinal when he was taking leave of his comrades in his lecture room, advised them earnestly to make Master Giraldus their lecturer and teacher in his place; and this he did with much commendation of his talents. But though all the scholars were eager in their demand that he should do so, he none the less refused their request, since he proposed shortly to visit Bologna that he might yet further improve his knowledge in that faculty. Yet at

---

[1] The normal course was three years on civil law and three on the Decretals.
[2] A reminiscence from Jerome, *in Ezek.* xiii. c. 45.

DE REBUS A SE GESTIS

their urgent entreaty he daily gave two lectures in his house to his comrades on the decrees of Gratian, one dealing with the 'Distinctions', the other with special cases.[1]

CHAPTER III

How the Canons of Mynyw protested the rights of the dignity of their Church at the Lateran Council

I HAVE thought good here to insert an account of the following event, how in the Lateran Council,[2] which took place about this time, the Canons of Mynyw, when their Bishop, though present, yet on account of his wicked and pernicious oath[3] kept silence, themselves openly and publicly protested the Metropolitan rights of their Church, making a synodal declaration in that great assembly. Wherefore, when Master Gerard, surnamed *La pucelle* and afterwards Bishop of Coventry, returned to Paris from the Council, to which he had been sent by Richard, Archbishop of Canterbury, he reported to Master Giraldus, among other things which had taken place at the Council, that the Canons of Mynyw had spoken there with great boldness and arrogance, in that august gathering protesting and proclaiming, both for themselves and for their Church, the Metropolitan rights which were their lawful due, most urgently demanding that judges should be given them to try the matter that a commission should be granted for the purpose. But since their Bishop, who was present, made no mention of the matter, the business did not at that time go forward.

---

[1] The Distinctions are the chapters or sections of the Decretals. He first interpreted the law and in the second lecture showed its application in special cases.
[2] March 1179.   [3] See I. xi (*ad fin*)

HE RETURNS HOME

CHAPTER IV

How Giraldus returned after long study, and those things which befell him on the way

BUT to return to our theme: after a long stay in the pursuit of his studies[1], Giraldus thinking it time to return to his country, since he had waited long beyond the appointed time for his messengers to bring him money at Paris, and since his creditors, to whom he was deep in debt, were impatient and importunate and pressed for payment more keenly every day, he betook himself, full of grief and anxiety and almost in the last extremity of despair to the Chapel of St. Thomas of Canterbury, which the Archbishop of Rheims, brother of King Louis, had built in the Church of St. Germain l'Auxerrois on the occasion of his canonization as a Martyr[2]. Thither he went with his companions as a last refuge that he might devoutly implore the aid of the Martyr to save him from his troubles; for he knew that, as Philo the wise has said, that when human aid fails, man must turn to the succour that comes from God[3]. And after hearing solemn celebration of mass in honour of the Martyr and making his oblation, he straightway received from heaven the reward of his devoutness. For in the same hour he received his messengers who brought him both joy and prosperity, thanks to God's wondrous dispensation, who from the things of this world, proceeding in their natural course, brings forth[4] praise for His saints and wills that the gifts, which are known to proceed solely from His grace, should yet be, as it were, obtained by prayer and merit. So he went on his way toward England and, when in the week of Pentecost he came to

[1] From end of 1176 to summer of 1179, approximately. [2] 1173.
[3] This quotation is clearly derived from *Hug. Flor.* p. 48; see *Girald, R.S.* 8, pp. 66, 67. [4] *laudem elicit.* The verb is omitted by Brewer.

Arras and was lodged on the market-place, there was a great stir in the city. For Philip, Count of Flanders, being then in the city, caused a quintain to be set up in the market-place, a great square in the midst of the town; now a quintain is a strong shield hung securely to a beam, whereon aspirants for knighthood and stalwart youths mounted on galloping chargers may try their strength by breaking their lances or piercing the obstacle — a prelude this to the exercises of knighthood. And Giraldus, who looked on from a lofty gallery in his lodgings (and would that he had been able to look down upon their sport as mere vanity!) saw the Count himself, and with him such a multitude of noble knights and barons, so many a fine horse galloping at the shield and so many lances broken, that, though he diligently watched each several thing, he could not sufficiently wonder at the whole. But when the sport had lasted about an hour and all that great space had been filled with such a throng of nobles, the Count suddenly departed, all his companions dispersed, and where a little while ago such pomp was visible, now neither man nor beast was to be seen nor aught save the market-place utterly deserted. Which in truth is a clear proof, as Giraldus himself is wont to say of these things, and their like, that all things under the sun are subject unto vanity and, as it were, phantasms swiftly passing away, and that all the things of this world endure but for a moment and are gone.

CHAPTER V

How, coming to Canterbury, he condemned those things which he saw in the Convent of the Great Church as deserving of correction

So proceeding on his way, he crossed the Flemish sea and came to Canterbury, where on the day of the Holy

GLUTTONY OF MONKS OF CANTERBURY

Trinity, at the Prior's invitation, he dined in the refectory with the monks of that place. And as he sat there at the high table with the Prior and the seniors, he noted two things, the multitude of the dishes and the excessive superfluity of signs which the monks made to one another. For there was the Prior giving so many dishes to the serving monks, and they in their turn bearing these as gifts to the lower tables; and there were those, to whom these gifts were brought, offering their thanks, and all of them gesticulating with fingers, hands and arms, and whistling one to another in lieu of speaking, all extravagating in a manner more free and frivolous than was seemly; so that Giraldus seemed to be seated at a stage-play or among actors and jesters. It would therefore be more consonant with good order and decency to speak modestly in human speech than with signs and whistlings thus jocosely to indulge in dumb garrulity. And as to the dishes and the number thereof, what shall I say, save that I have oft heard Giraldus himself declare that sixteen very costly dishes or even more were placed upon the table in order, not to say contrary to all order.[1] Finally, potherbs were brought to every table but were little tasted. For you might see so many kinds of fish, roast and boiled, stuffed and fried, so many dishes contrived with eggs and pepper by dexterous cooks, so many flavourings and condiments, compounded with like dexterity to tickle gluttony and awaken appetite. Moreover you might see in the midst of such abundance 'wine and strong drink',[2] metheglin and claret, must, mead and mulberry juice, and all that can intoxicate, beverages so choice that beer, such as is made at its best in England and above all in Kent, found no place among them. There beer among other drinks is as potherbs are among made dishes. Such extreme superfluity and extravagance might you behold both in

[1] *per ordinem . . . praeter ordinem.* [2] *uinum et siceram; Lev.* x. 9.

food and drink, as might not only beget loathing in him that partook thereof, but weariness even in him that beheld it. What would Paul the hermit say to this? What Antony, what Benedict, the father and founder of monastic life? Or what would Jerome say, who in the *Lives of the Fathers* extols with such praise the parsimony, abstinence, and simplicity of the primitive Church, saying among other things that as the Church grew in wealth, so she declined in virtue?[1] Giraldus would also at times recount a story, how the monks of St. Swithin of Winchester together with their Prior prostrated themselves in the mud before Henry II, and complained to him with tears and lamentations that Bishop Richard whom they had as their head in lieu of an Abbot, had deprived them of three dishes. And when the King inquired how many dishes were left them, they replied 'ten'. 'And I', said the King, 'am content in my court with three. Perish your Bishop, if he does not reduce your dishes to the number of mine!' 'To what purpose is this waste'[2] more especially in men professing religion and displaying it in their habit? 'For these superfluities might have been sold and given to the poor.' But this is the colour they put upon their behaviour, to wit, that the great number of courses served in their Order was invented for the sake of amplifying and increasing the alms they give to the poor. Nevertheless, scandal might have been better and more wisely avoided and provision made for their honour and simplicity of life, had they been content with fewer dishes and had they refreshed Christ's poor out of those superfluities; and thus they would curb their gluttony, lessen the scandal and increase their alms in a far more salutary way.

But setting out toward London, he found Richard, Archbishop of Canterbury, on certain lands of his not

---

[1] *Vita Malchi*, §1.   [2] Matthew xxvi. 8.

A DIVORCE PREVENTED

far from London, by whom he was welcomed for the night and received with honour as a well-loved friend. But in the morning he received a message that Richard, Bishop of Winchester, proposed on that same day at London by ban of the Church to separate one of his sisters from her husband, to whom she had been married in the diocese of Winchester. He therefore consulted the Archbishop on the matter and forthwith received a letter from him, in which he affectionately asked the Bishop to put off the divorce and not to stand in the way of a reconciliation betwixt husband and wife, if such a thing should be possible. So without delay Giraldus hastened to London, and there in Southwark at the Great Chapter summoned for the purpose he found his sister and her husband already standing before the Bishop and awaiting their divorce, which was on the point of being pronounced. But the Bishop, seeing him enter (whom he knew right well) and his comrades also, with little images of the Blessed Thomas hung about their necks, was filled with wonder at his sudden return; for he knew that he had been long away in France and thought him there still. Then, greeting him with a kiss, he placed him at his right hand and ordered his companions to be made welcome. And when he had read the letter of the Archbishop, which Giraldus had given him,[1] he replied that if the Archdeacon had come by himself without any such letters, he would gladly have heard his petition, yet he did so all the more readily because he had received the Archbishop's commands in respect of this matter. And so, the Chapter being dissolved on account of his unexpected advent and this unlooked-for event,[2] husband and wife, after discord bitter almost past healing, which must have ended in their having to pay a large sum to the Bishop for their divorce, were a little afterwards reconciled by the good

---

[1] *porrectas* (MS.) not *porrectus* (Brewer). [2] *aduentum ... euentum.*

offices of Giraldus. Which thing is a proof that God is ever near us in time of trouble and that no true believer, whatever his peril, need despair of the divine mercy, unless his sins are past forgiveness, and that often 'there comes at length past hope the hour of joy'.[1]

CHAPTER VI

How Giraldus came to Wales and, the Bishop soon after being driven from his diocese, by the Archbishop's commission took charge of the see, and how, to help the Charter of Mynyw, he resigned that office

So when he had traversed England and was come at last into Wales, it chanced not long after that Peter, Bishop of Mynyw, who on account of a quarrel betwixt himself and the Welsh had been driven or rather pretended to have been driven out of Wales, on the advice of the Archbishop of Canterbury committed the general care and custody of the diocese into the hands of Master Giraldus the Archdeacon, giving him full control of all things spiritual and temporal, save only those sacraments that are reserved for bishops alone. When, therefore, he had for a while wisely and modestly governed the Church of Mynyw, the Bishop presumed by letters and messengers from England, where he was residing in a certain monastery, impetuously and without due consideration to suspend some and to excommunicate others of the Canons and Archdeacons of St. David's, without summons or citation, and without their conviction or confession. And when Giraldus desired to set this matter right and could not, but the Bishop, spurning his advice, raged daily with greater violence against them, then

[1] *Hor. Ep.* I, v. 14.

QUARRELS WITH BISHOP PETER

grieving for his Church and filled with compassion he resigned to the Bishop the custody of the diocese which had been committed to him and, staunchly supporting the Chapter, he caused those who had been unlawfully suspended and excommunicated to be lawfully absolved by the Archbishop, and with prudence and discretion defended his Church against the outrageous oppression of the Bishop. Moreover when the Bishop sent a new officer to oppress the Church of Mynyw and the clergy of the country, he caused the clergy to repel him utterly to his great dishonour and to refuse submission. This is a proof of the love and devotion which he showed in such ample measure to his Church, preferring to assist and defend it in his private capacity rather than, when set in power over it, to oppress it or agree with its oppressor.

CHAPTER VII

Of a quarrel between Bishop Peter and Giraldus the Archdeacon, and how peace was made by the Archdeacon on behalf of the Chapter and himself

BUT not long after, a great dispute arose between the Bishop[1] and the Archdeacon, so great indeed that the latter was eager to write to Rome making a formal accusation against the Bishop and striving with all his might to secure his deposition. And though great men sought to make peace between them[2], he (since he set the peace of the Church of Mynyw above all things else) firmly declared that until the Bishop had made his peace with his Church, he would never hear of peace with him. At last, however, on a certain day, about Pentecost, on which the Archdeacon and the Chapter were summoned to a Synod at Mynyw, the last which the

[1] See Appendix II.   [2] Reading *laborarent* for the MS. *laborent*.

Bishop ever held, the Archdeacon then and there succeeded in securing an agreement to the effect that instant restitution should be made of all things which the Bishop had unjustly taken from the Chapter or the Chapter from the Bishop, or Canon from Canon, all parties taking a solemn oath to abide thereby. This done, the Bishop, that the peace between himself and the Archdeacon might be the more secure, there and then restored to him all the lands which he had seized at Llandduw in Brecknock and also certain lands belonging to the prebend of Mathry. But one, Pontius, Archdeacon of Pembroke, since these lands had not yet been effectively delivered, came and spoke secretly with Giraldus, bringing with him Philip de Barri, the Archdeacon's brother, an honest and prudent man, to bear him witness. And he began to point out that, if the matter proceeded farther, the Bishop's table would suffer no small detriment and his revenues would be impaired. Wherefore in all good faith he counselled him for his own interest to provide against this; for, he added, there was no one whom man more hoped to see as the next Bishop than the Archdeacon. But Giraldus replied that this hope should not persuade him to do anything that might hamper the fulfilment of the provisions which had been made so rightly and advantageously. And on this point, though Pontius the Archdeacon and his brother Philip dissuaded him, he was firm — so loyal indeed that a certain good Church of his, to wit, of Llanwnda had then among other possessions been assigned under oath to the Chapter, but none the less at his instance had been given as a canonry to a certain clerk of his own, one Martin of Lawhaden, whom the Bishop had instituted with the consent of the Chapter, which Church would in process of time return to the common use. He also asserted that, even if he had already been consecrated Bishop, he would not fail to do this, since,

ARCHDEACON'S YOUTHFUL BEAUTY

though it had come to pass to his own loss, he placed the common interests far above his own. This then is a proof past all doubt, that Giraldus the Archdeacon was most zealous to do what seemed to him right and was filled with a burning desire to secure the tranquillity of his Church.

After these events he visited Ireland with his brother Philip in 1183 (Exp. Hib. II, 20).

To the same period, probably a little earlier, belongs the following story from the Speculum Ecclesiae (R.S. IV, p. 104). *It cannot be later than 1183, since Serlo was no longer Abbot of L'Aumône in 1184* (cp. Gallia Christiana VIII, 1398), *nor can it be earlier than 1180, since Baldwin only became Bishop of Worcester in that year.*

Serlo's praise of Giraldus's youthful beauty has often been quoted, as though it referred to a much earlier date. That a weather-beaten Archdeacon should have preserved his youthful charms to the age, at the earliest of 35, is certainly surprising. It is just conceivable that Giraldus, writing more than 30 years after the event may have confused this with some incident of Serlo's earlier visit to Gloucester (see below).

Moreover, Baldwin, afterwards Archbishop of Canterbury[1], having been promoted from being Abbot[2] to be Bishop of Worcester, since I was travelling from the midlands to the march and border of Wales, hearing that the Bishop was at his manor of Blockley not far from my road, I turned aside to visit him; for I was known to him and he loved me well. And he received me with liberality and kindness and I stayed with him for two days and was shown much honour. Now I was then a young man and remarkable for beauty of face and form, a boon of nature that endures but for a moment and is gone. And when he called me to sit by

[1] 1184. [2] Of Ford, a Cistercian Abbey in Devon.

him, a certain Abbot of the Cistercian order, Serlo[1] by name, who was seated on the other side and had received the Bishop's welcome a little before, after gazing at me for a while on my coming thither, said, 'Think you that such youthful beauty could ever die?' — words which, brief as they were, none the less moved me deeply ... (*a hiatus in the MS.*) Now there was being read aloud in the presence of the Abbot and the Bishop, when I came upon them, a certain treatise concerning the Cross, which the Bishop — though I then knew it not — had composed for the canons of Waltham at their instance — for they enjoyed the privilege, unique in England, of possessing relics of the Cross. The reading being done and having received from the Abbot the praise which it deserved, I asked the Bishop in a low voice by whom the book was written; and he, that he might not seem boastfully to ascribe the authorship to himself nor falsely attribute it to another, murmured confusedly between his lips some words which were neither audible nor intelligible.

Then, after the reading, there ensued a serious and sober conversation between them on divers topics, and among them they fell to speaking of the Cluniac Order and the Black monks. Whereupon the Abbot openly and positively asserted that he would far sooner die and would await the stroke of death with greater confidence if he were a black mastiff than if he were a Black monk! ... But the Bishop when he heard this cried, 'Peace, brother, peace. Speak not so loud against that holy Order, in which there are so many holy men'. For the Bishop was a man of dove-like simplicity, in all things showing an innocent kindliness both in word and deed; nor would he ever open his lips to say aught that might wrong or offend any man ... But the Abbot spoke thus out of the fullness of his heart; for he knew the sins

---

[1] Abbot of L'Aumône (1171) a Cistercian Abbey in France; see p. 140.

THE STORY OF ABBOT SERLO

of those monks right well, having lived long with them and having removed himself to another Order that his character might not be defiled by their company.... Now on the third day after I had come and on the second of the week, having taken leave of the Bishop and received his blessing, we travelled together in joyous company to Evesham, passing over the Cotswold hills; and we beguiled our journey by talk on many things, at last falling to discuss why he had left his first Order and transferred himself to another. And of this he gave the reason at once, namely that he might the more effectively win his home in heaven, the crown incorruptible and the palm of victory by pursuing the narrow way that leadeth to life everlasting.[1] I asked him also whether it was due to excessive abstinence and immoderate mortification of the flesh that he had now become so lean and wasted, whereas when he wore his former habit in his first Order he was so well fleshed and corpulent. For as I then told him, long ago when I was in the years of boyhood and the days of my green youth studying in the Abbey of St. Peter at Gloucester under that most learned scholar Master Haimon, during the abbacy of Amelin the Frenchman ... (*a hiatus in the MS. makes the exact circumstances of what follows obscure. It is not clear whether Giraldus had seen Serlo at Gloucester or had only heard of him from Haimon*) ... He was then wearing the Cluniac habit and very well fleshed both in face and body. When therefore these two had long discoursed in pleasant and cheerful talk concerning their delightful comradeship when they were in the schools together both in England and in France, at length at their parting they commended themselves devoutly to each other's prayers. And as Serlo was bidding Haimon farewell he concluded his adieus with the ending of a

[1] He was an accomplished poet and certain of his poems, which we may hope belonged to the days preceding his entry even of the Cluniac Order, are far from edifying. See Raby, *Secular Latin Poetry*, II, p. 111.

SPECULUM ECCLESIAE

line of Ovid,[1] 'When we are dead all envy is at rest'. And these words though they were spoken so long ago, the Abbot remembered as though they had only been spoken the day before. But to my question as to his former corpulence and present leanness, he replied that it must not be ascribed to his great abstinence or mortification of the flesh (for he did not wish hypocritically to claim any merit that was not his); but that when he was sent to Brittany a few years before to visit the houses of his Order, as he was preparing to leave a house by a very narrow and low gateway, being mounted on a large and powerful horse, the beast made a rush to get out; and since he was holding the reins carelessly and failed to pull him in, he was badly crushed between the upper lintel and the saddle and as soon as he got outside fell from the horse to the ground as though dead, many of his ribs being broken and the blood gushing violently from mouth, nose, eyes and ears and all the windows of his head. And when after a long trance, the very image of death ... he at length recovered his senses, he could scarce summon back his vital spirits to control his limbs, his sinews and bones being enfeebled to the very marrow and his whole body so weak and withered, that the doctors were with one accord of the opinion that he had fallen into an incurable decline ... So he was wont to declare in his utter weariness of such a life that he 'would sooner die than lead a life of death'.[2]

Moreover, whereas in the days of his youth he at times took pride in his tall stature and the care and cultivation of his flesh, perchance being enslaved to the desires thereof, now he most patiently endured the suffering of that same flesh and the affliction which God in his mercy had sent upon him for his salvation, weeping past sins with penitence unceasing, and with devout heart

[1] *Am.* I, xv, 39.
[2] A hexameter. Both Serlo and Giraldus were poets: the line may be due to either.

GIRALDUS THE KING'S CLERK

acknowledging the mercy of his Father in heaven, until at last, by the grace of God, he was able to find joy in life once more.

CHAPTER VIII

How the Archdeacon became a follower of the Court

Now, as the fame of Giraldus increased and became more widely known from day to day, King Henry II, who was then in the March intent upon the pacification of Wales, summoned him to him on the advice of his magnates; and although he was most unwilling (for as he values the scholar's life above all others, even so he detests the life of a courtier), yet by reason of the King's urgency and also of his promises and commands, he at length became a follower of the Court, and the King's clerk. When therefore for several years he had rendered faithful service by following the Court and had been of great assistance in the pacification of Wales, none the less on account of his kinship with Rhys ap Gruffydd and other princes of Wales, he received of the King, who enriched and promoted so many unworthy persons, nothing save empty promises void of all truth. Yet in secret the King praised him mightily in the presence of his counsellors and approved his character, his self-restraint, his modesty and his fidelity, saying that, if he had not been born in Wales and bound so closely by ties of blood to the magnates of Wales, and more especially to Rhys, he would of his bounty have exalted him by the bestowal of ecclesiastical dignities and rich rewards and would have made him a great man in his kingdom.[1]

---

[1] Probably his service at Court began in 1184. See Lloyd, p. 561, n. 131

DE REBUS A SE GESTIS

CHAPTER IX

Concerning Rhys ap Gruffydd and how Giraldus discoursed with him in the presence of great men

Now it happened that about this time Rhys ap Gruffydd, Prince of South Wales, came to Hereford to meet the messengers of the King, namely, Baldwin, Archbishop of Canterbury, who had now succeeded to Richard,[1] and Ranulph de Glanville, Justiciar of England,[2] that he might parley with them. And when the Prince was sitting at breakfast in the house of the Bishop of Hereford, William de Vere, by whom he had been received with great honour and hospitality, as he sat between the Bishop and Walter FitzRobert, a noble baron and, like the Bishop, of the house of Clare, Giraldus the Archdeacon drew near and standing before them, the table only being between, thus addressed Rhys in courteous jest. 'You have cause for rejoicing, O Rhys, and glad may you well be, that here at this feast you sit between two great men of the great house of Clare, whose inheritance you hold.' For Rhys then held the whole of the land of Cardigan, which he had recovered from Roger, Earl of Clare. But Rhys, being a man of excellent wit and quick in repartee, at once replied, 'It is true that long since we lost our inheritance to the house of Clare; but since we had to lose it, we are glad to have lost it, not at the hands of sluggards of obscure birth, but to men of such high fame and renown'. The Bishop thereupon added, 'And we too are well pleased, since it was our fate to lose the lands we had possessed so long, that they are now held by so good a man and of such high birth as Rhys'. But after the midday sleep, when the day was already declining, the Bishop and the great men

[1] 1184.   [2] Justiciar, 1180-9.

THE LANDS OF THE SONS OF NEST

entered a certain garden-close, taking Rhys with them, and sat down together; and when Giraldus and others came in and sat down, Rhys, giving way to merry speech and jocularity and taking the matter of his words from Giraldus, as though he wished to pay him back for what he had said at breakfast, spoke as follows: 'This Archdeacon and those of his family who are called Giraldines descend from Nest, my aunt, the sister of Gruffydd my father, and are great and good men, but only in a corner of Wales, to wit, in the cantref of Pembroke . . . (*The MS. is clearly defective, since what follows is obviously Giraldus's reply.*) . . . 'Nay, the sons of Nest held seven cantrefs in Wales. The Eldest, William Fitzgerald, held Pembroke and Emlyn;[1] Robert FitzStephen held Cardigan and Cemais; Henry, the King's son, held Narberth and Pebidiog (Dewisland); Maurice held Llanstephan; William Hay held St. Clare, and Howel and Walter held Llanbedr and Velfrey,[2] together with other lands. And the two daughters of Nest, Angharad my mother and Gwladus, were married to the Barons of Rhos and Pembroke. Beside these six or seven barons, she had a son named David, the Bishop of Mynyw, who held episcopal sway over almost all South Wales. Moreover though they held such great portions of Wales, none the less, as their offspring increased, Robert and Maurice, the sons of Nest, with their nephews Raymond and Meilyr and their sons and kinsfolk, crossed the Irish sea and by their valour began the conquest of that Kingdom; and they kept for themselves and their folk thirty cantrefs and more of the Irish realm. . . . Since then the offspring of Nest have held some seven cantrefs in Wales, besides Cardigan of which they once possessed the greater part, and since they acquired thirty or more in Ireland, it cannot be said with truth nor ought it to be said in earnest, that the children of Nest are not to be found save in a corner of

[1] MS. *Ginelin*.   [2] MS. *Welfrei* not *Swelfrei* (Brewer).

DE REBUS A SE GESTIS

Pembroke. But it can be most truly said that the sons of Gruffyd seem not to be found anywhere outside a small portion of South Wales; and whereas they now hold only seven or eight cantrefs therein, they yet claim the whole of the remainder as theirs by hereditary right, but none the less do not either invade the territory of others nor thus far seek to recapture their lost inheritance.'

Now since these things were said before a large audience, in the presence of the Archbishop and Justiciar and the Bishops also and Barons who by now had joined them in considerable numbers, for a brief space Rhys blushed for shame, but being a wise and discreet man, he answered in the same fashion, saying that in truth the descendants of Nest were, both then and now, good men and courageous, and that they had made a great conquest in Ireland, if they could only be sure of keeping what they had got. Now he added this last sally, because these two nations, the Welsh and Irish, feed continually on the hope of recovering all the lands which the English have taken from them. So when the messengers returned to the King and faithfully reported to him, among other things, the words that were spoken at breakfast and the answers that were made in the garden, the story was received with loud laughter, and the King began before them all with many words to commend and magnify Giraldus the Archdeacon for his honesty and prudence, saying that, were he not a Welshman, he would be worthy of high honour. But since 'Honesty is praised, but still goes cold',[1] although Giraldus, single-handed by his own labour and diligence, in addition to many other great services, had turned aside not a few of Rhys's great armies from the King's land, which the prince was preparing to invade, yet he got nothing from the King except such empty praise and flattery and great promises of future reward.

[1] *Juv.* I, 74.

THE EVIL MONKS OF LLANDOVERY

Wherefore, as was told him often by many of the King's counsellors during his life and by yet more after his death, nothing barred his way to high promotion save his nation and his kinship.

To this period also must belong the following story from Spec. Eccl. II (R.S. IV, p. 100).

When I was once sent into Wales by Henry II, King of the English, in the days when I followed the Court, to Rhys ap Gruffydd, Prince of South Wales, and found him in his palace of Llandovery in the province of Cantref Bychan, he himself forthwith, like the kindly and discreet man that he was, came down from the town into a strip of land that surrounded the castle; and when he had heard in full the message of which I was the bearer, and we were turning back, we saw three or four monks not far off seated on a hill within sight of us and waiting that they might by our intervention be reconciled to the Prince whom they had grievously offended, as they had entreated us to do on our coming thither. And when I spoke to him on this matter, he replied that if we had known what manner of men they were and how evil was their living, we should most certainly never have uttered a word on their behalf; he said also that the burgesses of the castle were ready one and all to leave his town and to retire into England, for the sake of their wives and daughters whom these monks frequently and openly abused. He showed us also a young and beardless monk among them, who to make himself chaste had castrated himself a little before that time, but to no purpose; for he asserted that he was notwithstanding far more given to lust and filthiness than all the rest of them. But at our instance and entreaty he granted our request that they might remain there in hope of the reformation that they promised and the mending of their ways. But a little after, since their vice abated not nor was the scandal

DE REBUS A SE GESTIS

removed these monks were one and all cast out, and clerks set in their place, by order of the Prince and of the Bishop of the Diocese.

CHAPTER X

How the Patriarch came to England and how King Henry sent Giraldus with John, the King's son, to Ireland

Now at this time the Patriarch Heraclius of Jerusalem, came to England and offered the keys of that city to the King, humbly requesting, but in vain, that either the King himself would come to defend the land of Jerusalem or that he would send one of his sons, of whom three were still living.[1] But the King would do neither one thing nor the other, but merely despised this messenger and was therefore himself also despised; and forsaking God and by God forsaken (for his glory which thus far had grown continually, from this time forth was turned to shame), he dispatched John with a great array into Ireland, sending with him Master Giraldus, because he had a great host of kinsmen there, sprung from the first conquerors of that nation, and because he himself had shown himself an honest and a prudent man. When, therefore, at Eastertide, his fleet sailing from Pembroke and Milford Haven, John crossed the seas to Ireland and landed at Waterford, he made no headway, for reasons set down by Giraldus in the book of *The Conquest of Ireland*.[2] Now of these causes I have thought it worth while here to insert the three most weighty. The first was that, when he ought rather to have been sent against the Saracens for the succour of the Holy Land, he was sent against Christians. The second that, being himself

[1] 1185. Richard, Geoffrey and John.   [2] *Exp. Hib.*, II, 36.

young and little more than a boy, he followed the counsel of the young men whom he took with him, who were utterly unknown in Ireland and themselves knew nought, whereas he rebuffed the honest and discreet men whom he found there who knew the customs and habits of the country, treating them as though they had been foreigners and of little worth. The third was that he was not disposed to render any honour to God and to His Church in those parts, as was clearly shown by the vision which Giraldus at that time saw and set down in the aforesaid book of the Conquest of Ireland. And yet it was more especially on account of this, to wit, that he might exalt and uplift the Church of Ireland and cause Peter's pence to be paid in that country as in England, that his father obtained leave from the Church of Rome to enter Ireland and subdue it for himself; as is openly declared in the Privilege of Pope Adrian[1] which he obtained concerning this matter....

To the same date belongs the following scene, recorded in the De Principis Instructione (II, 26).

Meanwhile it happened that when the King was hunting in the forest (a pastime in which he took great and frequent delight) and was about to drive the beasts from the woods at Clarendon[2], Henry, Duke of the Saxons, his son-in-law being with him, the author of this book thus addressed him in the hearing of many persons. 'O King, we have seen many visits of great men to England; but greater than all, not only in respect of your honour, but of the honour of the whole realm, we deem that of the Patriarch, both because so great a man has come from such distant lands and because, passing by all the Emperors and Kings of the earth, he has brought such great and glorious tidings to you and to your land.' To which the King made answer as in

[1] Repeated here from *Exp. Hib.* II, 5.   [2] Near Salisbury.

derision of him; for he did not take these words graciously or kindly that were uttered in the hearing of so many: 'If the Patriarch or any others come to us, they seek their own advantage rather than ours.' But the writer, emboldened perhaps by Welsh audacity, rejoined, 'O King, you should regard it great advantage and honour to yourself that you above all the Kings of the earth have alone earned the privilege of being chosen out by him'. But he, as it were turning from jest to earnest, replied, 'The clergy may well call us to arms and peril, since they themselves will receive no blows in the fray nor shoulder any burdens that they can avoid'. And when I heard this, all the high hopes vanished, which I had before conceived with great longing for their fulfilment. For I had hopes that he would redeem Israel in our day; and I call God to witness that I had greatly desired this not only for the retention of the Holy Land and its liberation from the infidel, but also for the honour of the realm and people; and the folk of all England also desired it most fervently.

CHAPTER XI

The Privilege of Pope Adrian

(*This Chapter is omitted as irrelevant save for the conclusion which runs as follows:*)

I HAVE also here appended the vision of Giraldus,[1] with certain things which he wrote by way of preface; and I have given it in his own words, that the vision may win the greater belief. For having brought forward many reasons for the disasters and misfortunes which he had observed with grief, he adduced this as weightier than all the rest. 'Now the greatest of all disasters was this

---
[1] As given in *Exp. Hib.* II, 36.

THE DREAM OF GIRALDUS

that in our new principality we bestowed no new gifts upon the Church, and not only did we deem her unworthy of princely bounty and the honour that was her due, but rather, taking away her lands and possessions forthwith, we strove to mutilate or abolish her former dignities and ancient privileges.'

CHAPTER XII

The Vision of Giraldus

'WHEN therefore I was not a little distressed in my heart concerning all the things which had befallen us, and above all many woeful thoughts rose into my mind concerning this wrong done to our Saviour, on a certain night I beheld in my sleep a vision (begotten it may be by what was left of my waking thoughts), which on the morrow I straightway revealed to John, the venerable Archbishop of Dublin, not without much wonder on the part of both of us. For I seemed to myself to behold the King's son, John, in a green plain, appearing as though he were about to found a church. And when, after the fashion of surveyors, he marked the turf making lines on all sides over the surface of the earth, visibly drawing the plan of a building, at length it became clear that, while the outline of the body or after-part of the church seemed ample enough, the presbytery was disproportionately small and ill-shapen, as though he had purposed to give a large part of the Island to the laity, but a very small portion to the clergy. And when I had argued with him (though all in vain), urging him to enlarge the presbytery and give it a worthier shape, the anxiety with which I strove to persuade him awoke me and banished sleep.' And even as he had done out of the fullness of his heart

DE REBUS A SE GESTIS

in the imaginings of sleep, so often in his waking hours Giraldus spoke to the Earl, giving like counsel, but all in vain.

CHAPTER XIII

How Earl John offered Giraldus two Bishoprics in Ireland and how he refused them

BUT in process of time the Earl gave the Archdeacon the choice of two Bishoprics then vacant, that of Wexford, also called Ferns, and that of Leighlin[1], and when he refused them both, offered him the two Churches and Sees, to be converted into a single diocese, if he were willing to undertake their government. To which he replied, that if he saw that the Earl's intent was to exalt and upraise the Church in Ireland, he would perhaps accept the honour offered him, that he might work with him and help him to that end. But since the Earl's heart was not set on this, he preferred rather to remain a private person than to be placed in power where he could do no good. Seeing then that the Earl made no advance toward that end, but that the state of Ireland was every day the worse for his coming, and considering the many strange and notable things that he observed in that country, things found nowhere else and utterly unknown, he set himself with great zeal and diligent inquiry to collect materials first for his *Topography* and then for his *Conquest of Ireland*, that he might at least by his own labour win some profit or conquest[2] thereby. So when the Earl, after spending the whole summer and part of the winter in Ireland all to no purpose, recrossed the sea and returned to Wales and England, Giraldus was left with Bertram of Verdun, the Seneschal of Ireland,

[1] A village in Co. Carlow   [2] *questum ... conquestum.*

to be his comrade and the witness of his deeds, and remained in the Island to the following Easter, that he might pursue his studies more fully, not merely gathering materials, but setting them in order.

Now when in the middle of Lent, to wit, at 'Laetare Jerusalem,'[1] John, Archbishop of Dublin, was holding a council in the Church of the Holy Trinity, having called together the suffragans of the province of Dublin, on the first day the Archbishop himself preached a sermon on the Sacraments of the Church; and on the second day Albinus, the Abbot of Balkinglas, who was afterwards Bishop of Ferns, preached at greater length on the continence of the clergy, heaping all the blame in this matter on the clergy who had come from Wales and England to Ireland, and setting forth how pure and blameless had been the life of the clergy of Ireland, until catching the contagion from the newcomers they themselves had been corrupted, since manners are formed by intercourse and 'he who touches pitch shall be defiled thereby'[2]. Moreover, to crown their confusion, when the sermon was finished, our clergy of Wexford accused each other continually before the Archbishop and the whole council, concerning the concubines whom they had publicly kept and taken to their homes and wedded with all ceremony; whereupon the Archbishop by the advice of Giraldus urged that witnesses should be summoned and heard against the accused, that justice might be publicly done without delay; whereupon, after hearing the evidence, the Irish clergy convicted them with much mockery and insult, while the Archbishop, to check the insults of the Irish and to prove that such impurity and lawlessness were displeasing to himself, passed sentence at once on those who had been convicted and suspended them from all office or benefice in the Church. And on the third day he ordered Giraldus to preach; and he,

[1] The *Introit* for the fourth Sunday in Lent.   [2] Ecclesiasticus xiii. 1.

taking pastoral duty as his theme, began by saying all that might be said with truth in praise of the Irish clergy, then proceeded to speak of their vices and excesses, more especially censuring them all for the sin of drunkenness, and finally turning to their prelates, by irrefutable arguments convicted them of carelessness and negligence in their pastoral duties. Wherefore I have thought it not beside the mark here to insert in the same words the portion of the sermon which is to be found in the last book of the *Topography of Ireland*.[1]

CHAPTER XIV

The sermon of Giraldus in the Council at Dublin

Now in respect of religion the clergy of this land are sufficiently to be commended, and among the divers virtues in which they excel, chastity is pre-eminent and outstanding. Also they are most vigilant in respect of Psalms and Hours, in reading and in prayer; and, keeping themselves within the precincts of the church, they do not neglect the divine offices with the performance of which they are charged. They indulge also to no small extent in abstinence and fasting, so that commonly most of them fast even to twilight, until they have fulfilled all the offices of the hours of the day. But would that after these long fasts they were as sober as they are late, as faithful as they are strict, as pure as they are austere,[2] and that they were such in reality as they are in seeming. For among so many thousands you will scarce find one, who after this unceasing instancy in prayer and fasting does not make up for the labours of the day by drinking

---
[1] *Top. Hib.* III, 27-39, interrupted by a passage from III, 19.
[2] *tam sobrii quam seri, tam ueri quam seueri, tam puri quam duri.*

wine and other liquors at night to an extent beyond all bounds of seemliness. And so, dividing the twenty-four hours into two equal parts and dedicating the hours of light to the spirit and the hours of night to the flesh, even as during the day they indulge in the works of light, so also in the darkness they turn to the works of darkness. Wherefore we may well marvel that, where wine has dominion, Venus has no dominion . . . Yet there are some of them who are most excellent and most upright without such leaven of excess. For all this people is immoderate in the most part of its actions and most violent in every passion. Wherefore, as the bad are most wicked (and nowhere may worse be found), so you will not anywhere find more praiseworthy persons among them that are good. But among the oats and tares there is little wheat. You will find many that are called, but few chosen, little grain, but much chaff. And among the Bishops and Prelates, I find this especially worthy of blame, that they are exceeding slothful and negligent in the correction of a people whose transgressions are so extravagant. Therefore, because they neither preach nor chide, now in my preaching I proclaim that they themselves deserve chiding. Because they accuse not, therefore I accuse; because they are slow to blame, therefore I blame. For, as Gregory says, whosoever rises to the priesthood, undertakes the duty of a herald.[1] Therefore if a priest knows not how to preach, how shall a dumb herald cry aloud? For if the Prelates from the days of Patrick, through so many rolling years had manfully, as their office demands, given themselves to preaching and instruction and likewise to rebuke and chiding, then would they have rooted out some of the great enormities of the nation and assuredly have set some stamp of virtue and religion upon them, more particularly seeing the especial need there was of good

---

[1] *Past. Cur.* II, 4.

DE REBUS A SE GESTIS

Prelates and good preachers. For that we may not omit all mention of the perjury and treachery, the thefts and robberies in which the people with few exceptions so outrageously indulge, nor of their divers vices and most unnatural filthinesses (as are set forth in the *Topography*)[1] this nation is the foulest, the most sunk in vice, the most uninstructed in the rudiments of the faith of all nations upon earth. For they do not yet pay tithes or first-fruits, nor yet wed within the bonds of matrimony. They shrink not from incest, nor do they frequent the Church of God with due reverence. Nor do their priests catechize the children, as they should, at the church door, nor do they honour the bodies of their dead according to the rites of the Church with the obsequies that are their due. Nay, further, a thing which is most detestable and most contrary not only to the faith, but to any form of virtue, in many places brothers, I will not say, wed the wives of brothers but take them over,[2] knowing them foully and incestuously, in this not cleaving to the core of the Old Testament, but only to the outer rind, and desiring to imitate the men of old in their vices rather than their virtues. There has, therefore, never been a Prelate among them to 'lift up his voice as a trumpet';[3] not one to rise up against them and 'set himself as a hedge for the house of Israel';[4] not one to fight for the Church of Christ, which he won for Himself with His most precious blood, nor to suffer banishment, much less shed his blood for her sake. Wherefore all the Saints of these lands are Confessors and there is not a Martyr among them; a thing which it will be hard to find in any other Christian realm. It is, therefore, a marvel that in a nation so exceeding cruel and thirsty for

---

[1] From this point to 'rather than their virtues' comes from *Top. Hib.* III, 19 (except 'nor do their priests ... are their due'). The text then returns to *Top. Hib.* III, 28.
[2] *non dico ducunt sed traducunt, immo uerius seducunt.*
[3] Isaiah lviii. 1.   [4] Ezekiel xiii. 5.

blood the faith that was founded long ago is continually so lukewarm that no crown of martyrdom has ever been won in the service of Christ's Church. And so there has never been found in Ireland one bold enough to cement the foundations of the rising Church with his blood, no, not one! For there are shepherds who seek not to feed, but to be fed; there are Prelates who desire not to profit their flocks, but to rule; there are Bishops who care naught for the essence of their office, but only for the name, and seek the title, while they shun the burden it should entail. Therefore the Prelates of this land, following ancient custom, keep within the precincts of their churches and for the most part indulge in contemplation alone, wherein they are so delighted with the beauty of Rachel, that they scorn the sore eyes of Leah.[1] And so it comes to pass that they do not preach the word of God to the people nor tell them of their sins nor uproot their vices nor ingraft the virtues in the flock that is committed to their charge. For since almost all the Prelates of Ireland are chosen from monasteries to be clerks, they sedulously perform all the duties that beseem a monk, but neglect almost all such as beseem a clerk or prelate. Caring always for themselves and anxious for themselves alone, they negligently omit to be anxious for their flock, or put by their anxiety to another day ...[2]

'But it is wonderful, when there have always been so many careless of the salvation of those subject to them, that so many of them are regarded as Saints in the land and are devoutly honoured and venerated, as such, by the inhabitants. Whence it is certain that one of two conclusions must be true: for either it is proved by those that have written concerning the Saints, both as regards the duties of the pastoral office and for our

[1] Genesis xxix. 17.
[2] A number of quotations, mainly from *St. Jerome*, with which Giraldus emphasizes his point, are here omitted.

DE REBUS A SE GESTIS

instruction concerning many other things of diverse nature, that much is sent upon us to affright us and that, since 'the earth is full of the mercy of the Lord',[1] there is more to hope from his clemency than there is to fear from his justice; or else rather that the Church Militant is deceived in many things, whereas the Church Triumphant is never put to scorn. Wherefore there are some whom the Church Militant receives and the Church Triumphant despises ... The latter also not undeservedly honours many among the elect, whom the former none the less wholly ignores. For some seem to be within the fold who are cast out, and others to be cast out who are none the less within. For that which is exalted in the sight of men is often abominable in the sight of God, while the contrary also is not seldom true.'

CHAPTER XV

Concerning the confusion of the Irish clergy and the exultation of our own

WHEN the sermon was ended, there arose a murmur of applause from our clergy. It was not as it had been the day before, since now the tables were turned; the Irish clergy were covered with much confusion, while ours lifted up their heads, insulting their foes and exulting in their own victory. And on the same day, when Felix, Bishop of Ossory, a monk and a eunuch, was supping with the Archbishop, and the latter asked him what he thought of the Archdeacon's sermon, he replied that he spoke much evil well. 'He called us drunkards,' he said, 'and in truth I could hardly restrain myself from flying at him or at least giving a very sharp answer in retaliation for what he had said.'

[1] Ps. xxxiii. 5.

GIVES THREE DAYS' READING AT OXFORD

The Archbishop of Cashel also commented on the sermon. 'Henceforth Ireland will have plenty of martyrs,' he said.[1]

CHAPTER XVI

Concerning the composition of the Topography of Ireland *and its reading at Oxford in England*

So having won great name and fame in the island, between Easter and Pentecost Giraldus crossed the seas from Ireland to Wales, where he turned his whole mind to the completion of the *Topography of Ireland*, which he had already begun. And when in process of time the work was finished and corrected, not wishing to place the candle which he had lit under a bushel, but to lift it aloft on a candlestick[2] that it might shine, he determined to read it before a great audience at Oxford, where of all places in England the clergy were most strong and pre-eminent in learning. And since his book was divided into three parts, he gave three consecutive days to the reading, a part being read each day. On the first day he hospitably entertained the poor of the whole town whom he gathered together for the purpose; on the morrow he entertained all the doctors of the divers Faculties and those of their scholars who were best known and best spoken of; and on the third day he entertained the remainder of the scholars together with the knights of the town and a number of the citizens. It was a magnificent and costly achievement, since thereby the ancient and authentic times of the poets were in some manner revived, nor has the present age seen nor does any past age bear record of the like.

[1] Cp. *Top. Hib.* III, 32.   [2] Matthew v. 15.

DE REBUS A SE GESTIS

CHAPTER XVII

Of the taking of the Cross in England, both Peter, Bishop of Mynyw and the Archdeacon Giraldus being signed therewith

ABOUT that time the land of Jerusalem[1] having been conquered by the pagans and Parthians under the leadership of Saladin, Richard, Count of Poitou, was the first of all princes this side of the Alps to be signed with the Cross, and King Henry, following the example of his son, took the Cross together with Philip, King of the French, at Gisors in the presence of and at the persuasion of the Bishop of Tyre. After a brief stay in Normandy the King came to England about the first day of February and straightway summoned a council in the neighbourhood of Northampton at Geddington.[2] There Baldwin, Archbishop of Canterbury, preached and displayed the sign of the Cross, and Gilbert, Bishop of Rochester, also delivered a sermon and, the King also labouring to the same end, the magnates of England, both clergy and laity, there took the Cross upon their shoulders. But that he might allure and bind good men of Wales as well as of England to the service of the Cross, the King sent Baldwin, Archbishop of Canterbury, to the land of Wales. And, about Ash Wednesday, he came with Ranulph de Glanville, who had been sent with him, to Hereford, and entered Wales by Radnor, there meeting Rhys ap Gruffydd and many of the chief men of Wales; and after a sermon had been delivered by the Archbishop concerning this adventure for the sake of Christ crucified, Giraldus, the Archdeacon, setting an example to others, at the urgent request of the King before their departure and at the instance of the Arch-

[1] 1187.
[2] Feb. 11th, 1188. *Gattedun* (not *Garcedun* (Brewer)) is the reading of the MS.

PREACHING OF CRUSADE IN WALES

bishop and the Justiciar in the King's name, and moved not less by his own devotion than by the exhortation of such great men, was the first to take the Cross at the hands of the Archbishop. And Peter, Bishop of Mynyw, at once followed the Archdeacon's example, and many others were bound to the service of Christ crucified, the Cross being taken and sewn upon their shoulders. But as for the deeds of each day during the circuit of Wales and the things that took place both in ancient and modern times in those places they are fairly set forth in the *Itinerary* which Giraldus himself wrote.

CHAPTER XVIII

How Baldwin, Archbishop of Canterbury, preached the Cross throughout Wales and how Giraldus the Archdeacon, was attached to him to be his faithful associate in preaching

So the Archbishop, proceeding on his way and taking with him Giraldus the Archdeacon as his inseparable companion in the task of preaching, proceeded along the south coast of Wales through the diocese of Llandaff towards Mynyw, everywhere in such places as seemed fit, preaching the Cross and the service of Christ crucified. And when at last he entered Dyfed and approached the region of Mynyw, he himself first delivered a sermon to the clergy and people of those parts whom he had summoned to Haverford as being in the centre of the province, and then enjoined upon Giraldus that he in his turn should preach the word of the Lord. And in that same hour God gave him such grace of speech and of persuasion that the greater part of the young men, the flower of the knighthood of those parts, took the Cross, but those of the common folk that did so were past counting. Now when the Archbishop saw that, when he himself spoke, so few out of so great a multitude had taken the Cross, he was filled with grief and wonder, saying, 'O God, what a hard-hearted people is here!' And when he gave the Cross which he had in his hand to be taken to the Archdeacon that he might support himself with it, the latter, who was sitting beside the Archbishop, asked that his Bishop, Peter, should be enjoined to speak. But the Archbishop replied that for such a purpose rank should not be regarded, but only the man to whom God had given His grace. Now the Archdeacon had divided his sermon into three parts and reserved his strong power of persuasion for the close of each of these. Wherefore thrice there was such a throng of those who came and eagerly seized a Cross, that the Archbishop could hardly be protected from the crowd of those who pressed upon him, and on each of these occasions the Archdeacon was forced to be silent in mid-speech and pause by reason of the tumult. Now a certain knight, named Philip Mangonel, a kinsman of Giraldus, had said to him on the day before in the presence of many, in all seriousness and not in jest, that not one good man in all the country would take the Cross for all his preaching or that of the Archbishop, and that therefore they had come thither for nothing. To which the Archdeacon made answer that this rested with God and not with man. Now it happened that as oft as he thus paused and was silent, he beheld that knight, who sat within sight of him, weeping so that he was all streaming with tears. And afterwards at the sermon's close he with five or six other knights, good men and valiant, were adorned with the sign of the Cross. From which it is clear that the Spirit bloweth when and where it listeth. And often on that journey the Archbishop would say that he had never seen so many tears as on that day at Haverford. Now, as Jerome[1] says in a

[1] *Ep.* LII, 8.

THE EFFECT OF HIS PREACHING

book of his letters, the tears of the people are the glories of the preacher.

Moreover, many were amazed that, though the Archdeacon spoke only in French and Latin, the common people who knew neither tongue wept in untold numbers no less than the rest and more than two hundred ran all together to receive the sign of the Cross. The like also befell in Germany in the case of the blessed Bernard, who speaking to Germans in the French tongue of which they were wholly ignorant, filled them with such devotion and compunction, that he called forth floods of tears from their eyes and with the greatest ease softened the hardness of their hearts so that they did and believed all that he told them; and yet when an interpreter faithfully set forth to them in their own tongue everything that he said, they were not at all moved thereat. Wherefore at the sermon's close, when the Archdeacon sat down again, a certain Hospitaller who sat near him said to him, 'In truth the Holy Spirit has manifestly spoken by your mouth this day'. But John, Count of Mortain, who afterwards succeeded his brother Richard on the throne and at that time held the Earldom of Pembroke at his father's gift, as soon as he saw Giraldus in England, assailed him with bitter words in the presence of many, because by his preaching he had emptied his land of all the strength of men that was his defence against the Welsh; and that he had done this, not so much that he might succour the land of Jerusalem as that he might destroy the Earl's land, in order that when he had emptied it of its men he might hand it over to his kinsmen the Welsh. To which the Archdeacon briefly replied that God, who searches out the hearts and intentions of all men, knew his purpose in so doing, wherefore let God judge between them!

DE REBUS A SE GESTIS

CHAPTER XIX

How the Archbishop enjoined upon the Archdeacon the duty of preaching at Mynyw and what things happened in Cemais and Cardigan and also in Gwynedd and Powys

Now the Archbishop, coming thence to Mynyw, since he himself was in haste to go to Rhys, Prince of South Wales, who was waiting for him at Aberteifi[1], deputed the Archdeacon to sow the word of God there. And many indeed ran up with great devotion to take the Cross, when they heard him; but many who had been much moved by his words and were firmly resolved to take the Cross, yet when they heard the words of his interpreter, which were far less well-ordered and persuasive, immediately recoiled from the vow that they had taken. For as Apollonius the rhetorician says, 'Nothing dries quicker than a tear'.[2] But on the next day in Cemais, not far from the bridge of Aberteifi, when the people of those parts were called together in the presence of Prince Rhys, a vast number were drawn to hear first the Archbishop and after him the Archdeacon. Wherefore on that same day a man named John Spang, a jester who by his pretended folly and his witty tongue was wont to give the court much entertainment, said to Rhys, 'O Rhys, you ought greatly to love this kinsman of yours, the Archdeacon; for to-day he has sent a hundred of your men or more to serve Christ; and if he had spoken in Welsh, I do not think that a single man would have been left you out of all this multitude'.

Now it happened on the same day, when a certain man had been signed with the Cross, an only son and his mother's sole solace in the decrepitude of her old age,

[1] Cardigan.
[2] Cp. *Cic. Part. Or.* 17, 57. *Cito enim exarescit lacrima, praesertim in alienis malis.*

A MIRACLE AT CARDIGAN

his mother, as soon as she beheld him, cried aloud as though inspired from heaven, 'Thanks be unto Thee, most dear Lord Christ, from my inmost heart, that thou hast granted me to bear such a son as thou mightest deem worthy of serving thee!' And there was another woman there, a matron of Aberteifi, who was of a very different mind. For, firmly holding her husband by his cloak and girdle that he might not go to the Archbishop and take the Cross, lost to all shame she dragged him back in the presence of them all. But on the third night thereafter this same woman heard in her dreams a terrible voice crying, 'Thou hast robbed me of my servant; wherefore from thee also shall there be taken that which thou most dearly lovest'. Now when she had told her husband of her vision to the wonder and the terror of them both, she fell asleep again and by a mishap no less grievous than her distress she overlay her little son, whom with more of a mother's love than a mother's care she had in bed with her. And straightway her husband told the Bishop concerning the vision and the vengeance of God, and took the Cross, his wife approving and of her own free will sewing it upon her man's shoulder.

After this they went through the wide province of Cardigan, and crossing the Dyfi entered Gwynedd, the whole of Lent having been given up to the service of the Cross and the words of Giraldus in all places having won acceptance past belief. And at length going round the outskirts of Powys by Whitchurch and Oswestry, they came during the days of Easter to Shrewsbury, where a great number of men were drawn to hear the persuasive speech of Giraldus, but very few to listen to the Archbishop and the rest. So, when the sermons were ended and the crowds were dispersing, a certain matron said to her neighbours and to other married women, as they were departing, in the hearing of the clerks of the

Archbishop and of Giraldus himself, who chanced to be following close behind them, 'Unless that Archdeacon had cozened and bewitched our husbands with his soft words and his simple looks, they would have got clear off, as far as the preaching of the others was concerned'. A certain man of that town also said, 'This Archdeacon does not need to trouble himself where and in whose presence he ought to speak'.

CHAPTER XX

Concerning the Archbishop's commendation both of Giraldus and his style

THIS praiseworthy mission thus accomplished, as the Archbishop was passing from the borders of Wales into England, some of his clerks who were travelling with him and talking in his presence concerning this pilgrimage to Jerusalem, asked him who could worthily cope with the glorious story of the recovery by our princes of the land of Palestine, and the defeat of Saladin and the Saracens at their hands. And the Archbishop replied that he had made good provision for that and had one ready who could handle the story exceeding well. And when they pressed him further and asked who it was, he turned to Giraldus who was riding at his side, saying, 'This is he who shall tell of it in prose, while my nephew Joseph shall record it in verse; and I will attach him to the Archdeacon that he may serve him and be ever at his side'. For the Archbishop hoped that the King would promote the Archdeacon and raise him to high honour. He began also highly to commend the Archdeacon's book, which he had given him as they entered Wales and which he had read from beginning

THE ARCHBISHOP PRAISES HIS STYLE

to end, to wit, the *Topography of Ireland*, extolling it with much praise both for its style and the manner in which he had handled the theme ... Moreover, the Archbishop enjoined upon him that he should not allow the excellent gift of style that God had granted him to lie fallow, but that he should continually employ it nor ever waste his time in idleness, but rather by unceasing study and laudable labour prolong the memory of his name to all eternity ... He said also that more than all earthly wealth that soon must perish, and worldly honours that so swiftly pass away, he should love the gift that God had bestowed upon him and be heartily thankful for it; for his works would be imperishable, and the longer they lived and the greater their antiquity, the dearer for all time and the more precious they should be to all men.

The next chapter opens with the statement that Giraldus went to France with the Archbishop. Some interesting details of the opening months of the visit are given in the De Principis Instructione, *III, 13 ff. (R.S. VIII, pp. 259 ff.) Whether he was actually at Le Mans with the Archbishop in March 1189, when Henry II was desperately ill is not clear. But he had joined the Court by April (ibid, p. 260). These passages are inserted here, in order not to interrupt the flow of the following Chapter.*

But God having decreed that recovering from his sickness the King should be reserved for yet greater woes, thereby setting a terrible example before the eyes of all the Kings of the earth, between Easter and Pentecost, that is, in the months of April and May, we went on several occasions to the fruitless parleys between the King and the Count of Poitou on the borders of the Marche — for at that time I too was following the Court. ...

DE PRINCIPIS INSTRUCTIONE

(Ch. 14.) Now it happened about that time, when many perished by reason of the distemperature of the weather and the inclemency of the air, Richard de Redvers, a man of noble birth and cousin to the King, fell desperately sick at Le Mans with a violent fit of that acute fever, which assailed so many great men at that time. And when that venerable man, Baldwin, Archbishop of Canterbury (in whose company I then was), came to visit him, the sick man, who lay in an inner chamber, whether awakened from sleep or rather recalled from the trance into which, by the will of God, the vehemence of the disease had cast him, suddenly burst forth into speech after this fashion. 'Where are my men?' he cried. 'Let someone go at once and tell the King without delay to make provision for himself and careful dispositions for his house, while yet it is in his power; for the opportunity will not return. For I go hence and beyond all doubt he shall follow me within two months and a half.' Now those that heard this were greatly amazed, but deemed that he wandered in his speech; a physician, however, named William Vacelin, who was then in attendance on him, bade him, more sharply than the rest to refrain from such words. But the sick man made answer, 'And you, William, I counsel you to make provision for yourself, since you also shall follow me within fifteen days after the King'. This said, William came out to us in the hall, and secretly whispered in the Archbishop's ear the words that had been spoken. And the Archbishop told us all with much marvelling, as we were on the way thence after he had visited the sick man. Now some of those that heard him paid no heed to the tale, but laughed at it as being wild and ludicrous talk, not to be seriously regarded, but some silently pondered over the matter and, noting carefully what happened thereafter, saw all things truly accomplished even as they had been foretold.

A FEARFUL VISION

To this must be added the following vision seen by Giraldus at Chinon a little later (Ch. 16, R.S., p. 264). *It is also recorded in almost the same words in* Exp. Hib. II, 29 (R.S. V; 367) *and* Symb. El. III, 27.

Wherefore I have thought it not beside the mark here clearly to set forth the vision which in this time of our misery and of the outrage done to the Cross of Christ was revealed to me, the most wretched and least of all men, who was yet thus visited by the Lord, who at times revealeth to the little things which he hideth from the great. In the days of that unnatural and most detestable quarrel between the King of the English and the Count of Poitou, as I sojourned with the King in the castle of Chinon, on 10th May and in the night, about the first cock-crow, I seemed to myself to behold a great throng of men looking up to heaven and as it were marvelling at some new sight. Wherefore I raised my eyes to see what it might be and I beheld a bright shining light in the midst of thick clouds. And suddenly the clouds were parted, as though this lower heaven were unlocked, so that through the window thus opened my gaze penetrated to the very empyrean, where the Court of Heaven appeared amid a great multitude, with weapons of all kinds threatening it on every side, given over to plunder and exposed to the slaughterous onset of its foes. Here you might see a head lopped off, and there an arm; some assailed by arrows from afar, others by lance and sword at close quarters, and yet again others pierced by daggers. And whereas many of those that beheld fell upon their faces either dazzled by the great blaze of light or moved to terror or pity by the things they saw, I seemed to gaze longer and more attentively than the others that I might see what the end would be. So when they had speedily vanquished all the rest, these bloody murderers turned one and all to assail the

DE PRINCIPIS INSTRUCTIONE

Prince of the Heavenly Host, who sat enthroned in majesty amidst his servants, as he wont to be shown in pictures. And dragging Him from the throne, his body bared to the waist, they pierced his right side with a lance. And straightway a very terrible voice was heard crying, 'Woth! Woth!'[1] Father and Son! Woth! Woth! Holy Ghost!' But whether this voice descended from above or was uttered by the people standing round about, I could not tell. And so at last the terror of the voice and of the vision awoke me from my sleep.

Wherefore I call Him to witness, to whom all things are open and laid bare, that straightway as I sat upon my couch and anxiously pondered over these things in my heart, for half an hour or more such a mighty shuddering possessed me, both of body and of soul, that being almost beside myself I feared to lose my reason and go mad. But with ready devotion betaking myself to that one refuge where man may find salvation, and again and again signing both breast and forehead with the Cross I spent a sleepless night until break of day. And thus, by the grace of God I came to myself, and was at last restored to my quiet mind. Yet never, not even to-day can I call that vision to mind without a mighty shudder. For what can be more terrible than that one of God's creatures should see his Maker pierced? Who could see the citizens of heaven, the household of God and the protectors of mankind dragged to the slaughter in confusion, without confusion to his own soul? Who could behold the Lord of Nature and the Moulder of the Universe thus suffering and not suffer with Him?

Now as to the meaning of this vision and that which it portended, I will set it forth in a few words. He who once suffered for His people in His own person, here

[1] *Exp. Hib.* lc. reads *Woth*; *De Pr. Intr. Woch.* The latter does not represent any German word (see end of vision). *Woth* however might represent *Worth*; cp. the German *Weh worth* (cp. our 'Woe worth the day!').

shows forth that once again He suffers, but in the persons of His own people. And whereas He, by the triumph of the Cross ascending to the right hand of the Father, entered His kingdom in victory, His creatures, now His foes in chief, strive to take away His Kingdom, to dim His Majesty and to overthrow the Church, which He redeemed by the outpouring of His blood. And therefore, as I think, this Passion was revealed not upon the Cross, but in His majesty, as though, the Cross being destroyed and swept away, His enemies now strive to rob Him of the glory which He had won for Himself upon the Cross. Or rather seeing that His faithful have now suffered, not on the Cross, but in arms and strife of war in that same Holy Land, which after the many and marvellous sacraments conferred by His bodily presence, He consecrated with His own blood, so now it was His pleasure, that this His passion, which in a sense He now endures where He reigns in majesty with the Father, should be made manifest not on the Cross but in arms and tumult of war. Even so did He once testify that He would Himself endure in Peter that same death which Peter should suffer at Rome, when Himself He said 'I go to Rome to be recrucified'. And thus He designed that the whole Court of Heaven should suffer like slaughter with Himself, desiring thus even by the manifestation of such grief to stir His people to vengeance.

(*He goes on to explain the admixture of the German tongue* ('*Woth! Woth!*') *with the Latin* ('*Pater et Filius*') *as indicating that only peoples of German and Latin speech showed any concern for the wrong done to the Saviour. But in the following paragraphs, written at a much later date and found only in the* De Principis Instructione, *he explains it as referring to the failure of the Crusade conducted by these two peoples.*)

DE PRINCIPIS INSTRUCTIONE

Though the events leading up to the death of Henry II, together with the death itself and the circumstances attending the funeral are vividly and most impressively described by Giraldus, there is no actual evidence that he was an eye-witness or that he was in attendance on the Court during this period. One more vision however dating from this period must be recorded (De Princ. Instr. III, 29 (R.S. VIII, 312)

Moreover, visions anticipating and foretelling this great event were seen by many a little before the King's death. And among these persons I too, who was then following the Court, beheld this. It seemed to me that the body of the King, as though then dead, was carried by night into the left aisle of a certain church; and suddenly there was a great flight of crows and daws, which had sprung forth from their hiding-places, as it were terrified by such a multitude of lights; and all at once every lamp that hung on high fell extinguished in fragments on the pavement; of the tapers also, the two which stood at his feet were cast down by the birds and extinguished. But the two which had been set up at his head, of their own accord fell from the candlesticks to the ground and were broken to pieces, before any of those who stood by could hold them up. Thus, therefore, all the lamps being extinguished, we, who seemed to be attending these nocturnal obsequies, straightway went forth, not in any order, but flying in haste and fear, so that in our dread and horror we left the body there, alone and destitute of all human comfort, as though it were beset by unclean things. Now this vision I told to the venerable Baldwin, Archbishop of Canterbury, while the King was still alive, though not long before his death; and when I had told it, he set forth to me a vision on the same theme which he had seen about the same time. Now it seemed to him that, having entered a certain church, he found in it the body of a dead man,

DREAMS OF KING HENRY'S DEATH

lying on a bier; and this body to the terror of all beholders suddenly raised itself upon its elbow and broke forth sharply into speech, crying, 'Where am I? and where am I lying?' And on being told that he was in a church, he replied, 'A church is no place for me; carry me out as quickly as you may'. And casting off the shroud with which he was veiled, he showed himself to be none other than Henry the King. Now, when he had been carried forth, the Archbishop, as though he had entered the church to hear mass with his priests, beheld the altar wholly bare and with a great cleft in the midst of it; and when he drew nigh he saw therein human excrement, and filth scattered all round about. And when he saw this he drew back in horror and shame and, beholding the priest of the Church standing on the other side, he called him to him and said, 'Are you the priest that ministers in this place?' And he made answer, 'I am'. 'Wherefore then do you keep the holy place and the altar of the Lord thus irreverently and in such dishonour?' And he replied, 'My lord, it is the man, whom you saw but now carried out, that did it this dishonour'. And the Archbishop forbade him to celebrate until he had cleansed and reconsecrated the place. And in very truth that man throughout his days, as far as in him lay, polluted the Church of God in his lands with filth and foulness by robbing it of its privileges and diminishing its dignities.

CHAPTER XXI

How Count Richard after his father's death sent the Archdeacon into England and Wales

MEANWHILE an exceeding great war having arisen between the Kings beyond the seas, Richard, Count of Poitou being the cause thereof, the Archbishop of

DE REBUS A SE GESTIS

Canterbury and Ranulph de Glanville the Justiciar went abroad, and by their advice the Archdeacon went also. But King Henry dying a short time after[1] and being succeeded by his son Count Richard, the Archdeacon Giraldus, by the advice of the Archbishop of Canterbury, was on account of the change of Kings sent with many letters to preserve peace in Wales. Now it happened that when he came to Dieppe to take ship thence to England, he could not sail because the wind was contrary; so leaving his baggage there with the drivers of his sumpter horses, he himself and certain knights, whose business called for like speed, made haste to travel unencumbered and without baggage towards Flanders along the coast, that they might cross thence more quickly. Wherefore I have thought it not beside the mark to insert a thing which the Archdeacon was wont to relate when talking of divers mischances that befell him. For it happened that owing to the general distemperature then prevailing, by which not only countless of the common folk, but even the King himself and many of his barons had been taken from this world, almost all the servants of the Archdeacon had either returned home in ill health or had taken to their beds through sickness. Wherefore having left a boy, the sole survivor of his folk who was whole and sound, with his driver and packs at Dieppe, he took as his servant a man whom he had never before seen and gave him the custody of his more precious possessions which he was carrying with him. Now after they had in the morning forded the river of Dieppe from the northern bank, an estuary of which the inflowing tide makes a harbour, they had betaken themselves to a certain hill[2], from which they could view the town which they had left behind together with the shipping in the port; and when,

[1] 1189.
[2] Clearly the hill on which 'Notre Dame de Bonsecours' now stands.

LOSES HIS BAGGAGE IN FRANCE

having halted there, they began to inquire of one another, as travellers are wont to do, whether they had with them all their comrades and all the things which they wished to carry with them, the Archdeacon's new servant was missing. And when they had waited for him a long time and he was nowhere to be found, the Archdeacon began (and no wonder!) to have doubts concerning him; for the man was an utter stranger and he had no surety for him; moreover, he remembered that the man himself had once said that, if he had not taken service with him, he was going to search for a brother of his in Hungary. And when the knights who were of his company heard that the man was a stranger and that he was carrying no small sum of money, they urged the Archdeacon to return and look for him not only at Dieppe, but at Rouen also where he had first come to him. But the Archdeacon, being alone and without a follower, doubted greatly whether he should find him, if he had run away, and chose rather to continue the journey which he had begun in their company, and to trust all to God.

When therefore they had passed Eu on the March of Normandy toward Flanders, they once more waited for him a long while upon a certain hill, but seeing him not, they lost all hope of him; for even if he followed them through the lands of Vimeu[1] and St. Valéry, which were full of robbers and footpads, he could not, since he was all alone, get through by any means without being robbed. And when the knights inquired the sum total of all that he was carrying and received his reply, they exhorted him yet more urgently to turn back and seek him. For there was forty marks worth in gold and silver and in spoons and cups and there was the good palfry that he rode and the clothes of the Archdeacon that he

[1] An ecclesiastical 'circonscription' between the Channel and the rivers Bresle and Somme, to the S. of Eu.

carried, besides a case, full of letters from the Count and great note-books[1] also, containing the *Itinerary*, a year's labour of which no other copy had been made. But he refused to turn back and committed all to God. So they hastened on their way and when they had come to Abbeville and found lodging there, the Archdeacon went to his room, full of sadness and thinking anxiously of the things that had befallen him. For, as he used to relate, the causes that made him grieve thus were three: first there was the loss of money, no light matter, yet trifling compared to the rest (for it is a common thing to lose money and then get more again); secondly there was the loss of the Count's letters, and the charge which had been committed to him thus brought to naught; this was a greater loss, but because he knew the gist of the letters, he might have found some remedy by getting others of like import from the Justiciar of England; the third and the greatest loss was that of his note-books; for he said that the loss of a book still to be published which those note-books contained, was not to be repaired, since (and it was that which grieved him most) the toil he had spent upon them could not be repeated either by himself or any other. While then he sat, exceeding sad and distraught, at last recalling the lover's remedy, ' 'Tis solitude that harms, shun solitude'[2], he betook himself to the hall, now joining the throng of knights, now that of the serving men, in order that by listening to one thing and another he might be able from time to time to think of something else than his loss, and thus assuage the vehemence of his grief. But very soon, since God is ever near in time of trouble, behold, a boy coming from the market-place sought out the Archdeacon and asked him what manner of horse his servant had; and when he heard that it was an iron-

[1] Scarcely 'maps' as Brewer takes it, though Giraldus tells us elsewhere that he had made a map.
[2] *Ov. Rem. Am.* 579.

THE LOST IS FOUND

grey, he said that he had seen a man riding such an one in the market-place with a great bundle in his charge and that he was asking for the lodging of the Archdeacon. Then, the boy being forthwith sent to fetch him, that servant was brought to the lodging and welcomed with joy by all. And when the Archdeacon asked if everything was safe, he replied 'Everything'. As to the cause of the delay (which the knights would not suffer to be told till they had breakfasted), he declared that after fording the river he had dismounted to rub down his horse and to secure and adjust the wrapper containing the goods, which was a large one, when he found that he had lost a girdle from the pack, which was worthy twenty marks. Wherefore he at once returned to the town and the lodging whence he had departed, but found it nowhere. And so returning and crossing the river for the third time, that he might follow his master, though he had lost all hope, he yet cast his eyes downwards along the stony shore, as he followed his former track. And there he espied the girdle lying among the stones, not unrolled, but still folded and tied as it had been before. Thus manifold were the workings of fortune and worthy also of wonder manifold; first because he found the girdle that he had thus lost; secondly in that having found it he did not take advantage of our absence (and we were then far away)[1] to go back with all the things he carried, more especially seeing that he was a foreigner; and thirdly that following alone and thus laden, by a road beset with robbers and footpads, he arrived without loss and with a whole skin ... So when they were come to the Flemish Sea, they crossed it and the Archdeacon made haste to London, where he found his boy and the driver whom he had left at Dieppe. And after delivering the Count's letters which were addressed to the Justiciar, he hastened on his way to

[1] One of the rare cases where he lapses into the first person. cp. p. 312.

DE REBUS A SE GESTIS

Wales, where he gave the Count's letters to those to whom they were sent, and by his coming and intervention did much to restore peace in his native land which was greatly disturbed owing to the King's death.

Soon after this Count Richard came to England and was crowned King in London, but after only a brief stay, crossed the sea[1] to Normandy that he might hasten on his pilgrimage to Jerusalem with Philip, King of the French, leaving William de Longchamp as Justiciar in England, to whom he attached the Archdeacon[2]. But the latter, seeing that King Henry, at whose instance he had taken the Cross, was now dead, approached the Cardinal Legate, John of Anagni, who was then at Dover on his way back from England, and obtained for himself and his Bishop, now worn out with age, the grace of absolution from their vows and the following charter, though the Bishop had not asked him to do so.

CHAPTER XXII

The letter in which the Cardinal granted absolution

'To the venerable father in Christ, Baldwin, by the grace of God Archbishop of Canterbury, and to all into whose hands these present may come, John of Anagni by the same grace priest Cardinal of St. Mark, Legate of the Apostolic See, health everlasting in the Lord!

'Giraldus, Archdeacon of St. David, has come to us and on his part and that of our venerable brother, Peter, Bishop of Mynyw, set forth that Henry, King of the English, had given them great hopes, if they would go with him to Jerusalem, in respect of the heavy

---
[1] Dec. 11th, 1189.
[2] He records his opinion of Longchamp in his *Life of St. Hugh of Lincoln*, in what is perhaps the most scurrilous of all his invectives.

ABSOLUTION FROM CRUSADER'S VOW

expenses to which they would be put by the aforesaid journey; but now since the King has been taken from their midst, they are wholly unable to perform the vow which they had made, since they have not the wherewithal to meet the expenses. We, therefore, have thought right that we should spare the poverty of the aforesaid Bishop and Archdeacon, as also of other Welshmen, who are not able of themselves to perform the vow that they had taken, after the following manner:—to wit, that since they cannot go in person, they should make contribution to those going to Jerusalem out of the possessions that God has given them and should bestow their labour and their aid upon the repair of the Church of Mynyw[1]. We also by the authority committed to us deem that the aforesaid Bishop and Archdeacon should, by reason of poverty or the weakness of age, be absolved from the said journey to Jerusalem, and we hereby declare them to be wholly absolved, but on this condition that they lend help and assistance to those going to Jerusalem. And we make the same declaration concerning the people committed to their charge.'

Now we see few archdeacons to-day, who do not rather seek or desire the removal of their bishops. This was, therefore, a clear proof that the Archdeacon had little yearning or aspiration to be his Bishop's successor. And in the meantime, Gwion, Bishop of Bangor, having died, that Bishopric was offered him by the Justiciar, then Legate of the Apostolic See; but the Archdeacon utterly refused it.

---

[1] Which the Bishop was doing so much to rebuild.

DE REBUS A SE GESTIS

CHAPTER XXIII

How the Archdeacon urged Earl John that he should not, in this time of universal pilgrimage, remain idly in England, but did not persuade him

Now the Earl John, who had sworn to his brother before his departure that he would not enter England within the next three years, boasted, though secretly and in private, to the Archdeacon, whom he treated as a close friend, that he had been absolved from his oath by the Chancellor, and said that in this he was most fortunate, since he could not forego the wealth and luxury of England. But the Archdeacon made answer that it better became his honour and reputation that he should be away during his brother's absence rather than present, and urged him that, when almost all other princes had gone forth on the expedition to Jerusalem, he alone should not abide at home in seeming sloth and idleness, but that he should rather go to Ireland, and wholly subdue it and build castles there, as became a man; for thereby he would gain great profit, since thus he would in the first place mend his fortune and not, alone of princes, sit idle-handed, doing naught; and further he would escape all taint of suspicion and gain great praise among men and great gratitude from his brother when he returned, because he had not seemed to be waiting for his death or aspiring to succeed him or to rob him of his crown. But the Earl did not regard his words with favour and replied that, not having so many kinsman in Ireland, he had not such a liking for that country as the Archdeacon.

The following incident is cited from the 'De Instructione Principis' (Bk. I, R.S. VIII, p. 127). *The date for Giraldus's visit to Glastonbury was 1192-3; for in the expanded version given*

THE DISCOVERY OF ARTHUR'S TOMB

in the Speculum Ecclesiae (Bk. II, R.S. IV, p. 47) Giraldus states that Abbot Henry (de Sully) showed him the 'tomb' and the relics of Arthur and his wife. Henry was Abbot 1189-93 and R. de Coggeshall (p. 36) states that the grave was discovered in 1191. As the new tomb in the Abbey was already in being at the time of this visit, the date can scarcely be earlier than 1192. This passage would seem to be the earliest description of the discovery and to be the source of later descriptions, which add little or nothing to our knowledge.

Now the body of King Arthur, which legend has feigned to have been transferred at his passing, as it were in ghostly form, by spirits to a distant place and to have been exempt from death, was found in these our days at Glastonbury deep down in earth and encoffined in a hollow oak between two stone pyramids erected long ago in the consecrated graveyard, the site being revealed by strange and almost miraculous signs; and it was afterwards transported with honour to the Church and decently consigned to a marble tomb. Now in the grave there was found a cross of lead, placed under a stone and not above it, as is now customary, but fixed on the lower side. This cross I myself have seen; for I have felt the letters engraved thereon, which do not project or stand out, but are turned inwards toward the stone. They run as follows.

HERE LIES BURIED THE RENOWNED KING ARTHUR
WITH GUENEVERE HIS SECOND WIFE
IN THE ISLE OF AVALON[1]

Now in regard to this there are many things worthy of note. For he had two wives, the last of whom was buried with him, and her bones were found together with his, but separated from them as thus; two parts of the tomb, to wit, the head, were allotted to the bones of the man, while the remaining third towards the foot contained

[1] See Appendix III.

the bones of the woman in a place apart; and there was found a yellow tress of woman's hair still retaining its colour and its freshness; but when a certain monk[1] snatched it and lifted it with greedy hand, it straightway all of it fell into dust. Now whereas there were certain indications in their writings that the body would be found there, and others in the letters engraven upon the pyramids, though they were much defaced by their extreme age, and others again were given in visions and revelations vouchsafed to good men and religious, yet it was above all King Henry II of England that most clearly informed the monks, as he had heard from an ancient Welsh bard, a singer of the past, that they would find the body at least sixteen feet beneath the earth, not in a tomb of stone, but in a hollow oak. And this is the reason why the body was placed so deep and hidden away, to wit, that it might not by any means be discovered by the Saxons who occupied the island after his death, whom he had so often in his life defeated and almost utterly destroyed; and for the same reason those letters, witnessing to the truth, that were stamped upon the cross, were turned inwards towards the stone, that they might at that time conceal what the tomb contained, and yet in due time and place might some day reveal the truth.

Now the place which is now called Glaston, was in ancient times called the isle of Avalon. For it is as it were an isle, covered with marshes, wherefore in the British tongue it was called Inis Avallon, that is 'the apple-bearing isle'. Wherefore Morganis, a noble matron and the ruler and lady of those parts, who moreover was kin by blood to King Arthur, carried him away after the war of Camlan to the island that is now called Glaston that she might heal his wounds. It was also once called 'Inis gutrin' in the British tongue, that is, the glassy isle,

---

[1] In his eagerness he fell into the tomb (*Spec. Eccl.* l.c.).

THE BONES OF ARTHUR

wherefore when the Saxons afterwards came thither they call that place Glastingeburi. For 'Glas' in their language has the same meaning as *uitrum*, while 'buri' means *castrum* or *ciuitas*.

You must also know that the bones of Arthur thus discovered were so huge that the words of the poet seemed to be fulfilled:

'And he shall marvel at huge bones
In tombs his spade has riven' (*Virg. Georg.* 1, 497).

For his shank-bone, when placed against that of the tallest man in that place and planted in the earth near his foot, reached (as the Abbot showed us) a good three inches above his knee. And the skull was so large and capacious as to be a portent or prodigy; for the eyesocket was a good palm in width. Moreover, there were ten wounds or more, all of which were scarred over, save one larger than the rest, which had made a large hole.

CHAPTER XXIV

How the Archdeacon out of his love for study refused the ecclesiastical dignities that were offered to him

BUT in process of time, when the Chancellor had been deposed by the Earl and cast out of England, and the Earl himself held, as it were, the position of Viceroy, he offered the Archdeacon the Bishopric of Llandaff, whose Cathedral Church with the greater part of the diocese was in his lands of Glamorgan; but he refused with the same constancy as was his wont. Therefore besides the Church of St. David, to which he had been nominated and especially called in his youth, four Bishoprics had now been offered him, two in Ireland and two in Wales;

yet all these offers he trod underfoot with lofty and untroubled mind, since he coveted no such thing. For then he wished to have no more than he already had, since it would hinder his studies, which he pursued with almost ceaseless assiduity. For it had been a marvel that, even when he followed the Court, he none the less wrote histories, and after long and laborious journeys, such as are the lot of courtiers, would keep vigil till dawn, working by candlelight and joining night to day, as though he were in the schools and set on naught save study. For he had read the saying of Pliny, 'Let no asperity of time rob you of time for your studies; for all time is wasted that is not spent on study'[1]. Wherefore his chief desire was this and this alone — to complete his studies and, above all, to perfect his knowledge of theology in the schools; and further that he might have an honourable competence to enable him to do this and to acquire and keep a fine store of books and authors such as that Faculty demands. For, as he was wont himself to say, studious minds should ever seek such a competence as may nourish and not impede study, and as may not by its abundance choke the diligence required by so noble a task, but sustain it by its attainment of the happy mean.

---

[1] An adaptation of Pliny, *Ep.* III, v. 16.

BOOK III

CHAPTER I

Concerning the deeds of his later and riper years

Now Giraldus, considering that his following of the Court was utterly in vain, vain too all promises, vain all promotions offered him, vain and unworthy of himself and his deserts, withdrew himself wholly from the turmoil of the Court as from a stormy sea, a course which he had long since conceived in his mind and now gradually begun to follow; and with salutary wisdom he resolved to transfer himself to the schools as to a calm and tranquil haven. For he oft recalled to mind the words of Plinius Secundus[1], 'Leave noise and useless running hither and thither and foolish toils, as soon as occasion offers, and give yourself up to study; for leisure is honourable and sweet, and study is a fairer thing than almost any business'. And again[2], 'Give mean and grovelling cares to others and claim yourself for study in some high and lofty retreat'.

CHAPTER II

How he visited his friend, the hermit of Llowes, and sought his blessing and his leave to go to the schools

WHEREFORE, his mind firmly set on this design, he went to his friend the hermit, a good and holy man named Wechelen, of Llowes in Elfael, a place within his Archdeaconry and near the Wye, that he might take leave of him and receive his blessing. And among other things he asked him with especial earnestness to pray for him,

---

[1] Plin. *Ep.* I, ix. 7.   [2] An adaptation of *Ep.* I, iii. 3.

that for his soul's health he might have power to know and understand the Holy Scriptures which it was his desire to study. And the holy man made answer, gripping the Archdeacon's hand with his own, 'Och, och, do not say "to know" but "to keep": vain, vain is it to know, and not to keep'. For such was the manner of his speech,[1] using only infinitives and disregarding the cases; yet he was quite easy to understand. Wherefore it was all the greater matter for wonder how a simple and unlearned man should have acquired such knowledge as to perceive that knowledge is in vain, aye, and perilous save for him that keeps its precepts; for he who sins knowingly and with his eyes open, sins most grievously. 'For unto whomsoever much is given, of him shall be much be required'.[2] For the better a man's knowledge, the worse is his offending . . . But the Archdeacon hearing this was put to shame and moved even to tears, and entreated him yet more earnestly to pray for him that he might not only know the Holy Scripture but keep it also. And when the Archdeacon asked him how he got his Latin, since he had not learned it, he replied as follows (I will set down his own words, as the Archdeacon would often gladly repeat them). 'I go', he said, 'to Jerusalem and visit the Sepulchre of my Lord; and when I return, I place myself in this prison for love of my Lord who die for me. And I grieve much because I cannot understand Latin nor the Mass nor the Gospel; and often I weep and ask the Lord to give me to understand Latin. And one day at the hour of eating I call my servant at the window once and again and many times, and he come not; and I for weariness and hunger go to sleep and, when I wake, I see my bread lying on the altar. And going to it I bless the bread and eat it; and straightway at Vespers I understand the verses and the words which the priest say in

[1] It is impossible to reproduce in a translation this diverting idiom, of which a faint suggestion alone is possible.
[2] Luke xii. 48.

ST. DAVID'S CATHEDRAL

A NEW WAY TO LEARN LATIN

Latin, and likewise at Mass, as it seemed to me. And after Mass I call the priest to my window with his missal and ask him to read the Gospel of that day. And he read and I expound, and the priest say I expound rightly; and afterwards I speak Latin with the priest and he with me. And from that day I talk thus, and my Lord who give me the Latin tongue, give it not me by way of grammar and cases, but only that I might be understood and understand others.' Such too was the saying of the prophet Esdras who thus writes concerning himself, 'The Lord said to me, "Open thy mouth". And I opened my mouth, and behold a cup full of water, but the colour of it was like fire. And I took it, and when I had drunk of it, my heart uttered understanding, and wisdom entered into my breast'.[1]

Now it happened that the Welsh were besieging Pains Castle in Elfael which had been built a little time before; and when a multitude of the English army had been gathered at Hay and in those parts, there came a woman in the likeness of a nun, who pretended that she had come from this hermit, and counselled them on his part that they should assail the Welsh without fear, promising them a certain victory. And since they believed him as being a holy man, they did so and in one day slew of the Welsh about three thousand.[2] Now when this saying had been bruited abroad throughout that province, the Archdeacon came to visit his friend the hermit, which he did most gladly when he could find occasion. And among other things the hermit told him concerning that saying, and that he was much grieved that such a thing should have been spread abroad concerning himself, swearing that he had never sent such a message to the English or known of it. For he said, as indeed became him, that he would rather seek to prevent than to cause

[1] *Esdras* II. xiv. 39.
[2] Aug. 13th, 1198. The visit to the hermit, recorded at the beginning of the chapter, took place in 1196.

such a conflict between Christians, of which bloodshed must be the outcome. But he said that the Devil, on account of the perdition of many that he saw must arise therefrom, and by reason of the great harvest of souls that should come to him from such a fray, had procured that such counsel should come to the English as from himself whom the English trusted; and that he might defame him as the instigator of so great a slaughter the angel of Satan had transformed himself, as it were, into an angel of light.

Now the hermit loved the Archdeacon most tenderly, so much indeed that he set before him his visions and the revelations which were made to him in secret; and when the Archdeacon was far away, desiring out of his great affection to tell all things to him, he would send a relation of these visions written on rolls. And so the holiness and blessedness of this man, beloved and elect of God, was miraculously shown forth by many signs and virtues during his life, and by still more after his death. Now once he had sought counsel of the Archdeacon, whether, when the halt and blind and men afflicted with divers infirmities came to him, in order that he might lay his hands upon them from his window and so cure them, he should drive them away, as certain monks of the Cistercian Order had advised him, or whether he should not do so. And he received this answer, that he should not check the grace of healing given him by God, but should rather charitably bestow it on those who sought him in their need; yet he should above all things beware lest because of this aught of pride or arrogance should steal upon him. The Archdeacon also recalled to his memory the example from the Gospel concerning the disciples who returned with joy to Jesus saying that even the devils were subject to them; and Jesus to repress their arrogance replied to them, 'Rejoice not that the spirits are subject unto you, but rather rejoice because your

GIRALDUS RETIRES TO LINCOLN

names are written in heaven'.[1] Thus much concerning the holy man, from whom it grieves me to depart, even as it grieved the Archdeacon when he spoke of him. But now let us return to our story.

CHAPTER III

How on account of the wars he could not go to Paris and so turned aside to Lincoln

So having collected from all quarters his treasure-store of books, concerning which he would say that it were a sweet and delectable thing not only to live but also to die among them, he set out for Paris forthwith that he might perfect himself in the knowledge of the Holy Scriptures. But as he drew near the sea, he heard for sure that the war between King Philip and King Richard, which he had been told was for the time being lulled to sleep by a five-years truce, had once more broken out; and since for this reason it was not possible for him to go to France, he resolved no longer to endure such loss of time, than which nothing could be more grievous to him. So for the sake of his studies, he went to Lincoln,[2] where he knew that the science of Theology flourished most soundly in all England, under that best of teachers, Master William de Monte, so-called because he had read in Paris at Mont Ste Genéviève, where the Archdeacon had known him. And having continued his studies there for several years, at last, since there is naught on earth that standeth sure nor aught in this life that knows no variation, Peter, Bishop of Mynyw, having meanwhile been taken from this world,[3] Giraldus was urged by letters and frequent messages both from the Chapter of Mynyw

[1] Luke x. 20. [2] 1196. See *R.S.* v, liii. n. 2. [3] July 16th, 1198.

DE REBUS A SE GESTIS

and from the barons of his native land, that he should at once go to the King, to whose father he had rendered such service, as well as to himself, and that, having the favour and assent of all, he should seek and obtain the Bishopric of St. Davids. But since he was wholly devoted to his studies and desired no other life on earth so much as this, he replied not once only, but often and always that a man worthy to be a Bishop should be sought by others, not seek it for himself; and that if he himself sought the Bishopric, he would thereby prove himself unworthy of the office, and further that, since what he had sufficed him, he was unwilling for any reason to leave his studies and the tranquillity of the best of all ways in which he then was living.

Now it happened that about this time, when there was a great famine in those parts, while the Archdeacon after his wont was sitting in his chamber, pursuing his studies, he heard the poor and needy at the doors and windows of his lodgings crying aloud for alms. And straightway he was filled with pity for them and looking at his cloaks and hoods and the pellices of foreign furs of rats[1] and conies, all hung upon poles, he ordered that whatever there was among them of vair and minever and cony should be sold and the money distributed for the benefit of the poor. This was done forthwith, and from that hour the Archdeacon was content with cloaks of lambskin.

---

[1] A generic term for squirrels, martens, etc. Cp. *R.S.* VII, 92, *mures siluestres qui scurelli dicuntur* (of the squirrels tamed by St. Hugh of Lincoln).

BISHOP PETER DIES

CHAPTER IV

How Peter, Bishop of Mynyw, having in the meanwhile died, and the Archdeacon Giraldus being sought beyond all others for his successor, many were very busy concerning that Bishopric

WHEREFORE the Bishop of Mynyw, having died about the beginning of autumn,[1] two Archdeacons and four Canons of Mynyw, a little before the feast of St. Michael, went with letters of ratification to Hubert, Archbishop of Canterbury, then Justiciar[2] of England, as he had strictly commanded them, to elect a Bishop. And they nominated three persons to him as follows: first, and at the head of the list they placed Giraldus the Archdeacon; second, Walter, Abbot of St. Dogmael; and third, Peter, Abbot of Whitland; and to these by way of precaution, to increase the number of nominees and that they might not seem wholly to exclude Englishmen, they added the name of Reginald Foliot, an Englishman, who could have no hope of success. But things which are believed to be done with caution and forethought often turn out to the contrary, as will be clear from what follows. Now the Archbishop, to begin with, rejected and persistently refused to accept the name which they had put first; and when the Canons asked why he refused a man of prudence and learning, who came of noble lineage and was born in lawful wedlock, he replied that the King would not have any Welshman as Bishop in Wales, especially when he was a blood relation of the princes of Wales. But there was another reason besides that which he alleged. For in respect of the Archdeacon, whose learning and courage he knew well enough, he feared, as by some presentiment, that which afterwards befell him. Nor

[1] He died July 16th (see above). The news must have reached Giraldus some weeks later.
[2] See Appendix IV.

DE REBUS A SE GESTIS

was that all; for the Archbishop received the news of the Bishop's death, while as Justiciar he was in the March of Wales with the English army that he sent against the Welsh when there was that great slaughter at Pains Castle; and when he inquired who there was who could take custody of the Church and Bishopric during the vacancy, and those who had been sent to him replied that there was Giraldus the Archdeacon, then in the schools of Lincoln, the Archbishop forthwith uttered vile and dishonourable words against the person of the Archdeacon, saying that never, while he lived, would he entrust him either with the Bishopric or its custody. For at that time he was much offended with the Archdeacon on account of William Wibert, Abbot of Biddlesden,[1] a monk of the Cistercian Order, and a most worthless gadabout, who had a little while before been deposed by means of the Archdeacon, whom he had grievously offended. For he had been a friend of the Archbishop and often put himself forward that he might be sent as his messenger both to Wales and to Scotland, and also to gad about in divers other places. Wherefore I have thought good here to insert the letter which the Archdeacon sent to the Archbishop on this matter together with the letter of the Archbishop in reply and the letter of the Archdeacon concerning the formal appointment of a Bishop.

CHAPTER V

The letter to the Archbishop of Canterbury

To the reverend Lord and beloved Father, Hubert, Archbishop of Canterbury, Primate of all England, Giraldus, Archdeacon of St. David, greetings in the name

[1] In N.W. Bucks, near Brackley.

LETTER TO THE ARCHBISHOP

of the Author of our Salvation! Blessed be God who has 'taught your hands to war and your fingers to fight'.[1] Blessed be God who by the hand of His anointed has given you such a glorious victory over your enemies. And blessed be His Holy Name who was ordained that this great realm should be ruled by law and pacified by arms through the unwearied labour of His Pontiff and Primate, strong both in spiritual and worldly warfare, fighting with either sword, and by his marvellous skill moulding himself[2] to meet the vicissitudes of these times. For from the time when King Harold so valorously with a host of foot-soldiers invaded Wales and almost utterly wiped out the whole nation and gave it over to destruction, the memory of ages holds no record of such an overthrow of a hostile people wrought in one encouner by any prince or leader. Therefore as the *Book of Wisdom*[3] teaches, 'Better is wisdom than strength and a prudent man than a valiant'. But since the evils of this world are never far from its blessings, and that which is sweet has always some sprinkling of bitter, honey is always mingled with poison, sadness clings ever close to joy and grief overtakes rejoicing (at least if it be to excess), even so a cloud and mist of untoward rumour hath taken away the brightness that filled my heart on the news of so glorious an event. For a thing was made known to me that I could not endure without grief, to wit, that I had incurred the grievous anger of my Lord; for so certain persons concluded from words of yours hurled forth against me with less circumspection than beseemed either my reputation or your magnificence. And I bore this all the more heavily and thought it all the more worthy of wonder, since for the past two years

---

[1] Psalm cxliv. 1. For the question of the command at the battle of Pains Castle see Appendix IV.
[2] *coaptante* MS.
[3] VI, 1. Found in the Vulgate, but not in A.V. *uires* not *uirtus* is the true reading: cp. *Symb. El.* xxviii.

DE REBUS A SE GESTIS

I have lived in all simplicity and innocency, given wholly to the study of theology and hurting no man in all the world either by word or deed or even by writing. Wherefore I am utterly at a loss to know to what thing I should impute it that I have incurred such indignation, beyond ought that I have deserved, on the part of my Lord, that he even pollutes his sacred lips with upbraiding and railing against his neighbour. Moreover, since there is no cause for this nor any guilt of mine, unless perchance as oft-times happens:

The sins of old awaken new-born shame.[1]

For a good man is wounded more grievously by words than by blows, and in truth noble hearts are far more vexed that their reputation should be torn in pieces than their worldly goods should be destroyed or dispersed. 'Be not in haste with upbraiding to publish that which thine eyes have seen, lest afterwards thou canst not amend what thou hast said, when thou hast dishonoured thy friend'.[2] And again in Ecclesiaticus,[3] 'Whoso casteth a stone at the birds frayeth them away, and he that upbraideth his friend breaketh friendship'. And a little later[4], 'The man that is accustomed to opprobrious words will never be reformed all the days of his life'. Concerning which the commentator says, 'He whose mouth is full of cursing and bitterness shall never prosper'. Therefore such things beseem not great and magnanimous men, nor do they even bring the small and puny to advancement. But since it is no great honour to the lion to pursue a hare, so may this anger, whatever the occasion of its conceiving, if it have not yet fully abated, nevertheless by the blessing of God soon abate and vanish away, since I am prepared to humble myself in all things before my Lord, and if I have offended in anything (though I

---

[1] An adaptation of Horace, *Ep.* I, xviii, 77, *incutiunt aliena tibi peccata pudorem*.
[2] Proverbs xxv. 8 (So in the Vulgate).   [3] xxii. 20.   [4] xxiii. 15.

call God to witness that I know not that I have offended in aught), yet am I ready to make such satisfaction as he may desire. And as beseems the clemency of so great a Pontiff, may the indignation that arose with the sun sink before its setting. For as Jerome says,[1] 'It is the weakness of man to be angry, and the strength of a Christian to put an end to his anger'. But if owing to the greatness of my transgression, I may not yet win the appeasement that I desire, nevertheless let him spare his words and let his avenging wrath rage its full against my revenues and possessions; let him destroy my substance as he pleases, but refrain from wounding my reputation. Wherefore be it granted to me to lie hid and to indulge myself with my books and writing for the rest of my days without vexation. I have thus far given too much time to ambition and my own perdition, wherefore my grief must be the greater. But from this time forth, God granting, I will follow the maxim of the poet Horace:

> Let me have that which now is mine — or less —
> And for myself live out what's left of life,
> If the Gods will that aught of life be left;
> Let me have store of books and garnered corn
> To last the year, nor waver anxiously
> In hope of days that fortune may deny.[2]

or of Ovid:

> Believe me, he who well lies hid, lives well;
> And each within his fortune should abide.[3]

or:

> If thou wilt trust a friend by fortune schooled,
> Live for thyself and shun the lords of earth.[4]

or once again of Flaccus:

> Shun greatness; and beneath a humble roof
> Find joys unknown to kings and friends of kings.[5]

[1] *Ep.* 12, *ad fin.*   [2] Hor., *Ep.* I, xviii, 107.   [3] *Ov. Tr.* III, iv, 25.
[4] Ibid., 3.   [5] Hor., *Ep.* I, x, 32.

Wherefore if by canonical election I were now called to some worthier See of England or of France that might chance to be vacant, God, the searcher out of men's hearts, from whom no secret is hid (for if I lie, in Him I shall find the heaviest of avengers) — God knows that even then, to obtain such greatness, I would not desert my study of the Holy Scriptures to which God helping me, I have given myself with all my strength. 'For it is a greater thing', as Jerome says, 'to possess a Bishop's virtues than to be a Bishop; and a greater thing to be worthy of a Bishopric than to be set on the Bishop's throne. For the former is the gift of righteousness, the latter of fortune; the first is a privilege of the good alone, the latter open to all.' Wherefore in the same book of his letters[1] he says, 'It is a less thing to hold the priesthood than to deserve it'. Why then is he who no longer seeks such honour or desires it, and is ready to lose without a murmur even that little which he has, why is such an one thus rent with words and torn with revilings? I confess that in my former days when the world and its ambitions held me captive, there were many things in me that were in truth most worthy of much rebuke. But in my present way of life, to which by the grace of God I have now devoted myself, I would not dare indeed to call myself free from sin, since no man that lives is sinless and even the just man falls seven times in one day, and all of us offend in many things; but this none the less I affirm with confidence and protest with truth unshakable, that I cannot remember that I have been guilty of any transgression so great and notable as should cause such offence to so great Majesty. And so in this new way of life, since a man of sound understanding is better known to himself than he is to others, though I have examined all that is in my heart with diligence and subtlety I can find no cause why I should be accused of any so great

[1] Cp. *Ep.* xlix, 4.

HE DESIRES LIFE OF PEACEFUL STUDY

transgression, unless indeed I am to be blamed for my vehement zeal in the study of sacred learning. Let others therefore seek favour, let others follow the Court, whereof I too of old was a misguided and unprofitable follower. Let them, I say, desire and run and mount the Bishop's throne. Only grant me permission to lie hid and indulge my study of the Scripture, in the knowledge of which I deem it desirable not only to dwell, but even to die and dying win salvation. Moreover, though ' 'Tis no mean glory to have praised the great,'[1] yet it were better, yea, far better never to have known a friend among the mighty than undeservedly to have fallen from his friendship once possessed. Wherefore Demetrius[2] says, 'I do not desire to have rich men for my friends'. And again Horace says:

> Sweet seems the courtship of some powerful friend
> To those who have not tried it; only try
> And thou shalt tremble.[3]

And so too Ecclesiasticus, 'Keep thee far from the man that hath power';[4] and again, 'He taketh a burden upon himself who hath one that hath fellowship with one that is of higher degree. And have no fellowship with him that is richer than thyself. For how agree the kettle and the earthen pot together? For if the one be smitten against the other it shall be broken'[5] ... [6]Again Jerome says, 'It is troublesome to have powerful friends; it is enough if they be not enemies to thee'. But would that this were granted also to me; for if I might not have my Lord for my friend, after his wont, I should at least not have him for my enemy. Therefore having oft experienced the fickleness of the great and endured enough and more than enough of vexation I now desire to be to them as one empty and unknown, neither hoping good

[1] Hor., *Ep.* I, xvii, 35.   [2] Perhaps an echo of Demetrius, the friend of Seneca.
[3] Hor., *Ep.* I, xviii, 86.   [4] IX, 13.   [5] VIII, 2.
[6] Further quotations from Ecclesiasticus to the same effect omitted.

DE REBUS A SE GESTIS

nor expecting evil. Wherefore may your fatherly piety and the God of mercy grant that I may pass the little that is left of life in pleasant quietude far from the cares and ambitions of the Court, that ever wound the heart and satisfy it not, and apart from the noise of the multitude, weeping and redeeming, as best I may, the time that I have wasted in the past, and that dividing my spirit between prayer and the reading of the Holy Scriptures, I may aspire throughout my earthly course to that life where vicissitudes veer not and vices vex not, where prelacy oppresseth not and domination dooms not and damns not, where there is quiet and peace everlasting and light unfailing, where joys are true, knowing no turmoil or sadness, world without end. And may your pious and placable Paternity prosper in the Lord for many a year, to be a blessing to many and a hurt to few, conforming to the praise that Maro bestows on Maecenas,

> Though blest with such a friend, thou might'st dare all,
> Yet not a man hath felt thy power to harm.[1]

CHAPTER VI

The reply of Hubert, Archbishop of Canterbury

HUBERT, by the grace of God, Archbishop of Canterbury, of all England Primate, to his beloved son Master Giraldus, Archdeacon of St. David's, health and blessing! You have ascribed to me the destruction of the Welsh, who fell by their own pride the other day, whereas their destruction must be ascribed not to me, but rather to God who casteth down the proud and humbleth them. For their foolish heart was so darkened by their pride, that though they were warned most urgently by us and

---
[1] *El. in Maec.*, I, 15, a poem falsely attributed to Virgil.

THE ARCHBISHOP'S REPLY

other men of great name and piety to desist from their purpose and turn to wiser courses, yet could they not understand our salutary counsel nor foresee that their own folly was dragging them to perdition. And that it was the hand of God and not my own nor that of any man which wrought these things, you may clearly understand from this, that in the encounter at that place neither their spear nor bow had power to wound to death one man of all our host. But concerning that which you tell me concerning yourself, that you now devote yourself to the study of the Holy Scriptures and that from henceforth you have resolved thus wholly to devote yourself, I commend you, concluding from this that you have learned that it is safer to sit and hear the word of God with Mary than to serve with Martha. And as for your protest that you have harmed no man nor deserved at all that you should be hurt by any other nor suffer upbraiding I answer that you know whether you have done that which you say you have not done. But I neither accuse you nor, as far as I remember, am I angry with you or any one else. Farewell'.

Now he added these words because the deposition of the said Abbot had been brought about by the Archdeacon whereby he manifested the rancour of his heart and the bitterness he had conceived against him.

At this point (to use a favourite phrase of Giraldus) we have not thought it beside the mark to insert the answer to the foregoing letter, which is contained in the Symbolum Electorum (XXVIII). *It has been much abbreviated for the purpose.*

'I think it proper that I should reply to My Lord's letter written in answer to mine, since in two points it seems to hint that I have given offence. In the first place, in the phrase with which I began I did not refer to hands consecrated by God or to the fingers of any man's hands, as is clear from what followed, more especially the passage

SYMBOLUM ELECTORUM

cited from the *Book of Wisdom* — 'Wisdom is better than strength and a prudent man than a valiant'. For that neither the hands of men (not to say of one man) nor the fingers of men of war achieved these things, but that the finger of God, who knows how to humble the proud and magnify the lowly, wrought this marvel, is clear (as my letter showed) from the fact that, when all the chosen youth of Wales was assembled to make trial of their strength and their whole pride was gathered there, and all the arrogance of a hostile nation had come to a head in that place, yet when the hosts met in battle, in rough and wooded country such as that race desires, so vast a multitude of them were destroyed, without a mortal wound to even one of our own, that it is difficult to tell the number of the slain with any certainty. Now it is known beyond a doubt to almost every man in those parts that my Lord himself was then almost thirty miles away,[1] where with a number of good and religious men of that region, whom he had summoned for the purpose, he prostrated himself in most devout supplication within the Church, lifting up his hands to God (as it were with Moses)[2] and praying that He would abate the fierceness of that barbarous people without slaughter and effusion of blood and would incline their hearts to peace and concord or would according to His good pleasure and infallible dispensation recall them from destroying the marches of the realm of England. It may be believed also that He dealt mercifully with those that fell, even as he did with those whom, at the prayer of Elijah, fire descending from heaven consumed in a moment. For both these men and those would have become daily worse and thus have merited yet deeper damnation. For if they had succeeded in their assault and fulfilled their desire by storming that town, without doubt they would

---
[1] At Bridgnorth. A pleasant thrust. Cp. Appendix IV.
[2] Cp. Exod. xvii. 11.

GIRALDUS RETURNS TO THE CHARGE

not have hesitated to occupy yet more of the realm of England and to exterminate the English that dwelt therein, until such time as they were driven back by the assembled strength of the whole kingdom. Since therefore Law and Justice permit men to repel violence with violence . . . blessed be God, who by the inspired vigour and virtue of one man freed the country from peril thus mightily and preserved the honour, integrity and peace of the realm by such a glorious victory . . .[1]

But I must speak also of that passage at the end of my Lord's letter, which hints that I have given him offence.[2] . . . I wrote that during the two years which I had given to study I had hurt no man by word or deed or even by writing. And in reply to this your notary[3] wrote that I knew well whether I had so hurt any man at any time: though it is, as you know, uncivil to judge any man after reading only a part of what he has said. For I did not say nor do I say now that I had never injured any one, since 'we all offend many in many things'; but this I do confidently assert that during those two years I wounded no man's feelings grievously by word or deed or even by writing for four years or more have passed since I wrote to Cîteaux[4] against my slanderer William Wibert, ex-Abbot of Biddlesden, who once so shamelessly thrust himself not merely upon your Court, but upon your intimacy. For after spending two years at Oxford[5] in your Court, just before I went to Lincoln, we were reconciled at Canterbury by the mediation of two monks, your personal chaplains, Alexander Abbot of Ford and another monk whose name I have forgotten. And I was the more

[1] A parallel from Judith, XIII, 22, is omitted.
[2] Quotations from Job and Boethius omitted.
[3] Another shrewd thrust.
[4] His letter to the head of the Cistercian Order is given in *Symb. El.* I. The gist of it is contained in the present letter.
[5] i.e., in 1194-5. There is no mention elsewhere of his stay at Oxford, but it is implied in Giraldus's attendance of Court; Hubert Walter, Archbishop of Canterbury, was made Justiciar at the end of 1193 and controlled the administration of the kingdom during the King's absence.

readily moved thereto, because I saw that our quarrel was displeasing to you and because I desired to have no rancour in my heart against any man; and I call God to witness that I have never sought to do him any harm. For as soon as I heard that the commission of inquiry into those things which I had written against him had been given to the Abbot of Garendon by letters from the Abbot of Cîteaux, I sent letters to Biddlesden with all speed, in which I warned him, and urged him to come to Lincoln that I might give him letters retracting what I had said against him and excusing myself for what I had done. But this he refused to do, presuming on his own defence and thinking that the charges I had made were false and frivolous, though I had made them in all good faith. And so in the following year he was deposed by the Abbot of L'Aumône,[1] as I heard, though he ignored his deposition. But in the same summer or rather at the beginning of autumn he was again deposed at Waverley and cast out in confusion by four Visitors sent for the purpose, who made strict inquiry into his life and behaviour. It is possible that my[2] former letters may have given occasion for this deposition. But the actual cause was without doubt his own wicked behaviour. It is, however, surprising that the wickedness of the man, which was known throughout the realm,[3] should have escaped the notice of one so wise and prudent as yourself. Marvellous indeed was his sorcery, who could thus as by art magic blind eyes so wise and keen. If the seniors of his order in England, to wit, the Abbots of Fountains, Rievaulx, Wardon and Waverley, were not set in judgment over him and did not proclaim him most worthy of deposition, why then, my Lord, I own myself to have

---

[1] A Cistercian abbey between Chartres and Blois, the mother house of Waverley.

[2] Reading *nostrae* for *uestrae* (Brewer).

[3] His misdeeds had been recorded in almost the same words, though with more lurid detail, in Giraldus' letter to the Abbot of Cîteaux (*Symb. El.* 1).

THE EVIL DEEDS OF WILLIAM WIBERT

been to blame in writing what I did concerning him.

'If any man should be curious as to my reasons for writing against a monk and, as it seemed, a man of religion, let him hear how the spark that kindled such discord came to be, and let him take warning thereby. In the year,[1] when our Lord the King was imprisoned in Germany, it chanced that in the Court of our Lady Queen Eleanor, mother of our Lord the King, I came upon this monk who a little while before had been deposed by certain Visitors[2] from his office of cellarer in his own house, and for this reason had betaken himself to gadding about. At his own instance, wherein he was most urgent and importunate, I took him once, twice and thrice with me to Wales, whither at that time I was often sent on business of state by the Queen and our Lord of Rouen,[3] who was then ruling the realm; and both going and returning, out of kindness, not to say folly, I maintained him at my own expense. And thus I made him known to the Queen and Court . . .[4] But he by his native malice, returning evil for good, secretly hinted to great persons at the Court, as I learned from them, not then, but later, that I ought not under any circumstances to be sent to Wales in the future, unless they sent some prudent man of their own following with me; for I was born in that country and a kinsman, too, of its princes; and he said that, had he not watched me so closely, I should have been false to all the commands placed upon me. And yet he was no more use than a ram in any matter of business when he was with me. For he would stand beside me mute and tongue-tied, revealing his religion by his garb and by nothing else, being wholly ignorant of the language and customs of the people. Finally to set a crown upon his malice, he accused me of treason. And since

[1] 1193.
[2] The Abbots of Neath and Margam. He had been guilty of scandalous dishonesty.
[3] Walter of Coutances.   [4] A number of quotations omitted.

he knew well how to bless friends after this fashion, he vomited out all the poison of his wickedness for my overthrow and destruction. For there is no quicker poison than intimacy, nor can any man hurt another more effectively than under the cloak of friendship. And so he asserted that it was owing to my machinations that the Welsh laid siege to a certain castle, and that every mishap that had befallen in the March had been brought about by my instigation. Thus by the infection of his venom he utterly brought to naught all my costly labours, which with such waste of time (the heaviest of my griefs) I had for seven years devoted to the service of the Court, at the very moment when I believed that my reward was at my very door. And, worse than all, he inflicted such incomparable injury on my fair fame and reputation, till then without a blemish, and so damaged me in the opinion of many persons, that the scar of that wound may scarcely be closed by any lapse of years.

Last of all, I pray you to give a kindly or at least a just hearing to the story of a crime that moves me more than all the rest and has kindled me to avenge my wrongs and to write with special vehemence, so that, while you marvel at so unprecedented a crime, you may take warning therefrom and be rendered more cautious by another's injury. When a certain notary of mine chanced to lose the seal, under authority of which he should have obtained letters of summons from the judges appointed for the purpose, and was afraid to confess its loss to me, this my betrayer, who then was with me at London, persuaded him to affix false seals to letters of summons purporting to have been issued by the judges, but in fact composed by himself, and to present them to me as genuine; for which performance he exacted his price. And then after the summons had been duly, though not lawfully issued through these letters, and when my adversary was on the point of coming to terms with me as I desired, he revealed to him what had been done by his own fraud, though he placed the guilt elsewhere ... And for this he once more fixed and received the price of his treachery. And thus this most false and fraudulent of men both incited my opponents to resist me and, though I was innocent and ignorant of this offence, fixed upon me the charge of forgery to the great detriment both of my suit and my reputation; for he that touches pitch shall be defiled thereby[1] ... Wherefore on account of the wickedness of this monk,[2] though he is a demoniac rather than a monk, and of another who displayed the Cluniac cowl,[3] whose wickedness was less but yet great and unexpected (all of which I have endured beyond my deserts), whenever I repeat litanies, which I am now more used to do than was my wont on account of depravities of this sort, among other petitions, I most devoutly ingeminate this, and advise all my faithful and familiar friends to do likewise in the faith that their prayer will be answered, 'From the malice of monks, Good Lord deliver us' ...[4] 'As to the hopes of gain which inspired him to do this, and the reasons for this fabrication of these false charges against an innocent man who never deserved aught from him save gratitude, I will merely reply with the comic poet, 'His mind is evil and his heart is evil',[5] though it may be that he thought he would acquire fame and friendship for himself at Court by defaming me, whom formerly they trusted, so that by making me seem unfaithful, he might himself win the reputation of being a faithful friend of the Court ... But there was also a further reason why he was eager to slander me. For about that very time, when, having just secured his abbacy,[6] he presumed upon his services as courier to behave as though he was on familiar terms with the more important

---

[1] Quotations from many sources omitted.
[2] Reading *ob has* (with *Symb. El.* 1) not *Abbas*.
[3] Bishop Peter.
[4] Quotations from Augustine and Jerome omitted.
[5] *Ter. Andr.* 164.
[6] Secured on the request of Queen Eleanor.

SYMBOLUM ELECTORUM

members of the Court, he had promised Peter, Bishop of Mynyw — a credulous man, where the possibility of his own promotion was concerned and always eager for translation — that he would by his persuasive powers get him translated to the See of Worcester, his native place, which then happened to be vacant, which done, he himself would succeed him as Bishop of Mynyw. Having thus made and confirmed this collusive compact between them, they could find, as it seemed to them, no obstacle or impediment to the promotion of Wibert (as I afterwards learned from one who was privy to their designs) save myself alone. Wherefore they did all that they could to damage my reputation and turn my fair fame to ignominy, because it so chanced that I was better known than anyone else in those parts. Thus it came about that at that time my name was ever on their lips as that of a traitor, a Welshman, useless and unfaithful to the King and his realm, an expert in forgery, a skilful fabricator of false seals. And whatever dishonourable and unseemly conduct they could devise to lay to my charge, this they spread abroad and dinned into men's ears. But I call to witness the Supreme Craftsman, Himself a craftsman's son, that I was wholly guiltless of those crimes which the base self-seeking malignity of monks falsely contrived to lay to my charge....[1]

Moreover to-day I find myself in the same unhappy position as of old — placed between the hammer and the anvil. For as often as the wretched See of Mynyw is or is expected to be vacant, I am forthwith exposed to the sharp teeth of those who covet its wretchedness for themselves or for their friends; as though, if once they extinguished the sole lantern of my country, they would be able to walk secure in the darkness and to dispose all things to their hearts' desire. Would that neither Bishop's throne nor See had ever been, or rather that I had never

---

[1] A rhetorical paragraph omitted.

A PLEA FOR THE DIOCESE OF MYNYW

been born in that land to be exposed to the slanders and the gnawing jealousy of my rivals, because I desire that Bishopric, as now I do and as all may see. . . .[1]

But my spirit has suffered a yet greater wound than all these. For I have not merely to complain of the members of the Church, but that virulent viper has by his blind presumption and audacity tainted with the infection of his venom even my Lord, the very head of the Court. . . .[2] Patience alone now feeds and comforts me. For it is my duty to regard all my temporal adversaries as being in truth my helpers and to hope that all impediments to my worldly prosperity are aids to guide me to eternal life. Let my adversaries gnaw their fill, let them burst their sides! But I will not cease to walk in the way of learning and virtue on which my feet are set; for God is my guide and companion therein. Let them rend and tear and stone me, if they will! The Chapter of Mynyw will never consent to the election of a monk or a physician,[3] wholly ignorant of their native tongue and unable either to preach or hear confession save through an interpreter. For we seek a physician of our souls, not a conductor of funerals, nor do we wish to have a dumb dog or a tongueless shepherd set over us. Enough long since and more than enough have we endured from the follies of pastors fresh from the cloister's shade. But if a Bishop born in England must be set over us, I would gladly consent to one of two persons — that an end may be put to this strife — either the Archdeacon of Worcester,[4] a most learned man, a vessel capable of almost all knowledge and not ignorant of our language; or the Archdeacon of Oxford,[5] a man conspicuous in liberality, endowed with rich store of literary learning and polished eloquence and not unfamiliar with the habits of both

---
[1] A rhetorical paragraph omitted.
[2] Two pages, consisting mainly of quotations, are omitted.
[3] Geoffrey, Prior of Llantony at Gloucester.
[4] Peter de Leche.   [5] Walter Map.

DE REBUS A SE GESTIS

races; for he has often visited Wales and dwells upon her borders. To either of these would I consent and do all in my power to persuade our Chapter to accept him. May your Paternity fare well in the Lord.

We now return to the De rebus a se gestis. *The letter which follows, while dealing in part with the same theme, is very different in tone, free from the insulting irony which marks the foregoing. It is hard to discover the exact relation between the two letters or to account for the omission of the foregoing from the* Autobiography. *It is possible that the first letter was written in the heat of the moment on receipt of the Archbishop's letter, and that Giraldus postponed sending it, perhaps because of the illness mentioned at the beginning of the letter given below, which may have been sent in its stead, the Archdeacon's anger having cooled. But the later letter is not an answer to the original communication from the Archbishop, but is clearly an answer to another missive summoning Giraldus to his presence.*

CHAPTER VII

The letters of ratification which the Archdeacon sent to the Archbishop

I HAVE been afflicted by a long and grievous sickness and have twice suffered a relapse and have not yet fully recovered my health. Wherefore I could not appear before you on the day appointed. But that the absence of one man may not stand in the way of the necessities of our See now vacant, I would have your Holiness know that on whatever fit person our Chapter of Mynyw may agree with the assent of the King and yourself, that choice will be welcomed by myself as final. But by a fit person I mean one who, in addition to the other qualities that beseem a pontiff, will with pure and pious benevolence

ANOTHER LETTER TO THE ARCHBISHOP

condescend to minister to the poverty of our country, will recognize the ways and customs of both peoples, devote himself to his pastoral duties and not run hither and thither round about England, begging without cease to the no small reproach and confusion of our Church, once of such authority, though now so poor; and further I mean one who will deem it a vile and contemptible thing to aspire continually to the rich benefices of England, whether by means of translation or by adding them to that which he already has. But I make an exception of all wild beasts in black cowls. For from all monks and more especially Black monks and all-devouring plagues of that sort may God henceforth and for ever defend our miserable Church, lest from being miserable it become most miserable and perish utterly of starvation. 'Assuredly' says Jerome,[1] 'it is unjust for a man who has twice been shipwrecked to accuse Neptune as the cause.' May your beloved Paternity fare well in the Lord.

Now it was because the Bishop, who had now at last died, had been a Cluniac monk and had neither exercised his authority, as a pontiff should, nor worthily displayed the virtues of a monk, that the Archdeacon excepted all monks and more especially those of that order. But if any would read the letters of the Archdeacon against William Wibert, which he sent to the Abbot of Cîteaux, and the letters which he received in reply, let him turn to the book entitled *Symbolum electorum*.[2]

Now as the Archbishop had then rejected the Archdeacon, so he also rejected the two Abbots and all born in Wales. But he offered them two Englishmen, a Cistercian monk named Alexander, who had shared his board and been his personal chaplain,[3] and by his means had recently been promoted Abbot; and Geoffrey, Prior of Llantony, on account of his skill in medicine, of which

---
[1] A quotation from *Publilius Syrus*, LXIII   [2] 1 ff.
[3] Clearly the Alexander of Ford mentioned above. See p. 139.

the Archbishop held a high opinion; for he had often attended him in sickness and had become his intimate friend; wherefore the custody of the See of Mynyw during its vacancy was afterwards committed to him by the Archbishop. But the Canons who had been sent for the election would not depart from their nominations nor accept fresh names without consent of the Chapter, and knew not whether the King would give his assent, without which according to the custom of the realm nothing could be done; and since the King was in Normandy and the Archbishop had gone to him, they returned home leaving the matter in suspense. But, hearing this, Reginald Foliot, who was notary to William, Bishop of Hereford, forthwith conceived high hopes; for he had learned that contrary to all expectation he had been nominated with the others and that Giraldus the Archdeacon, concerning whom there had been the greatest expectations, had with all other Welshmen been rejected, while he himself was an Englishman and none the less Canon of Mynyw, having been appointed to a canonry by his uncle, the late Bishop. So though he was still beardless, unripe and in no wise fit to be a Bishop, he already assumed his horns or at least was confident in his presumption that they should soon be his,[1] and flew borne on the wings of ambition to King Richard, then in Aquitaine, to be his clerk and follow the Court, that by this ladder he might climb to his uncle's throne. Moreover, Adam of Dore,[2] a man not unknown to fame, the instant the Bishop died and immediately after that great slaughter of Welshmen in Elfael, which took place about that time, crossed the sea that he might bring the news of this matter to the King, while it was still fresh, that so he might be pleasing in his sight. And he took with him letters from magnates and barons of the March, in which they wrote to the King counselling his promo-

---

[1] i.e. the horns of the mitre.   [2] Abbeydore.

CANDIDATES FOR THE VACANT SEE

tion in the Church of Mynyw. And in order that he might please the King, whom he knew to be athirst for money, and might thus find an easier approach for the fulfilment of his desires, he gave a large sum of money to the King, who knew nothing about the place, for the possession of the wood of Treville,[1] near his own house, that he might cut it down, a Royal forest, very fair and remarkable, whose tall trees were a sight to feast the eye and wherein was a great multitude of wild beasts. And had not the King soon died abroad, more especially since he was always quick to perform anything that pleased him and above all to promote unworthy persons, great tribulation would have befallen the Church of Mynyw through the ambitions and quarrels of these two men. But the Archbishop, though far away across the sea, yet was much afraid concerning the said nomination and, desiring to take precautions concerning it, procured letters from the King to be sent to the Chapter of St. David in the form that follows.

CHAPTER VIII

The Letters of King Richard to the Chapter of Mynyw

'RICHARD, by the grace of God, King of England, Duke of Normandy and Aquitaine, Count of Anjou, to his wellbeloved, the Chapter of the Church of Mynyw, greeting! Know that we are well-disposed to consult for the welfare of your Church, which has been bereft of its Shepherd. Wherefore, on the petition of the Archbishop of Canterbury we desire, under God, to make provision for it. And therefore we command you to send to us in Normandy four of the more discreet of your Chapter, so that

[1] Details of the transaction are given in the *Speculum Ecclesiae*, III, 12.

DE REBUS A SE GESTIS

they may be with us on the fifteenth[1] day after the feast of St. Andrew with letters of ratification for the election of a fit Shepherd in accordance with the will of God and the dignity of your Church. Witness myself at the Rock of Andelys,[2] the ninth day of November.'[3]

But since these letters, on account of many impediments both by sea and in the March and on the rough road through Wales, were slow in reaching Mynyw, the Canons about Christmas received the following letter from the Justiciar, at the instigation of the Archbishop.

CHAPTER IX

The Letters of the Justiciar of England to the Chapter of Mynyw

'GEOFFREY FITZPETER, to his beloved in the Lord, the Chapter of Mynyw, greeting! Know that since you have not crossed the sea to our Lord the King by the appointed term for the election of a Shepherd of your Church, the King has commanded me to cause you to be summoned to go across the sea for this purpose. We therefore command you that, putting aside all other occasion, you shall be at Westminster on the octave of St. Hilary,[4] ready to cross the sea to the Lord King or to send either four or six of the more discreet of your Chapter to himself in Normandy. Witness myself, at the Tower of London, the eighteenth day of December.'

Thereupon they, after taking counsel on the matter, sent four Canons to London, sending also by letters and messengers to Giraldus the Archdeacon at Lincoln, strongly entreating him by the fealty he owed his Church,

[1] Dec. 15th. [2] Château Gaillard. [3] 1198. [4] Jan. 20th, 1199.

THE CHAPTER'S CALL FOR HELP

to hasten to meet his fellow-Canons who had been sent to the Justiciar in London, and that he would not fail his Church in such an hour of need. But first they sent him letters as follows.

CHAPTER X

The Letters of the Chapter of Mynyw to Giraldus

'To our Lord and beloved friend in Christ, Giraldus, Archdeacon of Brecon, the Chapter of Mynyw, greeting in the Lord! Thus far we have spoken together by letters and messengers; but henceforth necessity demands that we should speak face to face, so that by interchange of counsel we may set ourselves to further the welfare and honour of our Church. Therefore we charge and counsel you on your fealty that, so soon as you have received these letters, you should come to your Church, putting aside all other occasion and excuse. It is the counsel also of all your friends that you should come. Fare you well in the Lord.'

And again a little later they wrote thus:

'To our beloved friend and brother in the Lord, Giraldus, Archdeacon of Brecon, greeting and love bound with the cement of charity! Let your discretion know that on the 21st of December on which we received your letters, we received also the commands of our Lord the King in the following form: 'Richard, by the grace of God, etc.' [*as above*]. Also about Christmas we received letters from the Justiciar of England, to the following effect: 'Geoffrey FitzPeter, etc.' [*as above*]. We await your reply as to what should be done concerning such express commands as these. For our counsel is, if it appear expedient to you, that lest we should seem too Welsh or too rebellious, we should send to our Lord the King three of the more discreet of this Chapter with yourself making the fourth; we shall send three men with letters of ratification, that they may earnestly ask for you and elect you, if indeed our Lord the King should in any way refuse his consent in this matter, which God forbid! Know also that no schisms or dissensions have arisen amongst us, but that we are all of one mind and in agreement for your election, as far as in us lies; and nothing is lacking save means to meet our expenses. But do you send us petitions to the Lord King or the Justiciar, drawn in such terms as you know to be fit, and we will seal the same. Farewell, and let us have your reply on the day after[1] the feast of St. Hilary; for then, God willing, we are to hold a general Chapter.'

Now from these letters it is clear how great was then their desire that he sooner than any other should be their Shepherd. And when he heard these things and turned them over in his mind, considering that he owed no less to his own poor Church than if he were Canon or Archdeacon of the richest, he came to London on the appointed day a little before Lent. Now the Justiciar forthwith offered the Canons (who had presented themselves before the coming of the Archdeacon) those two whom the Archbishop had offered them, namely the Prior and the Abbot, bidding them take for their Bishop whichever they pleased; but his own leanings were rather towards the Prior. Otherwise he charged them to go abroad to the King with all speed. But they put off their answer till the Archdeacon was come, and then at last after taking counsel together replied that they had no authority from their Chapter to depart from their nominations or to accept others, and that, because they were poor and

[1] Jan. 14th, 1199.

from a poor and distant country, they had not the wherewithal to meet the expense of crossing the sea; and further that neither their own Church nor any other Church of Wales was accustomed to send their deputies abroad for the purpose of making an election. But they proposed to him that they should send two of their clerks to the King with letters to himself, that they might have clear knowledge of his assent concerning the Shepherd to be placed over them; and that they should have leave to make their election in England. This was granted by the Justiciar, because he knew that they were poor and also because he was unwilling to find the expenses for which they had asked, on account of the precedent that would be set if other Cathedral Churches were to make the same demand. So they sent one of the four, named Elidor, the son of Elidor, together with a certain clerk of their Church, across the sea. And they in pursuit of this business hastened through Normandy, Anjou, and part of Aquitaine, where they received news that the King had been killed in the province of Limoges,[1] where he was making an expedition. And forthwith after long days of travel, not without fear and peril, they brought their letters to Count John, his brother, at the castle of Chinon in Anjou, and there gave him first the letters of the Justiciar, and then those of the Chapter of Mynyw together with letters from the barons and abbots and priors of the country, with many seals attached thereto, all of which letters demanded that Giraldus should be given them to be their Shepherd. And when these letters had been received and given careful hearing in the presence of Queen Eleanor, the Count's mother and Berengaria, her daughter-in-law, and also of his secretaries, the Count straightway gave them a most kindly answer with much commendation of Giraldus the Archdeacon, saying that he had served his father and himself both long and faithfully. Wherefore

[1] At Chaluz, 6th April, 1199.

DE REBUS A SE GESTIS

on the next day they received three pairs[1] of letters, i.e. one for Giraldus, in which the Count told him that he had given favourable hearing to the petition of the Chapter of Mynyw and the counsel of the barons and clergy of the country urging that he should be appointed their Shepherd, and further told him that as soon as he had seen these letters, he should not delay to come with three or four Canons of his Church who should elect him; a second pair was addressed to the Chapter of St. David saying that he had given their petition kindly hearing and that they should send him three or four of their Canons with letters of ratification for the election of Giraldus the Archdeacon; and yet a third to the Justiciar telling him not to trouble the Canons about making their election, but to postpone the whole matter, till Giraldus, whom he had summoned to himself on this business, should return again.

CHAPTER XI

How King Richard being dead, Giraldus was summoned by Letters from Count John

So in the octave of Easter the letters of the Count were delivered to Giraldus at Lincoln. And when he had read them, in accordance with the counsel of the great men of the Church of Lincoln, to whom he was dear, he left the schools, but not his study, in which he was unceasing, and taking his books and his baggage, he prepared to go to the Count together with two Canons of St. David's, Elidor and Henry FitzRobert, who bore letters of ratification from the Chapter in accordance with the Count's command.

[1] This phrase (*paria literarum*) does not imply duplication, and means no more than 'letters', and in all subsequent passages, where the phrase occurs, it is so translated.

JOHN WITHHOLDS PROMISED BISHOPRIC

CHAPTER XII

How King Richard being dead, Giraldus was summoned by Letters from Count John

Now the letter was as follows:

'To their dearest and most desired Lord John, Lord of England and Ireland, Duke of Normandy and Aquitaine, Count of Anjou, the Chapter of Mynyw, greeting and prayers in Christ! We give your Highness thanks as manifold as they are loving, for that you have so graciously heard our petition and that also of the Barons and Clergy of the whole country concerning the Shepherd to be set over us. Let your Excellency therefore know that we demand Master Giraldus, Archdeacon of St. David above all others and that we elect him by the voice of those two or three of our Canons who shall present these our letters to you; and we shall hold as ratified and acceptable the election which they shall canonically make on our behalf.'

Now it should be noted that they call him Lord, because he was not yet King; and lest perchance the Canons whom they sent might be perverted to elect another, they say that they have already elected Giraldus; whereby is shown their great desire that he should be set over them.

But meanwhile the Count, coming swiftly and suddenly into England, was on Ascension day[1] crowned King at Westminster in London. This done, the Archdeacon came to the King with his fellow canons as he had been bidden. And having heard the King's will, which none the less, on account of the dissuasion of the Archbishop of Canterbury, he was unwilling to publish openly, the Archdeacon returned to Wales and, visiting Mynyw and the Church of St. David, which he had not seen for many

[1] May 27th, 1199.

DE REBUS A SE GESTIS

years, he was received by the Canons and clerks with great joy, as also by all the people and clergy. When therefore they had debated long and earnestly concerning the choice of a Shepherd and were all firmly resolved that the Archdeacon should be set over them, at length ... the election was put off for about fifteen days to the Feast of St. Peter and St. Paul,[1] to wit on the fifth day after the Nativity of St. John the Baptist, that all the Canons of the Church might be called together. And when they were all assembled on that day, either in person or by letters of ratification or by their proctors, after long debate the desires of all concurred in the choice of Giraldus the Archdeacon, and so electing him unanimously forthwith, they earnestly entreated him to go to Rome and receive his consecration at the hands of the High Pontiff, thereby avoiding that pernicious abjuration of the rights of the Church, so that by his laudable efforts in Rome he might vindicate the Metropolitan rights of his Church, fulfilling the unique and special hopes which they had conceived concerning him since his early youth.

CHAPTER XIII

How the fixed purpose of Giraldus was suddenly and unexpectedly changed

THE Archdeacon therefore considering the grievous desolation of his Church through its lack of a Shepherd, and how its ancient right had almost been lost for ever by reason of long silence, reflecting also how the desires of all the clergy and people were alike centred upon him, and noting too that 'the voice of the people is the voice of God', and remembering the saying, 'Will thou what

[1] June 29th, 1199.

THE CHAPTER ELECT GIRALDUS

God wills, else art thou not straight',[1] and knowing that it was not safe to resist the divine will nor so unanimous a call, though it was to a poor See and to great anxieties and toil beyond the heart of man to bear that he was so summoned, for all these reasons abandoned his firm-set purpose and his most blessed life of study, and at length, though scarce even then and most unwillingly, gave his consent. And forthwith such courage and heart grew within him that he delivered himself up without hesitation or delay to the task of re-establishing the former state of his Church and with it the honour of his country as though he had been born and appointed by God for this purpose. So on the day after his election, he made ready a ship and with a wind from the east crossed to Ireland, where he met and consulted his kinsman, Meilyr then Justiciar of the Kingdom, and other magnates of that country, and received high praise from all for his enterprise, and many promises of hands to help him in so great a matter.

It is probable that the following incident (recorded in De iure et statu Meneuensis Ecclesiae VII, 338) *took place during this visit to Ireland*

A certain clerk not in his perfect mind, who used to follow the Court of the Justiciar of Ireland, delighting the young men by his ribald jests, was wont often in public audience to address Master Giraldus and immediately answer on his behalf, as follows:

'Master Giraldus, do you desire the Bishopric of Waterford?' 'I do not.' 'Do you desire the Bishopric of Wexford?'[2] 'I do not.' 'Do you desire the Bishopric of Ossory?' 'I do not.' 'Do you desire the Bishopric of Leighlin?' 'I do not.' 'Do you desire the Archbishopric of Cashel?' 'I do not.' And then he would add, 'Do you desire the Bishopric of Mynyw?' and forthwith make

[1] Augustine, Serm. I in Psalm. xxxvi. 12, *si tu nolis quod Deus uult, curuus eris*.
[2] *Vis episcopatum Gueisefordensem? Nolo.* MS. (omitted by Brewer).

answer with a loud shout, 'I do!' thereafter bursting into a loud guffaw of laughter.

The De rebus a se gestis *continues*

And before the third week after his sailing was ended, he recrossed the Irish Sea and came back to Mynyw; and when on the next day he entered the Chapter, he learned from the Canons that in the meanwhile they had received letters from the Archbishop and orders from the Justiciar that they should appear before them to make their election on the Sunday next before the Assumption of the Blessed Mary[1] and should accept as their Bishop the Prior of Llantony who, even if they did not come, should be sent to them already consecrated. Wherefore, after deliberation, they sent letters from the Chapter against the appointed day, forbidding the officers of the Archbishop, namely the Bishops of London and Rochester (for the Archbishop himself had followed the King to Normandy), and interposing their appeal, that they should not presume to consecrate or appoint any man without canonical election; and they sent other letters to the Prior of Llantony and his convent, forbidding them as members of the Church of St. David and dwelling within the diocese, to meddle with such a reckless enterprise, no election of the Prior having been made. They then wrote two letters to be delivered to the High Pontiff by their Bishop elect, after the following fashion.

CHAPTER XIV

The Decree of the Chapter directed to the Lord Pope on behalf of the Archdeacon

'To the most reverend Father and Lord, Innocent, by the grace of God, High Pontiff, the Chapter of St. Andrew and St. David, greeting and homage of devotion!

[1] Aug. 15th.

LETTER FROM CHAPTER TO POPE

We make known to your Holiness that we have at length in our Church canonically and with one accord elected our Archdeacon Master Giraldus after many demands, wherewith by the common consent of the clergy and all the people of this country we demanded him in preference to all others both from the King of England and from the Archbishop of Canterbury. Wherefore since the Archbishop and the officers of the King, with violent intrusion against our election and our privileges, have desired to set over us a stranger, wholly ignorant of our native tongue and the customs of our country, and since from the oft refusal of our demands we found the will of the Archbishop wholly contrary to us and could not approach him by reason of the snares that were on all sides set for us and above all desiring that an unlawful oath might not be extorted from our Elect to the prejudice of the rights of our Church, such as had been forced more than once on our prelates, we have therefore appealed to your protection and with one accord have sent to you, that you may confirm and consecrate him, our Elect, a man well lettered, discreet and honourable, born in lawful wedlock and of noble lineage, who will as we surely believe, be of great advantage to our Church alike in things temporal and in things spiritual. And we entreat you earnestly with supplication that, deigning to lay the hand of consecration upon him, you will of your fatherly love apply remedies to those matters which our clerks, whom we have sent with him, shall make known to your Holiness on our behalf concerning the former dignity and liberty of our Church, which has been destroyed by the lay power as a punishment for our sins. May your Paternity fare well in the Lord for many a year to come!'

The same Canons on account of the Archbishop's threat to consecrate the said Prior to rule over them, and because he was wont to be hasty in such matters (as was

DE REBUS A SE GESTIS

clear from the case of Robert, Bishop of Bangor whom he consecrated, though no election had been made), wrote to the Lord Pope by way of precaution in the following terms.

CHAPTER XV

The Letter of the Chapter of Mynyw to the Pope against the Prior of Llantony

'To the most reverend Lord and Father, Innocent, by the grace of God, High Pontiff, the Chapter of Mynyw, greetings and homage of fidelity! If perchance it shall have come to your hearing that the Prior of Llantony has been consecrated Bishop and set over our Church by the Archbishop of Canterbury, know well that this has assuredly been done contrary to our election and our will. For from the beginning when our See was vacant we have demanded and to this day demand of your fatherly love that Master Giraldus, our Archdeacon, should be consecrated, whom we have already canonically elected in our Church, being willing, by the grace of God and of yourself, to agree to no other. Moreover, as at the outset, so continually and constantly we have appealed to your protection, that no man may presume to do anything to the prejudice of our Church and of this election canonically made with the assent both of the clergy and people of this country. May your Paternity fare well always and be a blessing to the whole world of the faithful.'

They sent two also from the very bosom of the Church, Master Martin, a Canon, and Ithenard, Dean of the Province and Vice-Canon, to go to Rome with the Archdeacon, their Elect, on behalf both of the Metropolitan rights of their Church and of the election.

GIRALDUS AND THE BEST OF BROTHERS

CHAPTER XVI

The counsel and consolation which he received from his brother

THESE dispositions made, he went to his brother, a good man and prudent, Philip de Barri, and secretly made known to him the journey that he was undertaking and the cause thereof, namely that he was going in all purity of heart on behalf of God and of the advancement of his Church. And this was the answer and the counsel which he received. 'Brother, it is a difficult matter and a laborious on which you are entering, very costly also and full of peril, inasmuch as it seems that you are contending not only against the Archbishop of Canterbury, but against the King and all England. Yet if, as you say, you are fighting for God and for the dignity of the Church of St. David, which you are striving to build anew, and not for greed of earthly pomp, then you may safely take up this labour, since in truth you shall win the reward thereof either here or in the life to come. For although the intent, that brings you such trouble and torment, is good, think not that all shall forthwith go well with you to the height of your desire. Nay, rather shall that ancient enemy, the hater of good desires, place many impediments in your path, and God will suffer that to be done, whether for your proving or for your purgation. And therefore when many evils shall be gathered in your path and shall assail you, despair not, but rather recall to mind how the Apostles, the disciples of the Lord, who preached to the world the faith of Christ and the way of salvation, were none the less afflicted by great adversities, enduring chains, scourging, prisons, and wounds, and, last of all, death for the sake of Christ.' Wherefore the Archdeacon was wont to testify that these same words of a good man, though a layman and unlettered, proceeding from his

DE REBUS A SE GESTIS

great wisdom, and love, had given him great consolation in the many afflictions, grievous and great, which he endured in this struggle. Often too, when tribulation assailed him more mightily and fortune fought against him, he would recall this saying of Gregory:[1] 'Adversity which opposeth virtuous desires is not a token of reprobation, but is ordained for the proving of virtue. For who is there that does not know how blessed was Paul's turning toward Italy; and yet he endured violent shipwreck, but none the less the ship of his heart stood unshaken in the midst of the waves.'

CHAPTER XVII

Concerning the first labour of Giraldus on his way toward the Roman Court and the assault that fortune made upon him even at his very door

THE Archdeacon, therefore, set forth upon his journey and, committing himself wholly to God and to St. David, whose soldier he was, came on the Vigil[2] of the Assumption of the Blessed Mary to the Monastery of Strathflur[3] with his companions and all his followers; and there on the same day he received his treasure-store of books, which had been brought from England to Brecon and thence to Strathflur, that they might be out of the power of the English, whatever should befall. And on the day after the Assumption, Ithenard the Dean, who had been sent by the Archdeacon toward Brecon with part of his money and the horses that had brought his books, lest he might be waylaid by the English in England, was plundered by the Welsh in the mountains of Builth[4] and

[1] *Ep.* IX, 122 (*Ad Recharedum*)   [2] Aug. 14th, 1199.
[3] The Cistercian Abbey of Strata Florida, SW. of Aberystwyth.
[4] *Buella* M.S. not *Ruella* (Brewer): *Buellt*.

THE JOURNEY TO ROME

avoiding Scylla, fell into Charybdis, 'From an unlooked-for foe receiving hurt'.[1] And because such troubles do not come singly, when Ithenard returned after being thus despoiled, he was stricken forthwith with grievous sickness and died, perchance because of the confusion caused him by this mishap. And so Giraldus at the very outset of his journey, was robbed both of his money and his follower, and was taught thereby bravely to bear the assaults of fortune and the outrage of adversity.

But proceeding from Strathflur and hastening through the mountains of Elenydd[2] towards Cwmhir[3] and thence, entering England at Kerry, he sped upon his way and crossed the Flemish sea from Sandwich. For fifteen days and more he waited at St. Omer for his messengers who were to come to him from the market of Winchester,[4] and there his second companion, Master Martin, was seized with grievous sickness, so that he was forced to send him home, a second outrage at the hands of fortune. But, finding two youths of his own Church, who were in the schools of those parts, one of them being a Canon of Mynyw, he took them with him that they at least might stand with him for the Metropolitan rights of his Church. Since therefore on account of the great war which had broken out between King Philip of France and Baldwin, Count of Flanders, who had taken sides with John, King of England, he could not go by the direct way through France, he followed a long circuit to the left through the lowlands of Flanders and Hainault; and thence through the great woods of Arden (Ardennes), which are both rough and horrible, he came at last after skirting Champagne and passing through Burgundy to the public causeway, whereon he travelled with pilgrims and merchants.

[1] *Ov. Her.* VI, 82.
[2] The hilly region S. of Plinlimmon. The old track still exists.
[3] A Cistercian Abbey E. of Rhayader.
[4] Probably bringing money of suitable currency for the journey. Cp. the money changers at the market of Troyes, p. 318.

DE REBUS A SE GESTIS

Now it is a marvel that, twenty-six years before, this labour had been foreseen by a certain man of Mynyw. For during the last days of David, Bishop of Mynyw, he dreamed that he saw a great procession there, and all the bells were pealing loud. And when he inquired what this might mean, he was told that it was the Elect of great Arden who was coming to the Church. And when he looked more closely, it seemed to him that it was Giraldus the Archdeacon who was coming with such pomp as the Elect of great Arden, and was received with much honour. But some who heard of this vision after the death of Bishop David, thought that, because Giraldus was the first and chief of those nominated, Wales had been called great Arden in the vision, because like Arden it is a land covered with forests. But the vision, more truly interpreted, had in view the time when he was truly and formally elected. And he was called the Elect of great Arden, because he was destined to enter upon so great and perilous a labour through great Arden, a pathless and circuitous journey, beset with footpads and robbers.

CHAPTER XVIII

How he came to Rome and gave the Pope books, not pounds

AND so crossing the Alps and passing hastily through Italy and Tuscany, he came to Rome about the Feast of St. Andrew[1] and, approaching the feet of Pope Innocent III, who was then in the second year of his papacy, he presented him with six books, which he had composed[2] with much study, saying among other things, 'Others

[1] Nov. 30th, 1199.
[2] Not 'bound' as Brewer seems to take it. Giraldus would not bind the books himself.

ARRIVAL AT ROME

give you pounds (*libras*), but I give you books (*libros*)'. Now the Pope, who was most learned and loved literature, kept all these books together by his bedside for about a month and used to display their elegant and pithy phrases to the Cardinals who visited him, and finally gave all save one to different Cardinals who asked for them. But the *Gemma Ecclesiastica*, which he loved beyond the rest, he would not suffer to be parted from him. And after no long delay, but about fifteen days before Christmas, a courier brought letters from the Archbishop of Canterbury to the Court, which a certain clerk, who came in the same company, stole secretly, suspecting that they were sent against Giraldus, and offered them to him for sale. Now twelve letters were there, sent to the Pope and to the Cardinals. But Giraldus, when he heard this, bade the clerk first show him the letters addressed to one of the Cardinals, that he might see whether it was sent against him or not. So the clerk showed him the letters addressed to Peter of Piacenza; and when Giraldus broke the seal and looked into the letters, he found that they were full of denunciations, bringing grave accusations both against himself and his election. Wherefore since he knew by this that the others were composed in the same tenor, he approached John, Lord Bishop of Albano, whom he knew better than any others who were then Cardinals, and consulted him on the matter. And he received the answer that he should give nothing for the letters nor accept them even as a gift; for to do this would be to wrong the Lord Pope and the Cardinals to whom they had been sent; and further that he should rather desire to have an adversary, than to make a long stay in the Court without one. But the clerk, when he could get nothing from Giraldus, betook himself to the courier and restored the letters to him for a price. Now the Pope, as soon as he received the letters of the Archbishop, summoned Giraldus and ordered that the letters should

DE REBUS A SE GESTIS

straightway be shewn to him. And when he had read them he answered, 'My Lord, this man has written rather as an Arch-adversary than as an Archbishop, sparing neither truth nor modesty, if only he might thus do me a hurt'. Whereto the Pope replied, 'Do you wish then to answer these letters?' And he made answer, 'I do so desire, if it please your Excellency'. Then said the Pope, 'So be it; do you answer these letters with letters of your own, after Christmas'. For Christmas was close at hand, and during those days they desired to be free from business of the Court. But on the day after Epiphany[1] (for they do not keep holiday beyond that feast), the Archdeacon in full Consistory declared that he was ready to reply to the letters which the Archbishop of Canterbury had sent against him; and the Pope replied, 'Let the letters of the Archbishop first be read, and then do you reply'. The letters were therefore read in the presence of all, and I have thought it not superfluous to give their tenor here.

CHAPTER XIX

The letters of the Archbishop sent against Giraldus[2]

To the most Holy Lord and Father in Christ, Innocent, by the grace of God, High Pontiff, Hubert, by divine permission the humble minister of the Church of Canterbury greetings and devoted reverence and obedience, such as is owed to his Lord and Father! The ordinance of divine Providence has set you over nations and kingdoms that the wisdom of your solicitude may according to the merits of each, tear out, destroy, dissipate and overthrow,

[1] Jan. 6th, 1200.
[2] This letter is found entire in *Invect.* 1, 1; the MS. of *De rebus* breaks off a little before the end.

build up and plant, so that the Son of the most High, through you whom he has made his vice-gerent here on earth, may eradicate and displant every plant that the Heavenly Father has not planted[1] and destroy those that scatter abroad, because they labour not to gather with Him.[2] For therefore has plenitude of power been given to you from above that the greatness of your Majesty, to which all things must bow, may reduce and bring to order those things which cannot be corrected by us who are called to share your solicitude.

Most Holy Father, I do not think that you are ignorant that the Church of Canterbury is the Mother and Metropolis of the Church of Mynyw and the other Churches of all Wales; as is testified by the confirmations and writings of your predecessors of blessed memory, Adrian, Eugenius, Alexander and Celestine, and as your own recent letter of confirmation makes manifest. None the less, of late, as I have learned on sure information, a certain Archdeacon of the Church of Mynyw, Giraldus by name, a Welshman by nation and the kinsman by blood or affinity of many of the magnates of Wales, encouraged perhaps by confidence in his lineage, though it would beseem him to rely on his virtue rather than on his blood, has procured his election to the Bishopric of Mynyw by the voice of three Canons only, whom (it is said) he had induced thereto in a manner far from right or seemly, though none of the other Canons showed him favour or gave their assent. Yet he, relying on such a nomination, has not sought or waited for the boon of confirmation by myself, to whom first he should have had recourse, but usurping both the name and the authority of Elect, when he found the Canon, who had charge of the seal of the Chapter, was not to be moved by prayers, terrified him with bloody threats. For the said custodian of the seal had placed it on the altar of the Cathedral Church, after

[1] Matt. xv. 13. [2] Matt. xii. 30.

first interposing an appeal, so that no one should presume to remove it without the consent of the Chapter. But Giraldus none the less, showing no more reverence for his appeal than he had shown compunction at his own intrusion, removed the seal, that he might be able to make instruments of patronage or evidence as often and of such a nature as he might desire. God knows, before whom I stand and from whom no secrets are hid, that, had I believed him a fit person, called to such high eminence after canonical election, I would with all goodwill have bestowed upon him the boon of confirmation, aye, and of consecration as well, if he had been willing to seek either one or both at my hands. But he, having little confidence in the validity of his election, unlawfully and uncanonically disregarding myself, has (so the rumour runs) made off post haste to the Apostolic See, that by false testimonies he may deceive you to whom the manner of his election has not yet been made known.[1] But you know, most wise Father, that oral witness deserves more credence than written evidence for more than one reason, since the will of those who are named as witnesses may not agree with the written evidence owing to the theft or violent seizure of the true seal or, as often happens, by the making of a fraudulent impression with the true seal.[2] These things I have thought fit to make known to you, most Holy Father, not (God knows) through any personal enmity, but in my zeal for justice and, it may be more restrainedly and temperately than is expedient or demanded by the truth, in order that, the truth not being known to you, you might not, so please your Holiness, by any means whatsoever be so far deceived as to lay the hand of consecration upon him or cause it to be laid by another. But we would desire

---

[1] Reading *quibus* for *cui* (*De Rebus*) or *qui* (*Invect.* 1, 1).

[2] The language is redundant and obscure. The corresponding passage in Giraldus's reply suggests that *expressa similitudo* not *expressa similitudine* is the true reading here.

DENUNCIATION OF GIRALDUS

that this also should be known to your Holiness, namely that if the Archdeacon, whom I have so often mentioned, should (which God forbid!) obtain from you the boon of consecration, he would not be content with this,[1] but since those 'who obtain what they had never hoped to obtain, conceive the most reckless hopes', would extend his efforts to more ambitious and nefarious schemes and, on the pretext of consecration by yourself, would irreverently seek exemption from the jurisdiction of the Church at Canterbury (a privilege which none the less he will never obtain, if God so will and your constant wisdom be to refuse), and would thus to the best of his power sow the seeds of perpetual dissension between the Welsh and the English for all time to come. For the Welsh being sprung by unbroken succession from the original stock of the Britons, boast that all Britain is theirs of right. Wherefore, if the barbarity of that wild and unbridled nation had not been restrained by the censure of the Church, wielded by the Archbishop of Canterbury, to whom it is known that this race has thus far been subject as being within his Province, this people would by continual or at least by frequent rebellion have broken from their allegiance to the King, whereby the whole of England must have suffered disquietude. May the most High long preserve your life and security.

That Giraldus's spirited and far more scholarly reply was contained in whole or in part in Chapter XIX of the De rebus a se gestis *is known from the Table of Contents ('De Archidiaconi responsione', a title which suggests that it may also have contained some account of the reception of the Archbishop's letter and the effect of the Archdeacon's reply). But it only survives to-day in* Invectiones, I, 2.

---

[1] Here the MS. of *De rebus a se gestis* ends.

INVECTIONES

The Reply of Giraldus, Archdeacon of Mynyw

Holy Father, as you know it is characteristic of the inborn insolence of dogs that, when they cannot bite, they bark without ceasing. Wherefore for the defence of my reputation, I have thought fit, with your permission to reply in your presence to the letters of that Archbishop of Canterbury, which have been composed to dissuade you from hearing me; and in his desire to have the better of me, he has composed them almost in the form of an Invective. I only wish he had written with his own pen and not with another's! I will deal with his arguments in detail as they occur, that he may know what a vain waste of effort it is and how it invites retaliation, to offend men of learning by letters such as these and by writing to provoke those who have the skill to write[1] a counterblast against them. From the beginning of his long and verbose letter to its very end, 'since out of the abundance of the heart the mouth speaketh',[2] his words are shameless, prompted by gnawing envy, so that almost every word seems directly or indirectly to besmirch my reputation. Nothing, it is true, is written directly against my character, but there are certain things suggested indirectly as if to defame me. But against the form of my election he openly inveighs, and with a shamelessness only equalled by his irreverence writes the falsest of charges to be read aloud before such an audience of distinguished persons as is here present. Yet, God helping me, I shall overthrow all these accusations by effective argument and by the living voices of my witnesses. Now at the very outset of his letter he says 'that through you the Son of the Most High may root out and displant every plant that the Heavenly Father has not planted'. He speaks boldly, not to say presumptuously, as if every

[1] *In scripturis eruditos.* The antithesis seems to demand that this should mean 'skilled in writings' rather than 'skilled in the Scriptures'.
[2] Matthew. xii. 34.

THE ARCHDEACON REPLIES

plant that is unworthy and unacceptable to God should be rooted up, and he alone stand firm and unshaken. But who shall boast that his heart is pure? What shall the reed that is in the desert do when the cedar of Lebanon is shaken? It is written, 'Happy is the man that feareth alway',[1] and elsewhere, 'I was afraid of all my works'.[2] Wherefore he seems almost to have said with the Pharisee, 'I am not as other men are'.[3]

He says also and boasts that he is fortified by the priviīeges of Adrian, Alexander III and Celestine. In regard to which I note that he does not begin with those remote in time, but only with the moderns, which seems to agree with what is said in the letters of the people and clergy of Wales, which you have received, wherein they assert that only three Bishops of Mynyw have been subject to the Church of Canterbury. But this also is worthy of note, that he calls those writings 'confirmations', not 'donations'. Nay, let him look to it, and his predecessors too, that by suppression of the truth they have not blinded the eyes of the Apostolic See. These things however require special treatment at the appropriate time, wherefore let me deal with the matter immediately in hand. He proceeds, 'A certain Archdeacon of the Church of Mynyw, Giraldus by name, A Welshman by nation, etc.' Once he knew my name well enough, though he strives now to extinguish both my name and fame. He would like to borrow some argument from my name if he could. But this name of mine seems to smack rather of France than of Wales. 'A Welshman by nation.' This argument he draws from the company he keeps and from his own nature. For he introduces it by way of insult and to do me a hurt, as if he were openly saying, 'Because he is born in Wales, he cannot be a prelate in Wales'. On which showing there should be no English appointed

[1] Proverbs xxviii. 14.
[2] Job ix. 28. So in the Vulgate; not in A.V.
[3] Luke xviii. 11.

prelates in England, nor French in France, nor Italians in Italy. Very well! give them Shepherds who are ignorant of the language, and you will find most excellent preachers! Again he says, 'He is kinsman by blood or affinity to many of the Magnates of Wales, etc.' He speaks truth; and he would not have written less, but more truthfully, if he had said 'all the great men of Wales of either nation — on his mother's side the Princes of Wales, and on his father's English Barons of the King, men who, fighting nobly for the King and for his realm, now by their castles hold the sea-coast of Wales against the Welsh' — but this he suppresses out of caution because it would help my cause. He himself acknowledges the nobility of my lineage and I do not deny it. It is for you to consider whether nobility in itself should prejudice my case, when it has other arguments to support it. Again he says, 'Encouraged perhaps by confidence in his blood, though it would beseem him rather to rely on virtue not on blood'. This is from Claudian, who says, 'On virtue not on blood should man rely'.[1] That is true because if a man cannot rely on both, it is better to rely rather on virtue. He concedes me one of these advantages. I concede him neither. Again he says, 'He has procured his election to the Bishopric by the voice of three Canons only, whom (it is said) he had induced thereto in a manner far from right or seemly'. It is a wonder that he has had the face to write such stuff to your Holiness and to such an assembly as this and to state what was so clearly contrary to the truth. But perhaps he thought that to write a lie was a very different thing from speaking a lie. For it is written, 'The *words* of a priest must be either true or sacrilegious'. The same ought to be true of his writing also, especially when it is sent as a statement of the truth to his Lord and Father upon earth. But to save his conscience he qualified his

[1] *De IV Cons. Honor.* 220.

HE DEFENDS HIMSELF

statement by adding the words 'it is said'. For all Wales knows, and no small part of the West of England knows also that for many years before the death of the Bishop of Mynyw, now at last deceased, all the people and clergy of the country, knowing that he was utterly useless, desired that I should rule their Church; and that desire was even stronger after his death. That good Bishop of Ireland (God be gracious to his soul!) knew it too and before his death testified thereto in the presence of yourself and the brethren; for in those last two years he was continually going and coming through our country and waiting for a breeze or a ship in the harbour of our Church, and had ample opportunity to hear and ponder the desires of the clergy and the people of Mynyw. So likewise the Lord Bishop elect of Bangor, before he died, bore witness to the same in this very Court. And yet for almost a whole year after the death of our Bishop, all the many letters and messengers both of the great men of the country and of the clergy from without, as well as the Chapter itself, could not recall me from the Schools, where I had taken my stand, until at last I received letters and messengers from the King of England now upon the throne, recalling me to Mynyw. But if I had been so eager to be the ruler of that Church, as to desire to enter it not rightly, but in any way I could, as he says in his letters, and to break in through the wall rather than go in by the door, I should doubtless have made greater haste. It is not likely for a revenue of twenty marks, and hard to collect at that, and at such a cost to my reputation, I should have been ready to forego a revenue of a hundred marks which I already possessed in peace and quiet. For I should have been a sorry merchant and have made a poor exchange. God knows, to whom all things are open and laid bare, that I should scorn to have obtained even his Archbishopric, which is so great and wealthy, by means such as those by which

INVECTIONES

according to him, I sought to obtain this Bishopric. Nay more, I say that I should scorn to have obtained it by such means as those by which he did actually obtain his Archbishopric. For unless King Richard had been detained in Germany and imprisoned there in many places, he would without a doubt have made very different provision for the Church of England.

Moreover, if, as he writes, I had been elected by the voice of no more than three Canons, all the rest being unwilling and protesting, he would assuredly, since we have almost as many English Canons as Welsh, have sent one or more Canons, won to his service by bribes or by entreaty, to give evidence against me in this Court. But he sent none, because he could not find even one. Again with no less shamelessness he has declared that I forcibly carried off the seal of our Chapter. But our Church knows, the whole province knows, our clergy know who took part in these proceedings and are here before you today, and more than all these He knows who knows all things, and would that in this grave conjuncture He might correct this liar by striking him with His vengeance! all these, I say, know how far removed this charge is from the truth. But which of these two things, I ask you, is the more worthy of belief? The letters of the Archbishop, whose conclusion clearly shows that they were kindled from the tinder both of jealousy and of fear, and in which his sole design is to defame me, seeing that he has sent no one hither to represent him and that he neither pretends or promises that he will prove a single one of all his statements either in your own presence or before such judges as you may appoint? Or the decree of our Chapter and the letters both of the clergy and the people of our country and the living voices of our clerks who stand before you, all of whom with one voice cry aloud in my favour, unworthy though I be?

Moreover, he has written this also: 'If he had known

HE DENOUNCES THE ARCHBISHOP

me to be a fit person, called after canonical election, etc.,' as though he would say, 'He is not fit'. I confess my insufficiency, for I recognize that I may be insufficient and unfit to rule even one small parish church. Let him, if he please, boast with pharisaic scorn that he is more than fit to rule almost the whole Church of England. But he is ready to regard as exceeding fit his monk or physician, a simpleton, an illiterate fool, whom with such vast, continuous and unceasing effort he strives to thrust upon us, that with him for Bishop he may 'enjoy his slumber all unvexed by care'.[1] But he refuses the name of canonical to this election which was made in a Church that is the mother and womb of Churches, with the consent of all and the applause of the whole people. Yet if four Canons or six, having been summoned to London with letters of ratification were forced by threats and spoliation of their property to elect his monk or physician or any other ...[2] he would, I believe, consider such an election to be just and canonical; for he is accustomed to such elections, though it was to prevent such scandals that his predecessor, the glorious Martyr, offered his head to the swords of impious assassins. But I cannot find that such a form of election has yet been approved by the law of the Church.

He also adds, 'that he would with all good will have bestowed upon me the boon of confirmation or of consecration or even of both'. But to this I will reply when I come to his conclusion, where he openly contradicts himself, though I would here interpose the words of Ovid, 'Sweeter is water from the fount itself'.[3] Again he introduces the following juristic argument against me: 'Since oral witness deserves more credence

[1] Perhaps an echo of *Virg. Georg.* III, 435.
[2] There are here two small gaps in the MS. Little is lost, but the text cannot be restored with certainty.
[3] *Ex Pont.* III, v. 18.

INVECTIONES

than written evidence.' But I would have him know that with the written evidence from the body of our Church I have brought witnesses as well. Still, if written evidence without oral does not deserve credence, then no credence should be given to his letters by themselves, since he does not produce any witnesses. Again he enumerates a number of forms of forgery of which I have never yet heard: 'Either the theft or violent seizure of the true seal or a fraudulent impression with the true seal'. He who enumerates different forms of forgery with such precision, is clearly well acquainted with them, and yet he has dared to hurl back at me the insinuation that I am a forger, that so he may deprive the decree of our Chapter and their letters of testimony of all credibility and authority. I would that he was as little liable to charges of incendiarism and homicide (witness the fate of Longbeard of London!)[1] as I am to that of forgery. For till now it has been my habit to make books, not seals; and if therefore he should desire to accuse my books of falseness, I should desire to have such a corrector as himself, who would neither remove anything of mine nor add anything of his own. My Lord, if it please you, there is nothing worthy either of wonder or of indignation, if being embittered by what he has written I should write bitterly myself. For I have not yet travelled so far on the road to perfection as not to be moved when accused of such disgraceful deeds. Our comic poet tells us that 'he who *will* say what he wishes, shall hear what he has no wish to hear'.[2] And the poet says:

> Nay, I love peace. Let no man wound me then!
> To him that stirs me, 'Touch me not'. I cry;
> You'll rue 't, and hear your name in mockery trolled
> By every ribald in the streets of Rome.[3]

---

[1] See p. 271.   [2] *Ter. And.* 920.   [3] *Hor. Sat.* II, i. 44.

HE REFUTES HIS CALUMNIES

And again he says:

> What if the man you bark at be a knave
> Meet for your shafts, and you are free from blame?
> 'Why then they'll laugh the matter out of court,
> Non-suit the rogue and send you home scot-free'.[1]

Moreover, at the end of his letter he adds that if your Grace should confer the boon of consecration upon me, I should not be content with this, but should extend my efforts to more ambitious and nefarious schemes and seek exemption from the jurisdiction of the Church of Canterbury. He does not say that I should seek to champion the rights of my Church and to revive its ancient dignity, but under the cloak of the word 'exemption' he has attemped to cast a veil over our rights and ancient dignity. But, look you, Holy Father, how clearly he here reveals the rancour of his heart and the tinder that has kindled all his hatred. For from the very outset he has opposed my promotion and has not ceased to this very day. And thus he contradicts himself. For he said earlier that he would gladly bestow the boon of confirmation or consecration or both upon me, etc. But ever since he has feared or suspected that I should champion the rights of our Church, it has been known to all that he would never confer either boon upon me or allow anyone in the world to do so, except perchance upon disgraceful terms, after I had first under compulsion given a solemn oath such as his predecessors have been accustomed to exact from us, namely that at no time whatsoever would we champion the rights of our Church against the Church of Canterbury. But here he has interposed a saying from Seneca[2] from his treatise on *Clemency* addressed to Nero — 'Those who obtain what they had never hoped to obtain, conceive the most reck-

---
[1] *Hor. Sat.*, II, i. 84.   [2] I, i, 7.

INVECTIONES

less hopes'. See how he has the philosophers and all the Scriptures ready to his hand. They are mistaken, then, who credit him with having little knowledge of literature! Yet if this saying of Seneca which is here cited in a mutilated form, be heard in its entirety, it may be applied to his fortunes rather than mine, seeing that it was by the power, not to say violence, of princes to whom he has cloven, after the fashion of the world, rather than by any merit of his own that he raised himself from insignificance and advanced beyond all hope to such high dignity and lofty eminence as now he holds. For Seneca says, 'Excess of good fortune makes them greedy, nor are eager desires ever so firmly controlled as to cease when they have gained their end. For great success provides a stepping-stone to greater yet, and having obtained what they never hoped to obtain, they conceive the most reckless hopes'. See how exactly this saying may be adapted to his own case, who from the Deanery of York climbed to the Bishopric of Salisbury and thence to the supreme glory of Canterbury,[1] and supported thus by chance rather than by skill, by fortune rather than by virtue, ascended step by step from great things unto greater. And since sudden and unexpected fortune makes men greedy beyond all bounds, he is not content with these achievements, but (so it is said) dares to aspire to the crown of Apostolic honour itself, and thus from the positive, nay from some lower degree, if that were possible, he strives to soar upon the wings of ambition to the superlative, or if that were possible, higher yet. Indeed only last year a flatterer, as though preparing to open a path to these ambitions and to set up a ladder whereby he might mount to their fulfilment (for the Archbishop had not only attempted to get himself made Cardinal of the Court of Rome, but had openly and publicly boasted of it), a flatterer, I say,

[1] York, 1186; Salisbury, 1189; Canterbury, 1193-1205.

THE ARCHBISHOP'S AMBITIONS

offered him this tribute in verse, not without profit to himself:

> Thomas' successor, in the days to come
> Thy hands shall hold the pastoral staff of Rome.
> (*Thomae successor, succedes baculo Romae.*)

Having rewarded the poet with ten pieces of gold, the Archbishop, to display the greatness of his erudition, on the morrow presented him with the following verse, forged laboriously as he burned the midnight oil, and further doubled his reward as well.

> Pray, I entreat thee, brother, pray for me,
> That worse than Thomas I may never be.
> (*Ora, frater, pro me ne sim deterior Thomae.*)[1]

But the saying of Seneca can by no manner of means be made to fit my case, since if I were to obtain that of which he makes such huge efforts to deprive me, it would not provide me with a stepping-stone from great things unto greater, but (save as regards my rank) a descent from greater things to less. But if he, so great a man and worthier than the worthiest has been able to conceive such high and lofty hopes, why should not I, so insignificant a being, conceive the most modest of expectations? Virgil in his *Bucolics* writes:

> To Mopsus Nisa's given!
> To what, then, may we lovers not aspire?[2]

as if he were saying, 'Since so noble a maid cleaves to such a worthless lover, why should any man despair?'

Finally, to clinch these arguments by a last hammer-blow ...[3] he tries to fortify his case by dragging in the

---
[1] The best that can be said for these astounding hexameters is that they are scanned by accent, not by quantity.
[2] VIII, 26.
[3] It is impossible to give a satisfactory rendering of the words omitted: *totumque negocium sub securi quadam et securitate concludens*; sc. 'to axe the whole affair and win security for himself'.

INVECTIONES

King as his ally, saying that, had not the Church of Wales been made subject by provincial law to the Church of England, 'that people would either by continual or at least by frequent rebellion have broken from their allegiance to the King'. But in this he seems, saving his authority, to have written with a certain lack of circumspection, as if the King of England with all his great forces could not subdue that little nation by the power of his material sword, without borrowing the spiritual sword to aid him. Hence is it, my Lord, that the princes of Wales make common cause in complaining to your Holiness that, as often as they meet their enemy in the field of battle to defend their country and its freedom, all who fall on their side, fall excommunicate, by the sentence of Canterbury, which is arbitrarily imposed in defiance both of common prudence and all ordinance of law.

Holy Father, as I have said, I am descended from both nations, from the Princes of Wales and from the Barons of the March, who defend the boundaries of the realm against the continual rebellion of the Welsh, and yet I hate injustice by whichever nation it be committed. And what can be more unjust than that a people, founded and rooted in the faith from days of old — for from the time of Pope Eleutherius who by the ministrations of Fagan and Duvianus, in the days of Lucius, King of the Britons, planted the faith of Christ in that island, long before the coming of the Saxons, who remained in their paganism even to the times of Gregory — what, I say, could be more unjust than that such a race, merely because they defend their bodies, lands and liberties against a hostile nation, repelling force with force, should forthwith be sundered from the body of Christ and delivered over unto Satan? It is an injustice unheard of till now.

Holy Father, a thing came to pass last year, so horrible that it is not right that you and your brethren should

JUSTICE FOR WALES

be left in ignorance concerning it. For when that man was still Justiciar of the realm, and had scarce held office for a year, the Welsh besieged a certain castle which the English had built not within the boundaries of England, but rather in Wales itself, to the end that they might rob them of their lands. And when he heard this, that Archbishop, that he might display his great power and courage, straightway mustered the English forces and coming to those parts, on the very same day on which he had ordered his men to give battle to the Welsh, called together the Bishops and clergy of those parts and, with candles lit for all to behold, excommunicated every Welshman that was arrayed against him. . . .[1] And it so chanced, such being the fortune of war, that about three thousand Welshmen were slain that day by the edge[2] of the sword; nor indeed would it be cause for marvel that signs and wonders should be vouchsafed to the successor of the Blessed Thomas. Moreover, on the morrow when he received the news of that great slaughter, forthwith through all the fortress of Bridgnorth, where he then was, he ordered the bells to be publicly rung and the 'Te Deum laudamus' to be chanted loud, like a good shepherd giving thanks to God that on that one day he had sent down to Hell the souls of so many of his sheep. But whether he ought more truly to be called a good shepherd of his flock or rather a ravening wolf, I leave as a matter of further inquiry. So on that occasion he made an evil use of both the swords committed to him and to speak truth it was an evil thing that he should at that time have had both swords at once in his grasp. Moreover, he has sent letters to many in this Court, more especially to those whom he thinks to be especially well-disposed towards him, earnestly entreating them to do him

[1] A short hiatus in the MS.
[2] Another hiatus which may with some certainty be filled by the Biblical *in ore* (a favourite phrase with Giraldus). He alludes to the battle of Pains Castle. See App. IV.

DE IURE ET STATU

great service and confer upon him rich reward by causing me to be sent back in confusion having accomplished nothing. But if I have ever desired to enter or rather to force an entry into our Church, after the manner which he depicts, then may God in his good time send upon me that confusion which he desires and with it yet greater chastisement. If, however, I have bowed myself to receive this burden in all purity and piety according to the will of God, then let that confusion return upon his own head and let Divine Providence, which cannot be deceived, proceed to deal with him as it deems best. Thus my Lord, do I reply to those letters and thus refute all that might in any way move you or your brethren. Of your good pleasure suffer, I implore you, that the decree of our Chapter and the letters of testimony and the living voices of these my witnesses may be given a hearing, so that, when all things have been fully debated in your presence, the truth may shine forth this day more brightly than the sun.

The story is now continued from the De iure et statu meneuensis Ecclesiae (Book II, R.S. III, p. 165). *This work does not contain all that was in the lost portion of the* De rebus a se gestis, *but the table of contents which precedes the latter shows that it contains the more important part, though a few picturesque incidents* (e.g. *his passage of the Alps in winter*) *have been lost.*

Now it happened on a certain evening, when Giraldus had gone to visit the Pope in his own chamber, he found him friendly and affable even beyond his wont. Wherefore, mention being made, at the very outset of their conversation, of the Metropolitan rights of the Church of Mynyw, the Pope ordered his Register to be brought, wherein the Metropolitan Churches of the pontifical dominion throughout the whole Christian world are set forth in order, kingdom by kingdom, together with

THE POPE'S REGISTER

the Sees subject to them. And when he turned to the realm of England the following was found therein and read aloud. 'The Metropolitan Church of Canterbury has subject to it the following Churches: Rochester, London', and so on in order, and when the suffragan Churches of England had been enumerated, after a rubric[1] 'Concerning Wales', the text proceeded, 'In Wales there are the Churches of Mynyw, Llandaff, Bangor and St. Asaph'. And on hearing this, the Pope said with a mocking smile, 'See, here is the Church of Mynyw enumerated with the rest'. But Giraldus made answer, 'Nay, neither it nor the other Churches of Wales are enumerated with the rest in the same way, to wit, in the accusative, as were the Suffragan Churches of England. If they had been in the accusative, then in truth they might be held to be subject to Canterbury.' And the Pope replied, 'You did well to note that. But there is another point which is likewise in favour of yourself and your Church, namely, the insertion of a rubric, which is never used in the Register save where there is a transition, either from kingdom to kingdom or from one Metropolitan Church to another'. 'True,' said Giraldus, 'and Wales is a portion of the Kingdom of England, and not a Kingdom in itself.' To which the Pope replied, 'You may be sure, then, of one thing, that our Register is not against you'. Moreover, when the Pope inquired whether the Church of Mynyw had any 'Privileges' dealing with the right which it claimed, Giraldus replied that once it had abundance of 'Privileges', but that, since the Church was situated in a corner of Wales upon the Irish Sea, it was often plundered by pirates coming thither in summer in their

---

[1] Cp. *The Papal Chancery*, R. L. Poole, p. 151. A Provincial of the type described exists in the Gesta of Cardinal Albinus, written in 1188 or 89, presenting the grammatical features and rubrication mentioned by Giraldus. But it is probable that the actual volume to which reference has been made was an earlier Register of the time of Alexander III. Cp. also op. cit. 193-5.

DE IURE ET STATU

long ships from the Isles of Orkney, and was often left desolate and almost in ruins, its books and privileges, its vestments, its phylacteries and treasures being carried away and its Canons also and clergy sometimes slain. And again when the Pope inquired how and for what reason the Church of Mynyw had been deprived of its pristine dignity, Giraldus in answer expounded to him how its Metropolitan rank had disappeared when Sampson, the last Archbishop of Mynyw, fled overseas to Brittany to escape the plague of jaundice (as is set forth about the beginning of this, the Second Book).[1] But when he heard this, the Pope replied, 'Nay, but Sampson of Dol was Archbishop of York'. But to this Giraldus replied, 'Nay, Father, saving your reverence, but the chronicles of Dol also bear witness that this Sampson was ours and not another's. Wherefore in a sequence of theirs concerning St. Sampson is found this verse:

> "Praesul ante Meneuensis
> dignitatis in Dolensis
> transfertur fastigium."[2]

The people of York have been deceived by the identity of the name; for they too once had an Archbishop Sampson.'

Again, when the Pope inquired how much time had elapsed since that Sampson fled across the sea, Giraldus replied that this happened in the time of Pope Gregory, the great Doctor, who sent Augustine and his comrades to England. At this the Pope said, 'Then the Archbishops of Canterbury are safe by long prescription'. But Giraldus made answer, 'Your objection is valid, Holy Father, as regards the recovery of the pallium. For as far as this is concerned, since the pallium was at

[1] *R.S.*, III, p. 151. 'The Yellow Plague' of epidemic jaundice.
[2] 'Once Prelate of Mynyw, he is transferred to the lofty honour of Dol.'

that time transferred and down to the time of Bishop Bernard was neither claimed nor recovered, we merely seek the expression of your fatherly pity and do not ask you to give judgment in our favour. But as regards the honour of our Metropolitan rank in its entirety, save only for the use of the pallium, you must know that the case is far otherwise, since down to the time of King Henry I of England, who subdued Wales and placed the Welsh Church under the rule of the English Church, the Church of Mynyw kept its Metropolitan right intact, save only for the use of the pallium, like the Scottish Church owing submission to none other save that of Rome alone and to her owing it directly.' To this the Pope briefly replied that there was nothing new or unprecedented in an ordinary episcopal Church owing no submission to any Metropolitan; as for example the Churches of Lucca or Pavia, whose Prelate, though but a simple Bishop, none the less, by indulgence of the Roman Church, enjoyed the use of the pallium and the privilege of having a Cross borne before him. And when once again the Pope asked how many years had elapsed since the alleged violence of that King, Giraldus replied that it was seventy years or more, but that the prescription, which might thus have been established, had been interrupted on many occasions; first, for example, by Bishop Bernard, who in about the twenty-seventh year after his promotion to the See raised the question of the Metropolitan right of his Church against Theobald, Archbishop of Canterbury, in the presence of Pope Eugenius[1] in France; and later, during the last days of Bishop David, the successor of Bernard, when he had been Bishop twenty-seven years or more, the Canons

[1] Bernard first urged the claim during the pontificate of Innocent II (1130-43). (See *Invect.* II, 7); next under Lucius II, 1144-5 (*Invect.* II, 3 and below, p. 200); continuing under Eugenius III (1145-53) (cp. *Invect.* II, 6), when he seems to have secured the pallium and lost it again (Hen. Hunt. 10); the dispute with Theobald took place at Meaux in 1147. See *Invect.* II, 1. 2, and below p. 192.

of Mynyw boldly raised the same question against Richard, Archbishop of Canterbury, before Uguccione, Cardinal of Sant'Angelo, then Legate in England;[1] and thirdly a synodal declaration was made in the Lateran Council by the Canons of our Church, who in that great assembly, firmly protested its rights in the presence of Pope Alexander III;[2] and fourthly we ourselves in your presence to-day, some twenty years after the Lateran Council, claim that same right for our Church and, taking up our quarrel against Hubert, Archbishop of Canterbury, will seek it and, by grace of God and of yourself, will seek it effectively'. And when he had heard all this, the Pope said, 'If what you say can be proved, it will be an easy matter to secure the right that you demand. Therefore I would have you write down and deliver to us all the evidence whereby the rights of your Church may be the more clearly proved'.

Now Giraldus, hearing this, showed himself no sluggard, but without delay applied his eager spirit to do that which the Pope had suggested; and so after a few days he placed the following writing in the hands of the Lord Pope, who received it with all kindness. It ran as follows:

There ensues a long disquisition on the History of Christianity in Britain, largely mythical. Most of it is here given in abstract the passages translated being placed in inverted commas.

When Fagan and Duvianus had converted Britain to Christianity, the country was divided into five Metropolitan Provinces, Caerleon, Dorobernia (Canterbury), London, York, and St. Andrew's in Scotland, each with a number of suffragans. When Augustine came to convert the Saxons, he divided England into two provinces, Canterbury and York. But in Wales Dubricius, Archbishop of Caerleon, gave place to David, who 'transferred the Metropolitan See to Mynyw, as was

[1] See p. 58.   [2] See p. 68.

A BRIEF HISTORY OF THE WELSH CHURCH

foretold by our prophet Merlin long before in the following manner, "Mynyw shall be invested with the pallium of Caerleon."[1] Now we had at Mynyw twenty-five Archbishops [of Caerleon][2] in succession, of whom the first was St. David and the last St. Sampson, who sailed to Brittany taking the pallium with him, as has already been described.' Then, turning to Bede's *Historia Ecclesiastica*, he points out that no mention is made therein of the Churches either of Wales or Scotland being subject to Canterbury. Augustine had been rebuffed by the Welsh Church when he asked their assistance in the conversion of the Saxons and, when the seven Bishops of Wales went to confer with Augustine, they publicly declared that they would not have him for their Archbishop. And there is no shred of evidence to show that the Church of Wales was ever subject to Canterbury down to the time of King Henry I. 'These facts, Holy Father, are acknowledged to be derived from authentic documents. And besides these, there are still in Wales many old men who have seen the days when the Church of Wales owed no allegiance save to Rome. Now since the pristine dignity of our Church is clear from all this evidence, the outcome of our suit, if it prove successful, will be as follows. In the first place it will greatly increase the honour of the Roman Church, if the Church of Wales (like the Church of Scotland) is directly subject to it, as it was in former times and still should be. There will also be this further gain to Rome, that Wales is ready to pay Peter's pence, each house contributing, as is done in England, which would bring in an annual revenue of two hundred marks and more. Further it will pay its "great tithe" to the Roman Church. Now they call it a "great tithe", when they pay a tithe of all their beasts, flocks, herds, horses, and all their

[1] Vaticinatio Merlini (*Geoff. Mon.* VII, 3).
[2] An interpolation from the previous line.

DE IURE ET STATU

movable property; and the total of this great tithe from all Wales would amount to more than three thousand marks. Further we may perhaps discern an omen in the fact that our claim is put forward in this Court in the very year at the beginning of which the Court deprived the Church of Dol of the pallium, though we were wholly ignorant of the fact at the time. Wherefore since all things should in due time return to their original state, just as the Church of Dol has already returned to its original standing, namely an ordinary Bishopric, even so the Church of Mynyw ought, in your time and at your gift, to return to its original rank of a Metropolitan See.'

When the Pope heard this, he replied, 'Since your adversary may be expected to appear before us, we will give you audience on his coming hither, and justice shall not be refused you'.

This done, since Giraldus's cause seemed to find no less favour in the eyes of the Pope and his whole Court than he himself had done, on a certain evening, when he visited the Pope in his chamber, as is the custom, the Pope called him to his side, saying, 'Come forward, Elect of Mynyw, come forward'. And when he heard this he fell upon his knees and kissed the Pope's foot and said, 'My Lord, such a word falling from your lips, seems to have the force of a confirmation'. And he with a smile made answer, 'I called you "Elect" because others call you so. The Pope calls no man "Elect" in all seriousness before he has been confirmed in his office'.

Now when Giraldus, who had come to the Court about All Saints and had sojourned there till 'Laetare Jerusalem'[1] and longer, there came to the Court a little before Easter, a certain Buongiovanni, a Lombard and a clerk of the Archbishop of Canterbury, bringing (it is believed) rich gifts, as is the custom, from the Archbishop to the Pope.

[1] i.e. from about Nov. 30 (1199) to past mid-Lent (1200). Cp. p. 164.

THE ARCHBISHOP'S REPRESENTATIVE

Some explanation is necessary with regard to the course of events after Giraldus's departure from England. This may best be given in Giraldus's own words (Invect. 1, 7).[1]

'When the Canons refused the Prior of Llantony as a person unknown and wholly ignorant of the language and customs of our country, the Archbishop immediately entrusted him with entire custody of the whole See, in order that he might thus win over the Chapter, either soothing them with gifts or terrifying them with wrongs. But I neither deem nor reckon this man among my persecutors, because though at first he greedily courted the honour offered him, yet later when he learned that I had been elected and had set out for Rome after interposing my appeal, he followed sounder counsel and resigned the custody of the See. But the Archbishop in his desire for victory ... since no English would at that time come forward ... procured the election of the Abbot of St. Dogmael, one of our countrymen, a fool and wholly illiterate, from whom he could have nothing to fear, and also my cousin, that thus he might withdraw the help of my kinsmen from me.'

The De iure *continues:*

Now Buongiovanni, being one day asked by the Pope in the Consistory, whether he had any special mandate against the Archdeacon of Mynyw, who had already stayed a long time at the Court, he replied that he had not; but that his Lord had bidden him say this to the Pope, if he should chance to find the Archdeacon at the Court, that there were four persons nominated for the Bishopric of Mynyw, of whom one was this Archdeacon; but that, since the King immediately refused him, the Canons had at London, with the King's assent, chosen a certain Abbot. And the Pope asking when this was done, he made answer, 'A little before Christmas'. And the

[1] From a speech delivered against Andrew on the second visit to Rome: cp. p. 196.

DE IURE ET STATU

Pope replied, 'But the Archdeacon was at that time in this Court'. And when the Pope asked whether his Lord had confirmed the election, he was silent. But, the Pope, pressing for an answer, he at length replied that he was not bidden to answer this; but that he believed the election was not displeasing to his Lord. Whereto the Pope rejoined, 'Such are the doings of your Lord; and we declare that whatever has been done against the Archdeacon since his hastening hither and since his appeal to us, is null and void'. Then turning to the Archdeacon, who was standing by, he said to him, 'And do you, Archdeacon, wait patiently for a little longer; for unless we hear something else, and that right soon, we shall take further action'. Therefore all that heard this thought that the Archdeacon would very soon receive his promotion, and so the Cardinals, when he visited them after this, as is the custom, said as though applauding him and offering their congratulations, that he had waited to some purpose and met with good success, since his effective promotion was assuredly hard at hand and almost within his grasp.

Now in the meantime the Pope was most friendly and well-disposed toward Giraldus; for he saw that he was fit for promotion to the Church to which he had been called, not only by reason of his personal character, but also of his rich store of learning; he considered also his high birth, of which the Archbishop had spoken in his letters and reflected that one who, having been thus deprived of such high honour, had striven so well and valiantly against such powerful and wealthy adversaries, would without doubt make a most useful Bishop and a doughty champion of his Church.[1] Wherefore, after he had deliberated on this matter with his brethren, it was at last resolved, as was secretly revealed to Giraldus by a

---

[1] The text is ungrammatical and perhaps corrupt. But the general sense is clear.

THE ARCHBISHOP'S BRIBE

Cardinal who was his friend, that the Pope, without regard to the Election that had been made and afterwards denounced as unlawful by the Archbishop, should of his own sole gift confer upon him the Church of Mynyw, which being in such a barbarous and hostile country was sorely in need of good governance.

This, then, having been decided, the said clerk of the Archbishop, forewarned not merely by the words of the Pope and the applause of the Court, but also by certain Cardinals who favoured his Lord, straightway set himself to hinder the proceedings, as he had been instructed, and cautiously and subtly to corrupt the Court. For the Archbishop, being a man full of worldly foresight and cunning, had enjoined upon him that, if he saw that Giraldus had won so much favour with the Court as to make it likely that he would be promoted then and there, he should forthwith suggest to the Pope that he should send an envoy from among his chaplains and the clerks of his Court to seek an aid from the clergy in England, while the Archbishop himself should further the business by setting an example to the rest, making a contribution himself and persuading others to do the same, so that a great sum should be forthcoming to the Pope as a result of this advice. Now this mission and his counsel proving acceptable, it seemed to follow that one, through whom such profit might accrue to the Roman Court, ought not to be offended or exasperated at this juncture; and thus the policy of the Court was changed, so much did this promised aid allure them. For it seemed better under these circumstances to appease the Archbishop than to irritate him by the promotion of Giraldus or of anyone else.

Therefore the Pope offered Giraldus a commission providing for the investigation by judges in England of the validity of his election, and forthwith sent a subdeacon named Philip to England, who in accordance with the promise of the Archbishop collected a large

DE IURE ET STATU

sum of money, in the first place from the Archbishop himself and also through the Archbishop from all the clergy of England.

Wherefore Giraldus, seeing the shifts, not to say the vices[1] of the Court and noting their fickleness, did what he could and demanded that to the Commission offered him to make inquiry into the question of his election there should be added another to investigate the question concerning the standing of his Church, since it was on behalf of this beyond all else that he had undertaken these labours. But the Pope, after taking counsel with his brethren, said that a Commission could not be granted to inquire into so difficult a question as the claim to an Archbishopric and the pallium, since no Privileges were put forward in evidence nor could they find anything on the matter in their Registers nor discover that it had ever been raised before. None the less, that after this rebuff he might do something to placate Giraldus, out of his generosity he granted him the administration of the Church of Mynyw both in things temporal and spiritual, so long as the See should be vacant. But the Archdeacon, far from being cheered by such an answer, was on the contrary much saddened and firmly replied that, if he could not obtain a Cormission to investigate the standing of the Church of Mynyw, he cared nothing at all about the other. But he also entreated the Pope to grant him brief access to the Register of Pope Eugenius, before whom he had heard that the standing of the Church had been debated in France between Bishop Bernard and Archbishop Theobald. This request being granted, he turned to the proceedings of Eugenius in France, a clerk of the Chamberlain being present to observe all he did; and in a short time he found the letters which he sought, and read them with no small exultation. These I have thought worthy to be inserted

[1] *uices ... uicia:* the pun cannot be reproduced in English.

here; for the Archdeacon at once got leave from the Chamberlain to have it copied. Now the letter from the Register of Pope Eugenius, addressed to Theobald, Archbishop of Canterbury, ran as follows:

'Our venerable brother Bernard, Bishop of St. David's, having come before us, has claimed in person that the Church of St. David was once Metropolitan, and has humbly demanded that we should restore it to that rank. Now when he had made a long stay in our Court to watch how his petition went, you, brother Archbishop, at length rose in his presence to oppose his claim and laid a complaint against him in our presence that he had withdrawn the obedience due to you as his lawful Metropolitan, and had shown himself rebellious and disobedient towards you, seeing that he was consecrated by your predecessor as though by his lawful Metropolitan and had both in speech and writing professed submission to the Church of Canterbury, and had in many things afterwards obeyed you and attended you like other suffragans. Now he, indeed, could not deny his consecration, but he utterly denied having made any such profession or rendered such obedience. And you, hearing this, produced two witnesses who testified before us that he, before their eyes and in their hearing had, after his consecration, made profession of obedience to the Church of Canterbury both in speech and writing. Therefore, having heard the arguments of both parties and having made diligent inquiry concerning them, carefully examined the witnesses and taken counsel with our brethren, we have taken their oath and have ordered that the Bishop should, as justice demands, render obedience and reverence to you as his lawful Metropolitan. But since we desire that every Church and every ecclesiastic should keep the dignity that is their just due, we have fixed a day both for him and you on the feast of St.

DE IURE ET STATU

Luke in the coming year, that we may then, both parties being present, discover the truth of the matter concerning the rank of the Church of St. David and its liberty, and that we may, under God, decide what is just. Given at Meaux on the 29th day of June.'[1]

His search having been thus crowned with success, to the height of his desire, the Archdeacon went first to the Pope's cousin, Ugolino, Cardinal Deacon of St. Eustace, who was later made Bishop of Ostia and whom the Archdeacon thought to be his friend; and when he had shown him the writing, the Cardinal congratulated him and counselled him to go with it to the Pope that very same night, promising that he would be there, ready to act as his friend. So on the evening of the same day, about twilight, when he was entering the chamber to approach the Pope, the latter saluted him as Archbishop and called him to his side. Now Giraldus did not catch what the Pope had said, but Cardinal Ugolino, who was sitting on the other side of the Pope, said, 'Did you not hear by what name the Pope called you?' And Giraldus replied that he supposed that the Pope had called him Archdeacon after his wont, as indeed was his belief. But the Cardinal made answer, 'Nay, in truth, he saluted you as Archbishop'. And when he heard this, Giraldus prostrated himself at the feet of the Pope and kissed them, saying that by the grace of God and of the Pope these words were in truth prophetic, as they should be, proceeding from the mouth of so great a Pontiff. And when the Pope went on to ask him whether he had found anything in the Register of Eugenius concerning the standing of his Church, he replied that he had, as indeed the Cardinal had already told the Pope. And when he gave him the writing, the Pope handed it to the Cardinal and bade him read it aloud. And when it had been read,

[1] 1147.

HE DEMANDS ADMINISTRATION OF SEE
the Pope replied that he was well pleased with it and granted the Archdeacon the Commission to inquire into the standing of the Church which he had desired, and bade Cardinal Ugolino to make out the Commission forthwith.

The letters, which dealt with both Commissions together, were originally contained in the Invectiones *(Book II, 5), but have been lost through the carelessness of the copyist. The heading alone survives; the Commissioners were the Bishops of Lincoln, Durham and Ely. At the same time Giraldus got a Commission to inquire into the qualifications of 'the Blessed Caradog, our noble Hermit and Confessor', for canonization, the Commissioners being the Abbots of Whitland, Strathflur, and St. Dogmael.*[1] *The text continues:*

'None the less these letters were suppressed owing to the envy and malice of two Abbots, Peter of Whitland and Walter of St. Dogmael; for owing to the corrupt incitement of the Archbishop they aspired, beyond all their hopes, to the Bishopric of Mynyw and therefore grudged Giraldus this glory. Nevertheless, both of them were cheated of the hopes which they had conceived and of the crafty promise which the Archbishop had made to them; nor did either of them escape the divine vengeance of St. David, since one died soon after and the other was deprived of his office.[2]

But when Giraldus requested letters for the administration of the Church of Mynyw, such as had been formerly offered him, but which he had refused, the Pope replied, 'You refused it when you might have had it, and therefore you shall not have it now that you desire it'. To which Giraldus made answer, 'Nay, my Lord, but if a father should offer his son bread, and the son in his folly and insolence refuse it, is he therefore to be deprived of

[1] See *Invect.* III, 7; the letter is dated from the Lateran, May 8th (1200).
[2] Peter of Whitland. See p. 265.

INVECTIONES

bread for the rest of his life'. And since a soft answer assuages fury and banishes indignation, whereas a harsh word kindles anger, the Pope soon after asked Giraldus whether the Church of Mynyw had a Dean; to which he replied that the Church had none to rule it but four Archdeacons; whereupon the Pope bade his notary make out letters giving the administration to Giraldus.[1]

In addition to these he obtained letters commending the Church of Mynyw to the Princes, Abbots, clergy and people of Wales,[2] and similar letters addressed to Meilyr, Justiciar of Ireland and to other kinsmen of Giraldus in that country; also letters to the King commending and excusing Giraldus,[3] and like letters to the Archbishop commending Giraldus and urging reconciliation.[4]

Some further explanation is required to show the position of affairs on Giraldus' return from Rome. The Archbishop had, as we have seen, caused the Abbot of St. Dogmael to be elected after the withdrawal of the Prior of Llantony. But he soon felt the need of a second string to his bow. Giraldus gives his account of the situation (Invect. I, 7) *as follows:*

But when the Archbishop heard that I was coming back from Rome with strict commands and a Commission from the Pope, he summoned two English intruders, false brothers of our Church, whom by his guile he enticed not merely to oppose me, but to oppose their own Church; and when he heard from them that the whole of our Chapter would support me against the Abbot on my return, he made diligent inquiry of them, whether they could by any means withdraw the Chapter from me. Whereupon they replied that, if he had caused the Abbot of Whitland, a Cistercian monk and a son of our Church, with sons and cousins and a number of kinsmen among the Canons, to be elected at the time when the Abbot of St. Dogmael was elected, they would

---
[1] See *Invect* III, I, dated from the Lateran, May 12th (1200).
[2] Ibid. 4, 5, 6, the last dated from the Lateran May 5th (1200).
[3] Ibid. 8. No date.　　[4] Ibid. 9. No date.

all have helped him against the Archdeacon, being moved thereto by the claims of the flesh. So when the Archbishop heard this, he called forth all the arts of his malice and forthwith sent letters and messengers to the Abbot of Whitland, summoning him to appear before him and promising that, if he would detach the Chapter from me, he would assuredly make him Bishop, despite the election of the Abbot of St. Dogmael. For that election must be regarded as null and void, since it was made while my election still stood and had for that reason been cancelled by the Pope in the Commission granted to me, a copy of which had already reached him. Now the Abbot, as befitted so religious a man, although he was at that time engaged upon a visitation which had been enjoined upon him in the remote parts of Ireland, on receiving this unexpected offer of promotion . . . borne on the wings of ambition, flew across the Irish Sea to Wales, in such haste that, passing through the gate of his Abbey on the Feast of the Assumption of the Blessed Mary[1] early in the morning a little before the hour of mass, he did not deign even to salute the brethren on his return nor to visit his Church either to celebrate or at least to hear mass, as would have been fitting on so solemn a Feast. But despising all such things as trifles and hastening without more ado to win his promised honours, he spared neither horse nor spur, but came panting to the Archbishop at Worcester, by whom he was received with rejoicing and honour. And forthwith they made a treaty between them, giving firm security on both sides; which done the Abbot was sent back to Mynyw, where the brethren were immediately called together and the letters of the Archbishop and the Justiciar were read out, but read in secret with hushed and trembling voice, that the other Abbot might not hear of it, lest he should perchance give up in despair,

[1] Aug. 15th.

but that each of them, the one openly and the other secretly might resist me in defence of his own promotion: and this done, he was elected. But I would have you remark the extreme scrupulosity of either Abbot in this matter. For the first, though he was my own cousin and was not only aware of my previous election, but had given his assent thereto and had even written on my behalf, and though he was in other matters simple-minded, yet now, disregarding the ties of blood and canon-law, sighed after the first place at the feast and the Bishop's throne. But the other, though before the world he had been my clerk and friend and had shared my board, and had often sworn ... to support me and knew that I had been elected and, after interposing my appeal, had set out to go to the Court of Rome, none the less, blinded by ambition, he put his trust in the empty promises of the Archbishop, whose aim was rather to damage me than to help him, and did not cease from doing his utmost to harm me by turning the Chapter from me and even inducing them to write against me. And further ... when after my return I spoke to him on this matter ... he swore of his own accord by every Church which we saw as we journeyed through England together, and finally with his hand outstretched over the altar and the relics of St. David, that he had never done me any hurt, either openly or secretly nor ever at any time, so long as there was any hope of my promotion, nor even while I was persistently pursuing my claim to be elected, had he sought to procure the election of himself or of any other in preference to my own. But, this done, feeling, that he could proceed with greater freedom and security than before, since what he had said was accepted for true and he had cleared himself of all suspicion, he did not cease to visit Courts nor to send messages and promises and bribes as well, that he might go forth mitre-horned. But he thought to conceal his design, because he pretended to be working for the other Abbot, and would frequent the Courts not only by himself but with the other also, on the pretext of helping him with the Archbishop, but in reality that he might supplant him.

BOOK III

THESE things accomplished, Giraldus at length after his long labours returned to his Church, and there he found that by the devices of the Archbishop the Church had been utterly corrupted, since in the meantime two Abbots, to wit, of Cemais (St. Dogmael) and of Whitland, had both been elected to the Bishopric, the first openly, the second by stealth.[1] Wherefore he showed the Chapter the letters granting Commissions to investigate the questions of his own election and the standing of the Church, together with the letter of Pope Eugenius concerning the latter, and likewise the letters concerning the inquiry to be made in respect of the holy Caradog. He gave them also a brief account of his own labours, though the false, dissembling brethren showed neither joy at his great success nor compassion for his labours, having been corrupted by the empty promises of the Archbishop. But none the less he watched diligently over the welfare of his Church and made careful inquiry whether any records were left from the time of Bishop Bernard, which concerned the standing of the Church of Mynyw. And at length he found the same letter, sealed with the seal of Pope Eugenius, though with a different heading being addressed to the clergy and people of Mynyw, together with others bearing the seal of Lucius II and addressed to Bishop Bernard. Both these letters were worm-eaten and almost worn to pieces, having been long mislaid, so that it was only after careful search that he discovered them.

The letter of Lucius II follows, dated from the Lateran on May 14th (1144). It is non-committal, asking for further information as to the claims of the Church of Mynyw to be Metropolitan.[2]

[1] See p. 196. [2] See also *Invect.* II, 3.

HE FINDS THE CHAPTER CORRUPTED

In addition to these letters, Giraldus, being in all things vigilant and vigorous on behalf of his Church, found divers others relating to its former Metropolitan dignity, which through neglect had been all but lost and forgotten; for example, letters of Bishop Bernard to Pope Innocent, of the Chapter of Mynyw to Pope Eugenius and also to Pope Honorius, and likewise of Bishop Bernard to Simeon, Archdeacon of Bangor, and of Owen and Cadwallader, Princes of North Wales, to Bishop Bernard, all of which are contained in the *Libellus Invectionum* and in the *De Gestis Giraldi*.[1]

During the absence of Giraldus on his first visit to Rome his beloved brother Philip died, as is clear from the Table of Contents of De Rebus (III, 45), *while a pathetic sequel, belonging to the present date, is preserved in* Invectiones VI, 25, *to which it has been transferred from* De Rebus III, 49-50. *It is here given in a slightly abridged form.*

When Giraldus departed from Mynyw, which he had found utterly corrupted and gone astray, he went, groaning in spirit, to see the tomb of that best of brothers and to bewail his death at Manorbier. But when time and reason had at last assuaged his grief, he read aloud in the place of his burial, letters, which at his brother's request, he had brought back from the Roman Court, and, this done, he laid them up in the Church. Now the reply of the Cardinal who at that time heard confessions for the Pope, was as follows: 'John of St. Paul, Cardinal of St. Prisca, to the noble Philip de Barri, greeting and love. As we have learned that you are pricked with doubt as to whether alms given to the rich acquire as much merit as those bestowed upon the poor, I will reply to

---

[1] *Invect* I, 8-12. *De Rebus* (Table of Contents, III, 45-6). The letters to the Popes set forth the claims to Metropolitan rank on much the same lines as was done by Giraldus himself and have no evidential value. The letter to Simeon merely begs his support before the Pope at Rome. The letter from the Princes acknowledges the claim of Mynyw.

INVECTIONES

you in accordance with the words of St. John Crysostom, that if the rich seek hospitality, no inquiry should be made concerning them. For if Abraham had made anxious inquiry concerning those who sought his hospitality, assuredly he would not have received the angels in his dwelling, but would have driven them away, it may be, with other persons as well. Therefore, inspired by consideration of his example, I tell you that you should bestow the works of hospitality and charity on rich and poor alike. For God will not reward you according to the persons whom you receive, but recompense is prepared for the giver according to his sincere intent, his pity and his kindness.'

For since this good man had his dwelling in a place midway betwixt two sea-ports, namely Milford Haven and a port in Devon, where there was a much frequented passage for voyagers in either direction, and since he welcomed all guests indiscriminately, both rich and poor, and owing to the great numbers of the rich that came to him could not bestow as much upon the poor as he desired, he had thought fit to consult the Roman Court upon the matter through his brother, Giraldus the Archdeacon. For if that which he spent on the rich, like that which he spent upon the poor, might be accounted a merit and accrue to the attainment of a heavenly crown then he would indulge his wonted hospitality without stint; but otherwise he would leave that place and his castle to his heir, and was firmly resolved to betake himself to some other place.

The De iure et statu Meneuensis Ecclesiae *continues:*

This done he departed from Wales, taking with him the documents he had collected,[1] and proceeded without delay to his judges in England. But since King John

---

[1] *gestis et congestis*, i.e., 'These things done and collected'. The play upon words defies reproduction in English.

thundered against him with violent threats, and the Archbishop either would not or could not obtain from the King letters patent of safe-conduct, as he had promised, after securing a statement from the judges,[1] he hastened to the Court of Rome and arrived there by the appointed day, to wit, the Sunday on which 'Laetare, Jerusalem' is sung.[2] And on coming thither he found two clerks sent by the Archbishop to oppose him, the one a clerk of the Archbishop's named Andrew, the other Reginald Foliot, a Canon of Mynyw, the most corrupted among all the corrupt, who had been made a Canon by Peter, Bishop and monk, who was inspired thereto by the flesh, not by the spirit. Now to this youth, a creature of fawning manners and lisping speech, so wholly beardless that from outward view none could tell whether he were man or woman, the Archbishop had given a solemn pledge that he should have the See of Mynyw, if he would go to Rome and there appear in court before the Pope to oppose Giraldus in both his suits, alike in the matter of his election and of the standing of his Church.

Now, as soon as might be, Giraldus went on a certain evening to the Pope and showed him the aforesaid letters of Popes Eugenius and Lucius concerning the standing of the Church, which by diligent search he had lately found at Mynyw; and when they had been examined and read aloud and the seals had been noted, the Pope gave orders that the Cardinals should be called together on the morrow and that the letters should be read aloud in open Consistory and public audience, that the whole Court might be fully informed concerning the suit relating to the standing of the church of Mynyw, which had more than once been brought before them,

---

[1] Perhaps a mere statement that Giraldus had appeared before them and had produced certain documents; possibly, however, including a statement of the difficulties arising out of the King's persecution and the Archbishop's failure to fulfil his promise.
[2] Mid-Lent. March 4th, 1201.

and that henceforth it might not be regarded as a new matter and without precedent, as it had seemed on the first coming of Giraldus.

But afterwards, Andrew and Foliot came forward with letters from the Archbishop of Canterbury, whereby Andrew was appointed the Archbishop's proctor in the suit concerning the election, while Foliot was appointed proctor both of the Abbot of St. Dogmael and of the Chapter of Mynyw by letters from both parties, since the Chapter had been corrupted and led away to oppose Giraldus, as has already been related. Now when, these letters having been read, inquiry was made whether Andrew or the other was the Archbishop's proctor in the suit concerning the standing of the Church, Andrew replied that he had no letters to that effect, since they had been taken from him at Parma where he alleged he had been robbed; and when he was asked why those letters had been taken from him rather than the others, he was unable to give any reason.

'Now when Giraldus had produced certain witnesses, his adversaries demanded a delay that they might produce witnesses from England.

But what was done or determined in this matter shall be made known from letters of the Lord Pope addressed to our judges in England, of which we quote the conclusion, as follows:

'Now the Archdeacon produced certain witnesses before those appointed to hear his suit, and when he demanded that their depositions should be made public, his adversary demanded that a delay should be granted in order that he might produce witnesses from England to support his case and to rebut the evidence produced by the other side. Now although it seemed to us from many indications that the Archdeacon had certain grievances, yet wishing to observe the due order of justice, we have thought fit to grant a delay. Therefore ... we instruct you by your messengers and letters strictly to enjoin upon the Archbishop and the Abbot of St. Dogmael and upon any other who thinks good to oppose the Archdeacon in the matter of his election, that he fail not within a year from the feast of All Saints next[1] ... to appear before the Apostolic See fully equipped and ready with his evidence, either himself or through a fit person who may answer for him. But if he disdain to come, we shall forthwith proceed with the business. But since the Archbishop, having been cited to appear before us both in the matter of the election and that of the standing of the Church of Mynyw, has only sent an accredited proctor for the former suit, whereas the Archdeacon has in person pleaded both suits, we desire and command that the Archbishop should make good to him at least half of his lawful expenses. And this you shall on our authority compel him to do, without right of appeal.'[2]

This done, Giraldus demanded fresh letters in respect of the administration of the Church of Mynyw;[3] and since he had been robbed of his revenues he demanded and obtained letters addressed to the Archbishop of Canterbury, commanding him to restore these revenues and to suffer Giraldus to administer the diocese in peace[4]. He further obtained letters close to the same effect for the Abbot of St. Dogmael, who had robbed him,[5] though he was his cousin; and letters patent for the judges concerning his spoliation and the restitution to be made to him and further enjoining them to make inquiry into the literacy of the Abbot, his despoiler;[6]

---

[1] Nov. 1st, 1202.
[2] This and the following letters are all written from Segni in 1201. The date of this letter is July 29th (*Invect.* III, 16).
[3] July 23rd (*Invect.* III, 2). [4] July 23rd (ibid. 13).
[5] July 23rd (ibid. 14). [6] July 27th (ibid. 15).

DE IURE ET STATU

also letters patent of protection[1] and letters close of commendation and protection,[2] addressed to the Archbishop of Canterbury ... and letters granting Giraldus the prebends and benefices then vacant in the Church of Mynyw;[3] and others again granting a second Commission to investigate the question both of his election and that of the standing of the Church, which may be found in the *Libellus Invectionum*[4] and in the *Gesta Giraldi*.

For the rest, both parties were ordered on a certain day to set forth the facts of each election before two Cardinals appointed to hear them, to wit, the Lords Suffredo and Peter of Capua. Whereupon the Archdeacon set forth his election and the day and hour on which it was made, namely on the Feast of the Apostles Peter and Paul[5], about the fifth day after the Feast of St. John the Baptist, together with all other circumstances, to the great approval of those that heard him. And after him Reginald Foliot rose and, obeying their commands, began to set forth the election of the Abbot of St. Dogmael, whose proctor he was. And, whereas liars should have good memories[6], he forgetting the lie in which he had been instructed, said in the course of his statement that the Abbot had been elected a little before Christmas,[7] though the Archdeacon had been elected almost six months before. Wherefore since, when two elections have been made in the same Church, the first is always held valid by the Roman Court and the second is annulled, all who were present and heard this, began to exult and cry aloud on behalf of the Archdeacon, whose cause and person had won their favour, as it had of all those who frequented the Roman Court. But Andrew, sighing anxiously, cried in a loud voice against all the rest that they had all misunderstood the dates and that he had never said this, doing his best to throw

[1] July 23rd (*Invect*. III. 11).   [2] July 23rd (ibid. 12).
[3] July 25th (ibid. 10).   [4] Lost through error of copyist.
[5] July 29th, 1199.   [6] *Quintilian*, IV, ii. 91.   [7] 1199.

everything into confusion. And so after much disputation Cardinal Suffredo put an end to the controversy by ordering both parties to write out their statements of the facts word for word in the order in which they had been delivered and which he remembered very well; and turning to Foliot, he bade him, under threat of his anathema, not to change or vary anything, 'For', he said, 'I shall remember the dates and everything else, and you will not be able to deceive me'. Meanwhile the week of Pentecost being over and nearly a whole month having thus elapsed since the last hearing, both parties at last appeared again before the Commissioners. And the statement of the Archdeacon, being read out first was found to agree exactly with that which he had made by word of mouth, whereas the statement of Foliot was found in the judgment of all to be most inconsistent. For after this long lapse of time, that they might make the first election last and the last first, thanks to the elaborate subtleties, not to say falsehoods, of their advocates, they now pretended that there had been two elections of the Abbot, one before the election of the Archdeacon and the other after. Their statement concerning the Abbot's election was, then, written as follows: 'When on the death of Peter, Bishop of Mynyw the Archdeacons and Canons, with letters of ratification from their Chapter for the election of a Shepherd, had come before the Archbishop of Canterbury about Michaelmas, and had nominated four persons, they then, being uncertain concerning the assent of the King, at that time abroad, placed the election in the hands of the Archbishop, saying that they would accept as their Elect, whomsoever he might choose on behalf of the Chapter with the King's assent. Wherefore in course of time on the day after Epiphany in the Isle[1] of Andelys he elected the Abbot of St.

---

[1] Jan. 6th, 1199, at Château Gaillard; 'Isle' is used with reference to the spur of the hill on which it stood, a use found both in English and French place-names.

Dogmael with the King's assent. And a little before the following Christmas the Chapter solemnized the election made by the Archbishop.' And when all who had heard the first, cried out that the written statement was obviously different, and the Lord Suffredo said the same, yet none the less, when the adversaries loudly protested and raised a tumult, since the other Cardinal favoured the Archbishop and since it seemed that owing to lapse of time the facts might have been forgotten, the written statement was accepted, and no punishment was imposed upon them for their falsehood and disobedience. And so the opponents of Giraldus to the very last directed all their efforts to prove this fiction by false witnesses.

The Archdeacon therefore produced three priests and two clerks as witnesses to make good his claim and prove his election. And since many pilgrims from Wales were at this time flocking to Rome in divers companies, they all of their own accord appeared before the Commissioners and bore witness to the priority of the Archdeacons' election and more especially concerning the common report in their country. And they, no less than the eye-witnesses, were received, sworn and examined; for strong presumptions often afford no little support to proofs.

But meanwhile there was great wrangling before the same Commissioners between the Elect of Bangor and Andrew, who opposed him with all his might, since the Archbishop favoured Robert, Bishop of Bangor. Now this Elect was a Cistercian monk and Sub-Prior of the monastery of Aberconwy in Gwynedd, who said that he was the lawful Elect of Bangor and that Robert had been forced upon them by the Archbishop. Now the Archdeacon, both on his first visit to Rome and on this, finding this man at Rome, strove with all his might to help him, both to bring odium on the Archbishop, whose action the monk, like himself, was attacking, and because this

ANDREW'S ELOQUENCE

man also was a Welshman and might help him in the suit concerning the standing of the Church of St. David. So when this monk entreated the Archdeacon to reply some time to Andrew, who so often in public audience inveighed with foul abuse against the Welsh, on a certain day in the presence of the Cardinals and a great audience, since Andrew in the course of his speech had reiterated the phrase, 'You shall hear wonderful things', he began, as follows, in words that redounded to the glory of the Welsh and the confusion of the English: 'Master Andrew has promised and daily promises that you shall hear wonderful things. But if his procedure were that of the harper[1] (*psallendi*) and not of the dancer (*saliendi*) he would come to *Defecit* before reaching *Mirabilia*.[2]' Now these words were the more noted by all and were regarded as prophetic, since Master Andrew soon afterwards did in truth 'fail' (*defecit*) and died of a mortal sickness at Segni.

The Speech is given in its entirety in Invect. I, 4.

Master Andrew has promised us and daily promises that we shall see 'wonderful things', but if he will follow the order of the 'harper' and not of the 'dancer', he will come to the word 'failed' before he reaches 'marvellous things'. He continually in your presence utters shameless invectives against us and our nation, laughing at us in derision, and making himself an object of derision to all good and honourable men. But how has he the face to venture to set the English nation above ours or even to compare it? for the English are the most worthless of all people under heaven; for they have been subdued by the Normans and reduced by the law of war to perpetual

---

[1] i.e. the psalmist. The reference to 'dancing' may perhaps allude to Andrew's extravagant gestures.
[2] It is impossible to reproduce the point of this jest in English. Giraldus alludes to two sections of Psalm cxix. sc. vv. 81-88 beginning *Deficit*, and vv. 129-136 beginning *Mirabilia*.

slavery; and our own Merlin[1] testifies thereto, when he says of that same people, 'They shall wound their mother with mattocks and shall bear the yoke of perpetual slavery'. The English in their own land are the slaves of the Normans and of all slaves the most worthless, while in our land we have no cowherds, shepherds, cobblers, skinners, mechanics, or cleansers of our sewers, save English only. I pass over the fact that the betrayers of the Britons were first called in as mercenaries, men respecting neither oath nor treaty, for to this very day they are above all other peoples given to treachery and are the most bloodthirsty also of manslayers. Wherefore in Germany whenever any man commits some specially atrocious crime, of whatever nation he be, they say in their own tongue, 'Untriwe Sax', that is 'faithless Saxon'. I say naught of the fact that they are beyond all others given to gluttony and drunkenness and have defiled a land that of old was sober with the vice of intoxication, that above all others who frequent the Court they make use of forged letters and false seals at Rome, and have won a shameful reputation there for faithlessness and falsehood, and that in France, at Paris, in their movements and hissing speech they are like to geese and ganders. But our British race, now known by the false name of Welsh, is like the Romans, sprung of Trojan blood, and defending its freedom both against Norman and Saxon with ceaseless rebellion, and remembering how,

for freedoms sake
Aeneas' sons were rushing on the steel,[2]

have to this very day shaken the yoke of slavery from their necks. Wherefore let Andrew cease to compare slaves with freemen, the wretched with the great, the vile and

[1] Vaticinatio Merlini (*Geoff. Mon.* VII, 3).
[2] *Aen.* VIII, 648.

abject with the noble and the brave. Otherwise the words of Virgil may most aptly be cast in his teeth,[1]

So whelp to dog and kid to dam, thou knewest,
Are like, and small with great things wouldst compare.

Nor is it to be wondered that he mangles and lacerates us and our race with biting tooth, for he does not fear, when full-fed and drunk as an Englishman, to provoke and exasperate even cardinals in their lodgings, wrangling with them as if he were their peer. But whence come his horns of pride? Assuredly from the Archbishop's purse. For there is naught that begets such violence as 'living on another's loaf'[2], as the comic poet bears witness when he says:

Behold
The fruit of idleness and other's fare.[3]

Moreover, he contends in this Court against the Archbishop of York in respect of the Primacy, and against us too in the matter of our Church's liberty as well as of my own election. And this is not enough for him; he must oppose the Lord of Bangor on behalf of that wandering exiled Robert, a bishop without a city, though he has no general or special mandate to that effect and is not formally associated with that suit, but merely offers security.[4] But let us consider who Andrew is that he should be able to give sufficient security in so important a case, when he has no mandate. He holds no benefice in the church, and such revenues as he possesses are very small and of little consequence. He may possibly be a good man and well-lettered. But this much is certain, that he has for some time been in the service of the Archbishop, though otherwise he is utterly unknown and as insignificant in fame as in form. For none of the seniors, none of the outstanding personages in the court

[1] *Ecl.* I, 22.   [2] *Juv.* V, 2.   [3] *Ter. Eun.* 265.   [4] *sc.* for his bona fides.

of their lord could be induced by anything or prospect which he could either give or promise them to undertake such a risk as the journey to this Court; for they were all terrified by the familiar examples of numbers who had undertaken such an adventure, such as Philip, Prior of St. Fridiswide's, Master John of Colchester, Master Remer, Master John Scot and very many others, all of whom the ambition of this man and the intestine strife, which he had with his own Church of Canterbury, delivered over to destruction... What is it then that inspires such boldness in Andrew who keeps running to and fro so often between Rome and England? It must be ambition. What was true of the hungry Greekling is true also of the hungry Englishman: 'and bid him go to heaven, to heaven he goes'.[1] Andrew is then a man of such character or of such importance, that he can give security in so important a case even though he has no mandate. Again he daily brings up foul charges against us, promising yet fouler still. Let him charge us with what he will, and let his charges be as serious as he pleases; we shall bring no personal charges against him, since in truth we know little about him either for good or ill. But this we say with confidence that he can bring no charges against us so foul or so false, but that we shall bring fouler charges and true charges against his Lord, whom we know through and through to his very marrow, and on whose behalf he brings all these accusations against us; and we shall be prepared to prove these charges, save that they are already notorious and known by reason of their very enormity. By his power and pertinacity he has forced us a second time to labour in this Court. It is true that we know and are well assured that, unless the Court of Rome fails to do us justice it will give no heed either to his person or his purse for the perversion of the truth. and if we have to labour yet a third time, he will have

---

[1] *Juv.* III, 78.

to labour here himself; for the business will reach such a pitch of difficulty, that he will not be able to settle it by his proctors, even though they be great men of high renown, much less if they be mean and obscure, nay it will be impossible, even though he send the most distinguished members of his court.

Further, Andrew calls us (that is to say, the Elect of Bangor and myself) ambitious, asserting that he wishes to force his way into the place of one who still lives, and that I am labouring to supplant the Abbot of a religious house. But let us see which is the greater, our ambition or the presumption of his Lord. When Gwion, Bishop of Bangor, died, this good man was elected by the unanimous vote of the Chapter. The Archbishop refused to confirm and consecrate him, because he was Welsh, and thrust into his place and consecrated, without any election at all, one Alan, an English Hospitaller, who finding no peace there fled to exile and banishment in England, where he was taken from the world in the very year of his consecration. Wherefore the moment they heard that he was dead, the whole Chapter of Bangor with one voice again elected this man. But when the election was laid before him, the Archbishop refused to confirm it, and had a certain Englishman named Robert thrust in and consecrated in his stead. And he, too, like his predecessor, is now a wandering exile, a Bishop without a city, who runs to and fro, begging at every Abbey in England, and going mitre-horned[1] hunts for Vicarships of vacant Sees... If therefore this Elect, this twice Elect at the unanimous entreaty of his people, his native land, his clergy and likewise his Prince, seeks to maintain his own right and the rights of his Church in due legal form, I ask you which is the greater, this man's ambition or the presumption of that intruding Archbishop who,

---

[1] Reading *incedens* for *incidens* (*mitratus incedere* is a familiar phrase in Giraldus).

INVECTIONES

with no less impudence than imprudence, so often thrusts so many others into his place.

But to turn to my own case: for about a year I remained immovable in the schools where I was studying, despite the frequent invitations which I received by letters and messengers from the clergy of my country and from its barons and princes, nor could any man stir me thence till I was summoned by the King himself. But after I had been elected, had interposed my appeal and set forth on my journey to this Court, the Archbishop caused a certain abbot of our land, my own cousin, a man of the highest literary achievements, and strongly resembling him in his philosophy, during whose Bishopric he might enjoy untroubled slumber — he caused this man, I say, by royal violence to be thrust in over my head, ousting me, who, whatever my character, of good reputation perhaps with some, of evil with others, pass like the apostle[1] through 'good report and evil'. Next he thrust in yet another Abbot, a Cistercian once a Canon of our Church, having among the Canons a son, a brother and cousins and many other kinsmen in that Church, himself a priest's son, who moreover had but a very little time before, under the very wings of the Church, in a cellar, a subterranean cave, acknowledged a child born him by his own cousin, as a witness to the brief endurance of his chastity. In the first case the Archbishop sought to cause a schism in my own family, in the second to cause a schism in the Chapter, in order that, being a marvellous contriver of such tricks and wiles, he might cast impediments in my way on my return ... His presumption therefore would appear to be greater than my ambition. But with what manner of ambition do they dare to charge me, seeing that the whole life of that Archbishop, the whole story of his promotion reeks with ambition? That good man, the elect

[1] 2 Corinthians, VI. 7.

THE RISE OF THE ARCHBISHOP

of Bangor was summoned from the cloister, and I from my studies. But whence came the Archbishop? From the Exchequer! And what is the Exchequer? A place in the public treasury in England — a square board, where fiscal imposts are collected and computed. From this study, from this exercise, in which he has grown old, he, like almost all Bishops of the Church of England, was called to all the various stages of his dignities. For he who is skilled in the computations of the Exchequer, is accounted to have skill in disputation, and a good calculator makes a good philosopher. Moreover up to this day, since 'once steeped, the jar still keeps the liquor's smack',[1] he has not learned to abstain from worldly cares and Courts. A year ago he was Justiciar, and when that office was taken from him by the Court of Rome, he managed at once to get himself appointed the King's Chancellor.[2] And when of late he lost that honour he spared no effort till he recovered it, though not without some disgrace and loss of reputation to himself. For as a fish cannot live out of water, so he cannot live without his Court and worldly cares, since he is either wholly ignorant of the words of the apostle or conceals the fact that he has ever read them, to wit, 'no man that warreth for God entangleth himself in the things of this world'.[3] He forgets also the saying of Jerome, 'That Bishop must be accounted as nothing worth, if he who is so high in honour, does not excel in knowledge and holiness,' since he, a man who deserves no praise either for religion or learning, and has presumed to rule, when he has not learned how to do good. O how unlike is he to the blessed Thomas, his predecessor, who (as I heard of late, at Clairvaux, from the lips of the Archbishop of Lyons, John Bellemain, himself a priest and scholar of most holy life) so soon as he had received consecration, straightway sent back to the King the royal

[1] Horace, *Ep.* I, ii. 69. [2] See Appendix V. [3] 2 Timothy, ii. 4.

INVECTIONES

seal of which as Chancellor he had the charge, saying that he was scarce able to fulfil the duties of the office conferred upon him by the Lord, recognizing his insufficiency therein, although in his former office he had been all-sufficient. But the King rejoined not without great indignation, 'If the Archbishop of Mainz or of Cologne is wont to be the Chancellor of the Emperor of Germany, why does the Archbishop of Canterbury refuse to be Chancellor to the King of England?' Thus, since the holy man could not be brought to change his purpose, there grew up between them a great crop of anger and discord.

Again Andrew casts in my teeth the fact that I am alone and unaccompanied by a single Canon of our Church. But will he nill he, nay though he burst himself, I have them all with me in heart and spirit, save only two, Osbert and Reginald, English intruders, false brethren of our Church, planted therein neither by adoption or by birth, who, though originally they supported me with the rest whither in person or by letters of ratification, are so far the only canons whom the Archbishop has been able to induce to give him open support, thanks to his threats and gifts already presented or promised for the future. And this is a sign and proof thereof, that though, fearing that they would be despoiled of all their goods, by order of the King, they did not venture to come with us, they none the less by clerks of the Church who had taken part in all the proceedings sent under their own seal both to the Lord Pope and our judges all such letters as they thought would be necessary to secure our promotion, and besides their own letters sent also the letters of the King and the Archbishop, but also the threatening letters that were sent at the bidding of the Archbishop by the Justiciar and officers of the public power, whereby they were forced either to act or write against us ... From which it is clear how unlike in all things to his predecessor

THE ARCHBISHOP'S TYRANNY

the blessed Thomas, who risked his life to check the tyrannic action of the Crown in respect of elections and the like, is this Archbishop, who not only makes no attempt as far as in him lies to abolish or weaken, but actually strives with reprehensible audacity meet for everlasting condemnation to foster the depraved and abominable customs which now prevail in the Church of Christ and from day to day become more and more frequent as this plague gathers fresh strength. Wherefore this fact must be regarded as having grave importance, seeing what confusion, and storm and horrible fear has fallen upon all the clergy. For it is dangerous to write anything about or against this man in whose hands is the power to proscribe his adversaries,[1] while to allege aught against him, who can banish the offender[2] is an act not to be thought of without fear. It is well known how at Gloucester[3] on the octave of St. Hilary the Archbishop, by means of the King's servants, forced our Canons and the clerks they had brought with them to write against our election. For to use my own words and not his own, which are only too well known, he relies on both his swords[4] together, that thus, as one who is ambidextrous or rather ambisinistrous, he may carry out by one power, what he cannot effect by the other. It is with this design that they are wont in Wales to set over us dumb dogs that cannot bark, since they are ignorant of our language, and have no desire to do so, seeing that just as they persecute our bodies owing to the inborn hatred that divides our nations, so also they have no care for our souls. And this they do that, as often as our people seeks to defend its lands and liberties against its enemies the English people, repelling violence with violence, they may at his command pass sentence upon us, so that he likewise may

[1] *scribere ... proscribere.*
[2] *legare ... relegare.* In both cases the play upon words cannot be reproduced in English.
[3] cp. p. 289. [4] *sc.* of State and Church.

not blush to use either sword against us in defiance of all law. This then is the cause, this the subtle reasoning, that makes him prefer worthless and abject[1] Englishmen to learned and honourable men of our own country. Hence a bad Englishman is a good Welshman, that is to say bad in England and good in Wales ... Holy Father we entreat you, deign with apostolic rigour to restrain all such errors and their like, nay all such madness as that man may employ against us. For unless a year ago you had to some degree humbled him, his follies would assuredly be beyond all bearing. But behold, once more he begins to abuse your patience and once more lifts up his horns. They require therefore to be blunted, lest they grow too long. For the rest, if those proofs which last year we set before you, to wit, the Decree of our Chapter, supported by three witnesses and by the writings, backed by four witnesses, which we now lay before you, and also by many letters testifying thereto, might suffice to prove the fact of our election, it may now justly so suffice, since all the evidence written against us, which they appear to possess, has been beyond all doubt extorted by the violence employed by the King. But all the evidence in favour of our cause is spontaneous and proceeds from freedom of heart. Above all, since by reason of this strife our See has now been vacant for three years, now, that our Church may not any longer lament that it is Shepherdless, we implore you to give us a prelate — it matters not who he be or whence he comes, provided always he is a fit person who knows how to stand up manfully for the freedom of his Church — and we beg you also to give us favourable and effective hearing in respect of our plea concerning the standing of our Church. For we would have you know this, the undoubted truth, that if we had been willing to yield to the Archbishop and abjure the claims of our Church, a matter in which he has many

[1] Reading *abiectos* for *obiectos*.

THE POPE'S DECISION

times presumed to harass me even since my return and the prohibition issued by you in your commission, I should already, if I desired, walk mitre-horned.

We now return to the De iure et statu Meneuensis Ecclesiae

This done, about fifteen days after Pentecost, the Pope gave judgment in the suit concerning the standing of the Church of Mynyw, condemning the Archbishop to pay the Archdeacon's costs, since he had not been defended in the suit, and again fixing a day, the feast of All Saints in the following year, whereon the parties should appear without fail. Also at the Archdeacon's demand, he appointed Judges in England to take the evidence of old and decrepit men on the claims of his Church to be Metropolitan, that the claim might not fail in default of witnesses, through lapse of time. None the less the following clause was added in favour of the Archbishop, that the Archdeacon should only be heard in that suit, if he was supported therein by the whole or the majority of the Chapter of Mynyw. For his adversaries knew that the Chapter might easily be corrupted and had indeed already been corrupted, by threats and bribes, in respect of both suits. Now about eight days later the Pope also gave judgment in the suit concerning the election. And since the opponents asked for a delay that they might produce their witnesses, he appointed the same day as he had already appointed for the other suit. But in favour of the Archdeacon, he ordered that adverse witnesses should not be received against him save in the Court of Rome; for knowing that the Archbishop could have a host of witnesses in England ready to assert anything he pleased, he held that such a decision was a necessary precaution. And since the Archbishop, though summoned to appear in both suits, had only been represented in one, he was condemned to pay half the Archdeacon's costs. But in the course of his speech the Pope, as though out of

DE IURE ET STATU

pity for the Archdeacon's labours, spoke as follows: 'If we could decide according to our conscience without regard to the allegations made, we should grant no delay'; and then turning to the Archdeacon he proceeded, 'And you, my brother, though it cost you both toil and expense, see that you return to us on the appointed day; for in truth, unless we hear something very different, you shall depart hence, not for consecration, but already consecrated'.

Now after the feast of St. John the Baptist and the feast of the Apostles Peter and Paul, the Pope, desiring to avoid the great heat of the season, departed with all his Court to Segni, which is about one day's journey from the city. But it was not till after a month's stay at Segni that the Archdeacon, who had followed him thither for this purpose, received all his letters both for the Commissions and the rest, Andrew being at this time mortally sick and at the last agony. And so returning to England in the company of the Elect of Bangor and one foreign servant, since almost all the comrades and serving men of both were dead, he caused the summons to be served upon the Archbishop and the letters of recommendation, together with those ordering protection and restitution, to be delivered to him.[1] Then hastening without delay to Wales, he came to his Church in the octave of St. Nicholas; and whereas he had found it corrupt before, now he found it most corrupt, so corrupt indeed that they refused to aid him even in the suit touching the standing and dignity of their own Church. For Osbert, an English Archdeacon and a false son of the Church of Mynyw, was playing the double part of corrupter and courier on behalf of the King, the Archbishop and the Justiciar as well,

---

[1] Some important events have clearly been omitted. See Table of Contents (*De Rebus*, III, 80-2), which show that he first went to the King in Normandy, that on his arrival in London he took steps to arrange for the hearing of his two suits by the judges appointed, that he had an altercation with the Archbishop and was once more forced to take the Cross (cp. p. 116).

GIRALDUS RETURNS TO ENGLAND

in this respect assuming the role which Foliot had been used to play, while the Abbot of Whitland, because he was a Welshman, escorted him round the country as he had escorted the other. For Foliot, having in the past year appeared at Rome against his own Church on the Archbishop's behalf, and knowing that for this reason he was hated by the Welsh, procured Osbert, corrupted like himself and like himself a pernicious son to his own Church, to run about Wales and to frighten the wretched Chapter of Mynyw with all the wonted threats or to tempt it with promises and gifts as before. Now as to the manner in which Giraldus went through Gwynedd and Powys and was received by the Princes of those parts with the greatest honour and concerning the help which they freely and generously offered him, all these things are clearly set forth in the *De Gestis Giraldi*.[1]

So returning thence and hastening to his own Church, he came thither on the day he had appointed for the Canons of Mynyw, namely, the octave of St. Hilary.[2] And when he had gathered together the Canons and clerks of the Church, he spoke to them of the promise which they had made to him in the beginning when he was about to go to Rome to plead the cause of their Church, as they had counselled him and implored him to do. And he charged them urgently that they should make ready to come with him to Worcester by the day appointed for him by the Judges, namely the day after the Conversion of St. Paul,[3] and that they should at least assist him loyally in the cause of the standing and dignity of their Church. Moreover, he offered to pay out of his own purse all the expenses of those that should come with him. The Princes of South Wales also, Maelgwn and Rhys ap Rhys,[4] by their letters and messengers counselled them to stand up firmly with

---

[1] See p. 233.   [2] Jan. 20th, 1202.   [3] Jan. 26th, 1202.
[4] Both sons of Rhys ap Gruffydd (d. 1197).

DE IURE ET STATU

Giraldus their Archdeacon on behalf of the dignity of St. David, saying that if they failed so to do, they would regard them and all the chief men of their country as their enemies for ever. Likewise Llewelyn, Prince of North Wales, by his messenger Laurence, Prior of the Isle of Saints (Bardsey), an eloquent man whom he had appointed for the purpose, invited them to follow the same course, informing them also by letters patent that, if any of the Canons or clerks of the Church of Mynyw lost anything at the hands of the English by so doing, he pledged himself to restore it twofold out of his own purse, and if any were driven out into exile on this account, he would receive them with honour in his own country and would liberally entertain them.

But on the other hand the Archbishop had procured that frequent letters full of terrifying threats should be sent to the Chapter from the King and the Justiciar,[1] while in addition, by means of Osbert he scattered among the Chapter golden rings, or rather I should say gilded rings from London, together with girdles tricked out with gold and ivory, and necklaces of gold entwined with silver[2] and divers like gifts, in which that luxurious city so abounds. And having sent these things in advance and promised far greater things to come, and having conferred ample revenues on some of them, he confirmed almost all the seniors in the previous corruption which he had wrought among them, to such an extent that being thus charmed with boons and blandishments they replied to the Archdeacon, neither respecting God nor fearing shame and infamy, that through fear of the King and the Justiciar, who forbade them in any way to support him in his suit concerning the standing of the Church, which they said was directed against the Crown, they did not dare to appear with him in support of that

---
[1] See *R.S.* I. 431 ff. for examples of the King's letters.
[2] cp. Song of Solomon, i. 11.

CORRUPTION SPREADS AT MYNYW

suit, since they dreaded their own destruction as well as that of their Church.

But the Archdeacon, knowing that under the pretext of fear they masked their own corruption . . . gave them this counsel, though all in vain, that they should preserve the loyalty they owed their Church by at least supporting him in the suit concerning its standing until they saw himself, the head of the controversy whom all his adversaries desired first and foremost to afflict with loss and wrong, deprived of all his revenues in England and Wales; and then they would be able to withdraw betimes and with less dishonour to themselves. With many divers words to this effect did he urge them, but persuaded them not. For the head of this corruption and of all corruptors, after the Archbishop, was the Abbot of Whitland, who was perverting the whole Church of Mynyw; for almost all the Canons were of his kith and kin, and at his instigation and that they might procure his promotion besides other things, they clung to him, being moved by the promptings of the flesh, and for this reason did not blush to oppose not only the election of the Archdeacon, but also the dignity of their own Church, like bastard and ungrateful sons, worthy not only of disinheritance but of extirpation. For that Abbot, who in the previous year had harmed him secretly, now opposed him openly with all the rest. For since the Abbot of St. Dogmael was waiting for the end and was no more than the shadow of a man, the Abbot of Whitland, whiter outside than within, in habit rather than in deed, in name rather than in truth, poured the poison of his malice into the Chapter of St. David and, being the cement that held together all this fabric of corruption, showed himself in manifold ways a pest most efficacious for harm, since he was an enemy in the house and at the hearth, infecting the Chapter, conducting the messengers of the Archbishop backwards and forwards, revealing the frailties of the Church of Mynyw, and, worst of all, betraying the secrets of the Barons, who loved the Church and for this reason favoured the Archdeacon, not only to the Archbishop, but to the King and the Justiciar as well. But the Archdeacon, sparing neither labour nor expense, journeyed through the rough lands of Ystradtywi towards England, and in the mountains of Cantref Bychan met a messenger sent by his Dean from Brecon, from whom he learned that all his lands of Brecon, both at Llandduw and elsewhere, that belonged to the Bishopric and which he held as custodian of the See, had been resumed into the hands of the King by order of the Justiciar and by means of the servants of William de Breos. And at Llywel he also received another messenger sent in haste, by whom he was told that not only the Bishop's lands, but all his own as well were shortly to be seized by the Justiciar with all their revenues, and that it was the counsel of his faithful followers and all his friends in those parts, that for the time being he should turn aside and avoid the fury of his persecutors, while it was fresh and in full career. For the courtiers and officers of the King were threatening arrest and imprisonment against himself in person, and against all his followers, if they could lay hands on them. But the Archdeacon went on his way unterrified and unslackened in his journey; and about a mile from Llandduw, between Aberyskir and Trallan, he met Richard his Dean, who had been his proctor in those parts for all his affairs, and now pale and trembling, repeated all that he had told him by letters and messengers, impressing each several thing upon him in language, if possible, more terrifying than before, and urging him in every way to turn aside for the present and not to presume incautiously to expose himself to the perils with which he was threatened. But he could not move him; for the Archdeacon, being a man dauntless and without fear, began to jest with him, saying, 'Have we not good beer at home? Let us go then and

HE IS ACCUSED OF HIGH TREASON

drink it before we are robbed of all'. So he came to his house and found his property and household undisturbed, and that nothing worse had happened than that Foliot and his accomplices, who were both few and contemptible, had spread terrifying threats through all the countryside to frighten the Archdeacon away.

Now the cause of this commotion and these insults on the part of his adversaries was as follows. The Justiciar, being at Shrewsbury a little after Christmas with the Barons of those parts, had received great complaints concerning Giraldus from Robert, Bishop of Bangor, and from all those whom he could induce to join him. For he said that Giraldus had favoured his adversary, who represented himself to the Welsh as being the Elect of Bangor, though he had not received the King's assent, and that he had lately restored him to the custodianship of the See of which he had been deprived;[1] he also asserted in public that he was in this matter and in all else, opposing the honour of the King, adding that he had just come to North Wales to ally Llewelyn and the Princes of Powys with the Princes of South Wales and to raise the whole of Wales against the King. And so the Justiciar, moved by these utterances of the Bishop, which being false should have been regarded as sacrilegious, caused the Archdeacon to be deprived of all the episcopal lands at Brecon, and passing through Oxford on his return, sent the following letter to the Archdeacon of that place:[2] 'Geoffrey FitzPeter, Earl of Essex, to his very dear friend, the Archdeacon of Oxford, greeting! Know that Giraldus, Archdeacon of Brecon, is an enemy of our Lord the King, wherefore we charge you to take into your hands all the revenues which he has in your Archdeaconry. Witness myself, at Gloucester, the 20th day of January.' Moreover, at the suggestion of the Abbot of

[1] He had however done something of the sort. cp. *De Rebus*, Table of Contents, III, 36, *electum Bangorensem reconciliauit et honori restituit*.
[2] Walter Map, a friend of Giraldus.

DE IURE ET STATU

Whitland, who had met the Justiciar with others at Shrewsbury, he sent the following letters to the said Abbot, that he might be able to deprive the Archdeacon of all advantage from the Cistercian Abbeys in Wales, where above all it had been his wont to seek help and refuge, when hard pressed by persecution.

The letter to that effect follows, threatening seizure of the religious houses if they have either 'counsel or agreement' with Giraldus.

Likewise the same Abbot, blinded by ambition, since he could not utterly forbid the Archdeacon from being received, sent a decree through all the Abbeys subject to his house, more especially to Strathflur, where Giraldus had stored his treasured books and whither he had most often betaken himself in the hour of violent persecution, that when he came thither he should not receive the honour due to the Archdeacon or the Elect, but should only be harboured in the public hall among the common guests and the noise of the people. He decreed also, which was more inhuman still, that neither monk nor brother nor even a servant of the house should escort him anywhere from place to place nor show him the way through unknown and lonely places, far from the paths of men, a boon which kind hearts are not wont to deny even to foreign travellers.[1] But a little later the Archdeacon repaid this same Abbot with full retaliation—nay, rather, God himself avenged the wrongs done to his Saint, whose Church and Champion the Abbot had assailed so vehemently, and caused the latter even on earth to be oppressed by means of him whom he sought to oppress, and to be deposed with ignominy and by just judgment to be deprived of the power which he presumed so recklessly to abuse, as shall be clear from what follows.[2]

[1] The MS. reads *uiatoribus* not *maioribus* (Brewer).   [2] See p. 265.

HE IS PERSECUTED

But to return to our story: after doing all that seemed necessary at Brecon, the Archdeacon proceeded to England and came to Hereford; but Foliot the runner had run before him[1] and had so terrified that city on his coming (for he said that Giraldus was soon to be seized and thrust into prison by the Castellans as an enemy of King and Kingdom, in virtue of letters from the Justiciar which he had received to this effect) that scarce any of the Canons or of his friends dared to speak with him for fear of the public power, and scarce any of the citizens would harbour him. But after all this loud talk and terror a servant from Foliot, delivered the following letters to him as from the Justiciar: 'Geoffrey FitzPeter, Earl of Essex, to Giraldus, Archdeacon of Brecon, once his well-beloved, greeting! We greatly wonder that you have so recklessly and of your own authority presumed, contrary to the Crown and Dignity of our Lord the King, to intrude upon the lands and properties belonging to the Bishopric of Mynyw. Wherefore we counsel and strictly enjoin upon you that, as you love yourself and all that is yours, you give over this presumption and for the future meddle in no wise with aught that pertains to the said Bishopric. Otherwise know that we shall punish you severely and shall seize into the hand of our Lord the King whatever of your property shall be found to be within the power of our Lord the King; and we shall cause your body, wherever found within the power of our Lord the King, to be taken and kept in safe custody. Witness myself, etc.'

None the less the Archdeacon pursued his way and on the day appointed by the Judges came in good time to Worcester on the day after the Conversion of St. Paul.[2] But he did not find there either his chief Judge, the Bishop of Ely, who had gone abroad with the Archbishop to go to the King, nor yet his substitute, the Arch-

---
[1] *cursor et precursor.*   [2] Jan. 26th, 1202.

deacon of Gloucester. Only the Prior of St. Mary, sent as surrogate by the Dean of London and the Archdeacon of Buckingham, sat solitary in a certain chamber in place of the Judge or rather of the Judges.[1]

But the Prior of Holy Trinity of Canterbury came with a throng of monks. Master Simon of Southwell, then the chief among the Archbishop's clerks and his general officer, had also come with a crowd of clerks to meet the Archdeacon, but rather out of ostentation and to make a show, so that it might be seen that the Church of Canterbury, though the Archbishop was absent, did not lack defenders. In such numbers did they throng together on the first day without any need for so doing.

So when the Court was seated, first of all the Prior of Canterbury addressed the Archdeacon as follows: 'It is a marvel that so discreet and learned a man should essay the task of draining a well which has no bottom, and that at the blind instigation of reckless men, he should strive to raise a suit which he can never bring to the conclusion he desires. For even though you should be able to overcome the Archbishop of Canterbury despite his great wealth and power, there would still await you a fresh contest with the convent of the Holy Trinity, who would assuredly risk all the lands and treasure of their Church sooner than suffer defeat in such a suit. But grant that you conquer both of these. A third conflict would still await you with all the suffragans of the Church of Canterbury. Further even though you were triumphantly victorious over all these three, there would remain a fourth struggle with the King himself, whose Crown you assail, a struggle beyond your power to sustain or carry to a successful conclusion.'

To this the Archdeacon briefly replied as follows: 'I grant that I am no match for all these adversaries and

---

[1] It is to be noted that the judges appointed by the Second Commission are different from those of the first (cp. p. 195). All now come from the province of Canterbury.

APPEARS BEFORE JUDGES AT WORCESTER

that I cannot in anything be compared with them; for to use the words of the poet:

> Not so mad am I
> That I should match me with such mighty names.[1]

Nevertheless if I did not to the best of my power champion the dignity of our Church in this hour of peril, I should most manifestly declare myself a faithless and bastard son. But he who directs all his effort and all his strength to obtain that which is his of right, ought not to be accused or upbraided whatever the issue of the day. Does not the poet say:

> Never may victory crown the man who deems
> That virtue needs the warrant of success![2]

or as he says elsewhere,

> Though strength may fail, yet shall the will win praise;
> With this, methinks, e'en Gods are well content.[3]

And again there is the saying of Seneca: "In arduous enterprises, even though they fail of success, yet the mere effort is worthy to be praised."[4] After long war and the hazard of ten[5] years, at length there followed the overthrow of noble Troy, wrought by the Fates or the unkind stroke of Fortune; and yet Hector, being a peerless champion while he stood in her defence, has obtained well-merited and immortal praise. And therefore the poet says:

> If Troy had prospered, who'd know Hector's fame,
> Whom hard-won honour led to headlong doom?[6]

---

[1] *Ov. ex Pont*, I, i. 25 (with *confero* for *comparo*). [2] *Ov. Her.* II, 85.
[3] *Ov. ex Pont*. III, iv. 79.
[4] He quotes the sense and not the actual words of some passage in Seneca, in whose works the sentiment is common. The nearest I have found is in *De vit. beata* xx, 2, *quid mirum si non escendunt in altum ardua aggressi? sed, si uir es, suspice, etiam si decidunt, magna conantes.*
[5] *duodenne* must be a slip for *decenne*.
[6] *Ov. Tr.* IV, iii. 75. The pentameter is taken from the preceding couplet and has *uadit* for *strauit*.

DE IURE ET STATU

Thus whoso fights with a feeble foe, if he be conquered, great is his confusion, and if he conquer, brief is his honour. But he who meets his foe in mighty war and in a just cause, if he fight well and leave naught undone that man should do, should never lose the meed of praise that is his due, however the fortune of war and the hazard of fate may fall. Wherefore it is my desire to fight bravely for our Church with all my might against stalwart adversaries, that so, even though I conquer not, I may at least escape the infamy that waits the coward. As for the King's Crown, I seek not to assail it, but with mighty effort to increase its honour by re-creating a third Archbishopric within his realm.'

For the rest, since none of the principal Judges were present and above all since the Bishop of Ely was beyond the sea, the case did not proceed farther that day. But the Prior of Holy Trinity in secret urged the Archdeacon with many words to renounce the suit concerning the standing of the Church and to make his peace with the Archbishop and the Church of Canterbury, yet could not persuade him. The Archdeacon therefore proceeded towards Oxford and on the way met his own servant whom he had sent with letters to the Justiciar, from whom he received the following answer: 'Geoffrey FitzPeter, Earl of Essex, to Giraldus the Archdeacon, greeting! We charge you that you should bear yourself towards the King otherwise than you have begun, and that you should hold no synod or Chapter in the land of our Lord the King save only within your Archdeaconry, as you love all that is yours and also your own body. But if you desire to speak with us, you may safely come. Witness, etc.'

Now the letters which the Archdeacon had sent him ran as follows: 'To the noble and magnificent Geoffrey FitzPeter, Earl of Essex, Justiciar of all England, Giraldus, Archdeacon of Brecon, health of body and of soul! I wonder that a man of your discretion and wisdom, the King's chief counsellor and Justiciar of his realm, should have given such easy credence to the words of enemies in the absence of their adversary, and should have been so readily moved to anger and indignation. For it is not customary, as you know right well, to form a judgment on the allegations of one party in the absence of the other. So I would have you know that I am not so much a wild man of the woods[1] as my enemies falsely assert, but that I am capable, when time and place demand, of living as an inhabitant of the more tranquil lowlands.[2] Wherefore, God willing, I shall shortly come from Wales to England, prepared, by the grace of God, to set forth the truth and make those songs unsung that my enemies have chanted concerning me with lying suggestion, and I shall show you that the words of a Bishop are not always evangelical, but when they lie, are on the contrary, sacrilegious. Good health and long be yours!'

So following the Justiciar, he came to London, but on the feast of the Purification[3] found him in Kent at Canterbury, whither he had proceeded. Now it happened that about the same time a messenger of Prince Llewelyn had come to Court; and when he was asked by the Justiciar what Giraldus had done in Wales, he repeated the whole story with absolute truth, saying that he had done all he could to win the Prince and his Lords to obedience and fidelity to the King. Wherefore the anger which the Justiciar had conceived at Shrewsbury was much appeased and mitigated.

So on the morrow at early dawn Giraldus heard Mass with the Justiciar in the Church of the Holy Trinity and, when Mass was over, being summoned by the Justiciar, he discoursed with him for a long time in private concerning the state of Wales. And when he had answered

[1] *Silvester*, a name sometimes substituted by his enemies for *Cambrensis*.
[2] *Campester*.   [3] Feb. 2nd.

DE IURE ET STATU

all his questions, he added that so great and discreet a man as he ought not to be moved by the words of his adversaries nor at their prompting to forbid him to hold synods and chapters, a matter which was no concern of the lay power. And further he strongly asserted that, though for the time being he would patiently endure to be deprived of the custody of things temporal, he would without question place under the ban of his anathema any man that, to his knowledge, stretched forth his hand upon things spiritual that had been entrusted to his charge; and that he would defer to no one save the King and his Chief Justice. So when the Justiciar, being a man of gentle and kindly temper, replied that he had given no order in these matters save by the King's command and in accordance with royal letters from abroad, the Archdeacon made answer, 'Since the Archbishop is there, who has charge of the King's seal, it is no matter for wonder if he causes such letters to be sent to you and persuades you to do such things contrary to the commands of the Lord Pope and to all justice, things moreover which he would never dare to do by himself or by means of his creatures. But it is matter for wonder that our Lord the King, contrary to his own honour, consents with him thus in all matters that concern the re-creation of a third Archbishopric in his realm.' To this the Justiciar briefly replied, 'I believe that it is fear rather than love that prompts these things'. Now this he said because the King, on account of the great war which he was waging against the King of France, did not dare to offend the Archbishop or any of his magnates. It was a wonder, too, that as oft as the King was moved against the Archbishop or when he was established in peace and prosperity, he sought the Archdeacon to procure the advantage of the Church of Mynyw, but when he was at peace with the Archbishop or at variance with Philip, he was suddenly hindered in so doing.

THE JUSTICIAR AT CANTERBURY

Now while the Archdeacon and the Justiciar were thus sitting and conferring together to the right of the altar, behold the monks of the Church stood by in throngs to gaze at Giraldus and to point him out to others; and noting this, the Justiciar said to the Archdeacon, who was absorbed in their conversation: 'Do you not see how these monks come crowding about us and gaze at you with wonder, as though you were some portent? I think the trouble you are causing the Archbishop is not too displeasing to them.' For he knew that there was no true nor sure love betwixt the monks and the Archbishop. So, since it is sweet when men 'Point with the finger, saying, "This is he!"'[1] Giraldus was wont to say to those who used to lament his toil and condole with him because he had undertaken so difficult and desperate a cause against such powerful adversaries, 'In this struggle I am sustained and uplifted by two wings, which lighten my toil and render it delightful. The right wing is the pure intent and the clear conscience, with which I have undertaken a pious and without doubt a meritorious labour on behalf of the honour of St. David and the dignity of our Church. But the left wing is the praise and glory, which I am sure to gain even on earth, both now and for all ages, because of this noble enterprise inspired by so firm a purpose'.[2]

Moreover, when on a certain feast day Llewelyn, Prince of Gwynedd, had called together all the magnates of his country and was holding a great court, there came forth at the end of the feast, one of those who are called Bards both in Welsh and Latin. Wherefore Lucan writes: 'Then gathered bards poured forth full many a song.'[3] Then proclaiming silence both with voice and hand he put the following question: 'I ask whether it were better and more honourable for the Elect of Mynyw' (for thus

[1] *Pers.* I, 28.
[2] See *Invect.* VI, 1. The incident was also recorded in the *De Rebus* (Table of Contents, III, 106).
[3] I, 449 (*longaeui* not *concreti* is the true reading).

DE IURE ET STATU

the Archdeacon was then called by all, though he called himself Archdeacon only) 'never to have raised the question of the dignity of St. David that had slept for so long, though it were never given him to bring it to a happy conclusion, or rather thus to have entered upon this enterprise and to have failed of its achievement?' And when there was a long pause and all were mute save for a certain whispering among themselves, the Prince at length broke silence and gave this answer: 'I will declare to you without prejudice what I think on this matter. I say that it were far better and far more glorious for the Elect to have vindicated the rights of St. David against such mighty adversaries and against all England, lest through silence overlong they should perish, even though victory might not be his. For as long as Wales shall stand, this man's noble deed shall for all time be noised abroad with worthy praise and honour, whether in written chronicles or upon the lips of poets. For he who does all he can and leaves nought undone that honesty and valour may venture, even though perchance he fail of his desire, has none the less deserved worthy praise. For neither a skilful dicer nor yet a valiant knight may always win what his heart desires. Moreover, thanks to his labours, the rightful dignity of the Church of Mynyw, so obscure before, shall through all time henceforth shine forth more manifest.' And universal favour and applause followed on the words of the Prince.

Also on a certain day about the same time Gwenwynwyn, Prince of Powys and Cyfeiliog, having summoned his nobles and the chief men of his country to sit with him in council, and mention being made of the labours of Giraldus, a common topic in those days both in Wales and England, the Prince himself thus spoke: 'Many a time and oft does our Wales stir up great wars against England, but never has it waged one so great and grievous as that now fought in these our days by the

Elect of Mynyw, who for the honour of Wales ceases not with long and pauseless efforts to vex and harass the King and the Archbishop and all the clergy and people of England. In truth, if our wars last through the summer, they return to peace in the winter season, and never continue more than a year at most, and often only half that time. But this man's warfare has already endured without cease for five years and more.'[1]

[1] See Appendix VI.

BOOK IV

THE Archdeacon therefore ... returned to Mynyw, coming thither for the feast of St. David, which is celebrated on the First day of March ... And on the feast-day itself he exhorted the people, taking as his text the words of Isaiah:[1] 'I have nourished and brought up children, and they have rebelled against me' ... For even so the clergy of the Church of Mynyw, nourished by their patron St. David under the wings of his Church and raised aloft to be Canons, Archdeacons and Abbots, despised both himself and his honour and with all their might hindered his sons and servants to restore its former dignity. Wherefore like ungrateful sons they showed themselves worthy to be cast out from their inheritance and to be utterly destroyed from off the earth. And on the same day, before he came down from the pulpit, publicly with candles lit he excommunicated Osbert, Archdeacon of Carmarthen, and Reginald Foliot as being rebellious against himself and disobedient to the commands of the Pope. But when the solemnities of the feast were done, on the morrow all the clerks and Canons of the Church, then present, were gathered before the Archdeacon who took from each one of them oaths of fidelity to himself as the administrator of the Church of Mynyw appointed by the Lord Pope. This done, those of our clergy who, having been corrupted and become the accomplices of the Archbishop, had gone out from among us and did not take their stand with us, when they saw this, groaned aloud, saying one to the other, 'See, we are of no avail; if we let him go thus, all our Church will go after him'. So straightway with common intent messengers of the two Abbots, who aspired to the Bishopric, crossed the sea to the Archbishop in Nor-

[1] Isaiah. i, 2.

HE RETURNS TO MYNYW

mandy, and, as is the way of mankind, speaking of big matters in even bigger words, hinted to him that the whole Chapter and clergy of Mynyw had sworn entire fidelity to Giraldus and had taken a solemn oath in person on the most precious relics of the Church that they would loyally stand by him in either suit ... And being not a little moved to hear it and filled with unbelievable consternation, the Archbishop, that he might cause the greater alarm, sent as from the King, whose seal was in his charge, letters close full of terrifying threats, addressed not only to the Archdeacon, but to the Chapter and the Bailiff of Pembroke, while to all others, to whom they might come, he sent letters patent. But if any man desire to see these letters, let him turn to the book *De Gestis Giraldi*.[1]

Moreover, that Giraldus might nowhere be free from vexation, he was in the meantime summoned by the Judges appointed by the Pope, to wit, the Abbot of Wigmore, John, Prior of Wenlock and Master Adam of Bromefield, to appear on an appointed day to answer the Abbot of Cemais (St. Dogmael), Osbert, Archdeacon of Carmarthen, and Reginald Foliot. Now this order was devised by the Archbishop, so that Giraldus, being harassed on every side, might be less able to devote his attention to the more important issue. But the Archdeacon was not a whit moved thereby, but as soon as he received a second summons (the first that was peremptory) in which was inserted a claim for a large sum of money on the petition of the three persons mentioned above, sent his clerks and his proctor who, hearing that the senior Judge, namely the Abbot of Wigmore, had by letters patent (as is the custom) deputed his office to one of his Canons without reserving final judgment to himself and his fellow-Judges, forthwith appealed to the Court of Rome. Now whereas the Judges wished to call

[1] III, 109-113 (Table of Contents).

DE IURE ET STATU

a halt and to defer to the appeal which had been lawfully made, as was their bounden duty, the Prior of Wenlock to do favour to the Archbishop, whose creature he was, and whom he had consulted on the matter, none the less proceeded with the case and did not cease from sending fresh, frequent and most peremptory summons, day by day, for the vexation of the Archdeacon. Wherefore, since the latter relied on the appeal, and for this reason on a large number of occasions appeared neither in person nor by proxy, the Judges, proceeding with strictness and severity, were prepared to pass sentence on him as guilty of contumacy; but the Bishop of Ely, who was the chief Judge in all the arduous and important suits of the Archdeacon, advised him to send proctors and advocates on each appointed day, despite the burden and the expense, that they might maintain his cause by legal remedies and postpone the sentence, due regard being had to the appeal, which had been lawfully interposed and was renewed on each occasion. For the Archdeacon had assumed (and had so informed the Bishop) that the severity of their proceedings was prompted by the Archbishop, so that in virtue of the Pope's authority, which they made use of just as they pleased without any regard to justice, they might with all speed pass sentence of excommunication upon him, and thus silence him and choke his fatal voice in all the arduous suits that he brought against the Archbishop. Therefore to counter their malice and to avoid the disaster which his adversaries and his unjust judges designed to bring upon him, he put himself to great expense, continually sending advocates from Oxford to the March of Wales, together with a large number of witnesses. Meanwhile, after some time had passed the following letter was sent by the Justiciar to the Bailiff of Pembroke in obedience to letters of the King sent from abroad at the instigation of the Archbishop:

PERSECUTION OF THE CHAPTER

'Geoffrey FitzPeter, Earl of Essex, to Ralph de Bendevill, Sheriff of Pembroke, greeting! We are informed that Pontius the Archdeacon and M. his son, and R. the son of Jonas and H. his son, and Meilyr, Samuel, Asser and G., Dean of Pembroke, Canons of Mynyw (who to the dishonour of our Lord the King and contrary to the dignity of his Crown and realm, support and cleave to Giraldus the Archdeacon and have taken oaths of fidelity to him against the King, suffering the seal of the Church to be given to him that he may do what he will therewith to the injury of our Lord the King) have lay tenements and lands and escheats, in which they openly keep their harlots, sinning against God and their order, and that they ought rather to be called luxurious laymen than ordained priests or Canons; and that in this cleaving to Giraldus they are no less manifestly the enemies of the King and his realm than is Giraldus himself. Wherefore we charge and command you, as you love yourself and all that is yours, to take into the hand of the King all their lay tenements and wards and escheats and chattels that may be found in their possession, and that you should also seize the bodies of their harlots and cause them to be kept in safe custody, until such time as you shall receive further orders from myself. Witness myself, etc.'

Thus from the tenor of these letters two things may be gathered: first, that all the seniors and sounder part of the Church of Mynyw would, if they were free to do so, support the Archdeacon; and secondly, that those false younger brethren and unfaithful sons out of their abundant malice revealed both to the Archbishop and the Justiciar all the frailites of the Chapter, and those things for which they are wont most to be assailed.

But the Archdeacon on the day appointed for the parties, to wit, on the day after the Feast of the Finding

DE IURE ET STATU

of the True Cross,[1] came without delay to Newport.[2] But since his chief Judge was still abroad, and substitutes had been appointed both for him and the Dean of London, of the original judges, only the third, namely the Archdeacon of Buckingham, was present, little progress was made in the suit for that day. Moreover because they feared the public power and were terrified by the aforesaid letters, not one of the Canons of Mynyw had come thither. The Archdeacon therefore received summons in respect of both his suits, that he should come to Brackley on the day after the feast of St. Botolph,[3] postponement having been made to that date of set purpose, that the Bishop of Ely, the chief Judge, might in the meanwhile return.

But in the meantime, the Archdeacon by the authority committed to him repeatedly summoned a General Synod of the whole diocese of Mynyw, first at Carmarthen, next at Pembroke, and thirdly at Mynyw; but on each occasion the assembly was prevented by letters from the King to the Justiciar, which were provided by the Archbishop, and by letters of the Justiciar to the Bailiff of Pembroke, prohibiting all synods and frightening the clergy away. Finally he summoned a General Synod at Brecon on the Octave of Pentecost, namely on the day after the feast of Holy Trinity,[4] and caused the following letter to be sent to the Abbot of St. Dogmael who, being an ignorant fellow, had despoiled the temporalities of the See contrary to the commands of the Lord Pope:

'Giraldus, Archdeacon of Brecon, to Walter, Abbot of St. Dogmael, greeting! ... We command you to the solemn celebration of our Synod at Brecon, which (God helping us) we purpose to hold on the Octave of Pentecost. Wherefore we charge you and by the

[1] May 4th, 1202. [2] Presumably Newport in Monmouth, not in Pembroke.
[3] June 18th, 1202. [4] June 10th, 1202.

GIRALDUS SUMMONS A SYNOD

authority of the Lord Pope committed to us, we strictly command that you should then appear before us and restore all the revenues of the Bishopric that you have received within the said term, in accordance with the command of the Lord Pope. Moreover we enjoin upon you that you shall on the following day deliver a sermon to the Synod and speak words of exhortation and instruction, as befits one in authority who boasts himself to be the Elect of Mynyw and calls himself by that name. Farewell.'

Moreover, since the Bailiff of Pembroke, by the command of the King and the Justiciar, whose letters he had received to this effect, had secretly and strictly forbidden all the clergy of the See of Mynyw, who had been placed in his power, to render obedience in anything to Giraldus the Archdeacon or to frequent his Synods or Chapters, the Archdeacon approached Master Simon of Southwell, who had been left in England as the general officer of the Archbishop, and obtained from him the following letters patent.

Letters follow in the name of the Archbishop forbidding the secular power to intervene in spiritual matters and ordering the faithful of Mynyw to obey Giraldus in all spiritual matters in accordance with the commands of the Pope.

Giraldus also obtained from him letters close in which he strictly forbade the Bailiff of Pembroke to presume to hinder the clergy of Mynyw from obeying the Archdeacon.

When, therefore, the two Abbots who aspired to the Bishopric and the other accomplices of the Archbishop heard that the Sheriff of Pembroke was already on this account ceasing to turn away the clergy from Giraldus and that the clergy of the country were already preparing to come to the Synod, they sent letters to the Archbishop

DE IURE ET STATU

in Normandy urging him with all speed to revoke the orders given by his officer. But the Archdeacon, omitting naught that required to be done, at last solemnly and publicly at Brecon held the Synod which had so often been summoned to so many places, but had always been prevented by the public power. But how the Synod was almost prevented and how the couriers of the Archbishop came with Reginald Foliot to bark against them and prevent them, and how they retreated, baffled and confounded, is clearly set forth in the *De Gestis*,[1] wherein it is also set forth how the aforesaid Judges of the March, regarding neither right nor wrong, strove more fiercely every day to vex the Archdeacon. Meanwhile, the feast of St. Botolph[2] drawing near, the Archdeacon came to Brackley on the appointed day, to wit, the morrow of the Feast, surrounded by hosts, not indeed of Canons, but of friends and advocates. And finding there the chief Judge, namely the Bishop of Ely, who had now returned to England, and two other Judges substitute, who were also clerks of the Archbishop, Master Simon of Southwell and Master John of Tynemouth, whom the Archbishop had appointed his proctor, and also Master William of Calne[3], the Archdeacon came forward into the midst of them and, since he had no one of his Church to support him, began as follows:

'Alone I am called to arms,[4] though he, who has God on his side, cannot be called altogether alone, nor is he wholly without following who has truth and justice to support him.' And he caused to be read aloud the letters close of commendation and protection which the Pope had sent to the Archbishop, whereby the latter was forbidden to entice the clergy of Mynyw by blandishments or to frighten them by threats or to inflict loss upon them,

---

[1] Table of Contents, *De Rebus*, III, 121.   [2] June 17th, 1202.
[3] *De Cauna*.   [4] Cp. *Aen.* XI, 442.

or by his own servants or by the ministers or officers of the King to prevent or suffer them to be prevented from supporting the Archdeacon in both his suits, if such should be their desire. Then he went on to tell how the Archbishop had first enticed the Chapter by paltry gifts and blandishments and had next proceeded to employ threats and the terrors of the public power, and lastly to plunder and despoil them, so that they were forced to swear and even to give sureties that they would not only refuse to support the Archdeacon, but would even, on behalf of the King and the Archbishop, oppose him constantly in both his suits. 'See', he cried, 'how obedient the Archbishop is to the Lord Pope; and yet in all his letters to him he calls himself his devoted son!' But afterwards, as the crown of all his wrongs, the Archdeacon read out the letters of the Justiciar to the Bailiff of Pembroke, in which he ordered him to seize the lay tenements and escheats of the Canons and even to lay hold of their concubines and keep them under watch and ward, until he should receive further instructions from him. Now these letters, like others, the Justiciar had sent by order of the King from overseas to terrify them. Wherefore it may be most strongly presumed that all this was done by the Archbishop: first, because he was continually at the King's side while he was abroad; secondly, because as Arch-Chancellor he had charge of the King's seal; thirdly, because he was an interested party; and fourthly, because he was not seeking to correct error, but was shown by clear proofs to be the oppressor of the liberties of the Church . . . But when the clerks of the Archbishop had answered these charges, as best they could, it was asked whether any Canons of Mynyw were present; whereupon those two English intruders, Osbert and Foliot, and two Welshmen, Martin, brother of the Abbot of Whitland, and Samuel his kinsman came forward. And being asked by the Judges, whether or no they were

DE IURE ET STATU

ready to support Giraldus in the suit concerning the standing of the Church, they replied as they had been instructed; for they had no head of their own and were unwilling to stir up so difficult a suit or to assist or assent to any other who did so, until they had a Bishop for their head. They also presented letters of their own Chapter, ratifying what these four should do or say there. But one of the Welshmen, namely Samuel, that he might not seem to have nothing to say on behalf of his Church, openly asserted that the Church of St. David had in truth been Metropolitan and ought so to be, but that time and place for the raising of this question were not yet come. They also testified abundantly, as though they were witnesses suddenly called and ready to assert anything, that they had never elected Giraldus the Archdeacon, and produced letters from the Chapter to that effect.

But to all this the Archdeacon replied that those who desired to oppose his election would have to go farther and visit the thresholds of the Apostles.[1] He also asserted that the two Englishmen had been excommunicated by himself, while the Chapter and the more discreet of the resident Canons had been compelled by violence and spoliation of their property to refuse him support and to write as they had done in respect of either suit; and he promised to prove this by witnesses who had been present at those scenes of violence, robbery and plunder, fixing the next day for their hearing by the parties to the suit. But with regard to those four canons, he said that they denied the fact of his election and opposed the dignity and freedom of their Church, solely that they might thus placate the Archbishop, by whom they had been seduced, and procure the promotion of one or other of the two Abbots who aspired to the Bishop's throne.

But see into what perplexity, owing to the burden of their own sins and the daily increasing malice of their

[1] Rome.

adversaries, they are brought who, if they defend their Church, as all know to be meet and right, are forthwith despoiled of all their goods; but, if they do the contrary, are perjured and foresworn. For it is a custom in the Church of Mynyw that, whenever anyone is made a Canon, he swears fidelity to his Church before he is installed, taking a solemn oath in person by the relics in possession of his Church. Wherefore the Archdeacon in the Consistory at Rome, before the Cardinals commissioned to hear his suit, impaled Foliot on the horns of a dilemma, which he stated as follows: 'Either our false brother here will with us support his Church in the suit concerning its standing or he will oppose it. But if he opposes it he is manifestly a perjured traitor to his Church. But if with us he supports the suit, he is a perjured traitor to the Archbishop, at whose expense and pay he has come hither and to whom he has sworn that he will on behalf of the Church of Canterbury oppose the Church of Mynyw in the Roman Court to the best of his power.'

'Wherefore,' continued the Archdeacon in the presence of His Judges, 'all the Canons of Mynyw who have presumed to oppose their Church and Mother for the sake of earthly gain, or rather for their loss, are for ever infamous and foresworn, most of all those two Englishmen, Osbert and Foliot, who have been hired and sworn to do this thing and to strive against their own Church, not out of sheer necessity, as many others do, but of their own free will.'

So after much debate on both sides, the suit was on the second day adjourned to the fourth day in the octave of St. James[1] at Bedford. And in due time when the parties came together there before the Judges, the Archdeacon produced as witnesses two priests and one clerk who had been present at the spoliation of the Canons and had

[1] July 29th, 1202.

witnessed the violence that was done them, on account of which they had dared to support him or to appear in court. But the four Canons of whom we have spoken appeared on this day also, as though the Chapter had sent them, and with their own lips, supported also by letters from the Chapter, denied that the Canons had been plundered or turned away by violence from the Archdeacon. But he asserted that this denial was due, beyond all doubt, to the fear lest, if they put forward their complaint, they might suffer yet worse from the public power. They also, moved by the same terror, declared that the letters of the Chapter on behalf of the Church of Mynyw or of the Archdeacon, were all of them either stolen or forged.

But when the Bishop of Ely asked why Giraldus strove with such vast effort to confer a benefit upon men who were unwilling to receive it and to rescue from slavery and subjection persons who were wholly ungrateful, he replied in public audience, making the following distinction: 'As you know, a benefit differs according as it consists in liberty, liberation or liberality. The first and second can be conferred upon the unwilling, the third never. For I can emancipate my slave and set my captive free from prison, however unwilling he may be. But I cannot give a book of mine to anyone, unless he is willing to accept it.' And he cited the saying of Jerome, 'Oftentimes boons are conferred upon the unwilling, when the giver seeks to profit them rather than to please them'; And again, 'he who binds a lunatic or wakens one who is sunk in lethargy, though he vexes both, yet loves them both'. He also added: 'The result of this corruption is in truth most wonderful; for here we have Welsh Canons, who used to rejoice in the honourable liberty that originally was theirs, and now, like the whole of their race, refuse to be snatched from the servitude and subjection which now oppresses them, even if the boon be proffered by a stranger, whoever he be and whatever the circumstances, not to speak of their refusal to be liberated by one of their own brethren who with such diligence and toil fights on behalf of the body of their own Church. It is not so amazing in the case of the English, long since reduced to servitude, which by now has become almost a second nature, if they refuse to depart from their habitual state of slavery... Wherefore the ears of those unwilling to be freed ought to be bored with an awl, after the custom of the Jews who used to manumit their slaves every seventh year'[1]... But the judges, postponing the reception of the witnesses produced by the Archdeacon to prove the violence used against the Canons and the spoliation of their goods, appointed the fifth day[2] in the octave of the Nativity of St. Mary for the hearing of both suits at St. Albans.

Meanwhile the storm of persecution growing more violent every day, it was ordered by public proclamation that no one in Dyfed or within the bounds of Mynyw should harbour Giraldus; so that when he went to those parts he avoided the houses of his kinsmen and nephews, lest they might incur peril or loss, and on the night[3] preceding the Feast of the Assumption of the Blessed Virgin he lay at his own prebend of Mathry six miles away, to which he returned after celebrating a solemn Mass on the Feast-day and delivering an exhortation to the people; for none at Mynyw dared harbour him and he was unwilling that any man should suffer harm for his sake.

So having accomplished all that had to be done in those parts, he returned to Brecon, where in the assembly of the clergy of those parts and in the Chapter at Aberhonddu,[4] that no time or place might be free from

[1] See Deut. xv. 12, on which he comments at some length.
[2] Sept. 12th, 1202.   [3] Aug. 14th.
[4] The Welsh name for the town of Brecon, which is at the confluence of the Honddu and the Usk.

DE IURE ET STATU

tribulation, lo and behold Osbert and Foliot, the buffoons of the Archbishop, proceeding in the most insolent manner, delivered a summons from the Judges together with letters from the Lord Pope to him, touching an alteration in the Commission. For the Archbishop, knowing that the Chapter of Mynyw, being thoroughly corrupt and therefore won to his side by a combination of threats and bribes, would bear just such witness against Giraldus as he might desire, had obtained letters by the messengers whom he had sent to Rome with the usual results, to the effect that witnesses should be admitted against Giraldus and his election not only from the Chapter of Mynyw, but from other sources, the old and decrepit, the poor and needy, although in the Commission granted to Giraldus it was expressly stated that any one who desired to protest against his election should come to Rome. But if any desire to see this summons and the various pronouncements with all the rubbish they contained and also the letters of the Pope sent to Giraldus on this matter, let him read the *De Gestis*.[1]

But the Archdeacon was not to be broken in spirit by all this nor crushed with despair. But rather with head erect and heart unshaken he showed that hope was still in him, spurned all the outrages of adverse fortune and with lofty courage trod underfoot the whirl of her turning wheel, remembering the wise saying:

> Yet yield not thou to ills, but bolder go
> Against them, while thy fortune leads thee on.[2]

Much too was he helped in all these straits by the wise counsel of that best of brothers, of whom we have so often spoken, who had urged him to bear his troubles with a cheerful mind.[3]

So by the devising of the Archbishop, letters from the

[1] Table of Contents, *De Rebus*, III, 133-4.
[2] Virg., *Aen.* VI, 95 (garbled).
[3] See p. 161. Philip de Barri died during G.'s first visit to Rome.

WITNESSES SUMMONED TO ST. ALBANS

King, the Justiciar and the Marshall were sent both to the Bailiff of Pembroke and to the Chapter of Mynyw, commanding all the Canons of Mynyw, young and old, rich and poor, as they loved the honour of their Lord the King, to come to St. Albans on the day appointed, making no excuse or evasion; otherwise their persons would be seized, as being enemies to the King and his realm, together with their concubines and all their chattels, and when they themselves had been cast into prison, their concubines would be outraged and all their goods confiscated. And with these letters were sent others from the Archbishop, which after their wont were half oil, half vinegar. Such was the terror thus inspired that the firm and faithful (as they would have been if they had been suffered to be so), no less than the corrupt, one and all prepared themselves to say whatever the King and the Archbishop would have them say. See then how perilous it is to fight against both these powers; for unless the violence of the King had pressed so hard and so continually upon him, the adversaries of Giraldus could have made little headway in either suit.

But the Archdeacon, employing fresh counsels to meet fresh circumstances, with his wonted vigour prepared a number of witnesses to support his claims and to prove his election before the Judges. And having completed these preparations with all speed, since he was unable to get the money promised him in North Wales and Powys, though he often sent faithful messengers to that end, (for the Archbishop infected even those parts and dissuaded them from fulfilling their promises by means of the Abbot of Whitland and other corrupters) Giraldus, making no delay, journeyed hastily through Elfael and Maeliennydd and Kerry and Cydewain on his way to Gwynedd, and penetrating the thick and shaggy forests of Powys and the land of Gwenwynwyn, he found the latter on an expedition against Llewelyn with whom he had been dwelling in peace. He received Giraldus with honour, but of all the Princes of Wales alone refused to give an aid to St. David in his own land, not only out of jealousy, because Llewelyn had been the first to promise aid, but also out of avarice, that he might appease the Archbishop and the English whom he had joined against Llewelyn. Wherefore the vengeance of heaven soon after followed; for he received such a hurt owing to his horse trampling on his foot, that he suffered from grievous lameness and weakness almost past cure.

It was probably at the outset of this journey that he met with a calamity recorded in the Speculum Ecclesiae, III, 5, *as follows:*

He came to the Abbey of Strathflur, because it was far from the power of the English and seemed to him a sanctuary and quiet place of refuge, bringing with him for the sake of security all those possessions which he held most dear, above all his treasure-store of books which he had so zealously collected from boyhood to his later years.[1] Wherefore when on the occasion of his third labour, by reason of his suits it became necessary for him to set forth to Rome that he might without fail be present on the day appointed for their hearing, the monks of this rich Abbey, seeing that he was anxious to get the money necessary for so costly a journey, devised a plan which, though it began with a show of kindness, ended in fraud, promising unasked that they would lend him money sufficient for his journey on the security of his books of theology; but to this they added the condition, that if he should at any time perchance desire to sell these books, he should sell them to none save themselves and their house. This offer he gratefully accepted, and promises were given on either side. But when, the time for his departure being already pressing, he came to the

---

[1] This first sentence refers to an earlier date. See p. 162.

PERFIDY AT STRATHFLUR

place to get his money, he found the monks converted and perverted to a deed of deliberate wickedness. For they said that in the mean time on looking into their *Book of Uses* they found that it was lawful for their Order to buy books, but not to take them in pledge; wherefore if he was ready to sell his books they would gladly buy them for a fair price. But the Book, which they called their *Book of Uses*, might more justly be called their 'Book of Abuses'. So when he accused them on the ground that they had already given their promise and accepted the books in pledge and had given him no warning on the matter, they replied that the prohibition had slipped their memory at the time. So this good man, who desired to walk uprightly and abhorred all double-dealing, seeing that he had been deceived by their guile and wickedly defrauded, and that time so pressed that further delay was impossible, while without the money he could do nothing — seeing this, I say, and being in sore straits, since he could not endure like a coward to abandon the suits which he had thus far pursued so manfully, at last — for necessity knows no law — he left his books for them to do with them as they pleased, feeling as though his very bowels had been drawn out of him, and exchanging for worthless coin that treasure beyond all price, which he had collected through so many years, he did as best he might and, full of sorrow and anxious past all belief, set forth upon his journey.

The story continues:

He therefore entered Gwynedd on his way to Llewelyn, together with the Elect of Bangor who had met him, and conversed with the Prince at Aberconwy concerning the money which had been collected and deposited with the Elect. He welcomed the Archdeacon with joy and cheerfulness; for he was a generous and kindly man and, if he had contracted any taint from the contagion of his

DE IURE ET STATU

neighbours, as soon as he saw the face of his friend, he cast all traces thereof aside and ordered the money to be paid to him, amounting, over and above that which he got from Powys, to the sum of twenty pounds.

This done he entered England by Whitchurch and Shrewsbury and, on about the fourth day after leaving Llewelyn, spent the night at the monastery of Haughmond. But on the morrow, before his departure, two messengers came to him from the parts of Mynyw, namely Philip, chaplain of his prebend at Mathry, and Aidan the chaplain of his church at Llanwnda, who told him that the hand of his persecutors had of late become so heavy against himself and his folk that after many threats they now had broken forth into deeds, nay into crimes and sacrilege; for Nicholas Avenel, who had succeeded Ralph de Bendevill in the bailiwick of Pembroke, being a cruel man sparing none, was with William FitzMartin, despoiling the Prebend of the Archdeacon at Mathry and the Church of Llanwnda, both within the churchyards and without, and leading captive both men and women, whom they cast into prison and forced to pay heavy ransom for their release.

But the Archdeacon, when he heard this replied courageously that this spoliation was a stroke of good luck for himself and that any fresh efforts of the Archbishop might be countered by putting forward a plea concerning this outrage. And so taking his chaplains with him into England to bear witness to these deeds, he was received that night on the land of a certain Baron, named William FitzAlan,[1] to whom he had once been dear and a familiar friend. But the Baron, returning from Worcester on that very day and having about that time spoken with the Archbishop and heard his loud complaints against Giraldus, when he learned that the

---

[1] William FitzAlan (the second), holding Oswestry and Clun. It was probably near Clun that this occurred.

Archdeacon was there, sent his chamberlain to him, telling him secretly to depart cautiously and without delay; for if certain of his folk, who loved the Archbishop, should find him there, he would be unable to prevent them from molesting him and plundering his goods; he added also that he was much grieved that it was not in his power to show him the love he bore him nor to receive him with honour at that time in his lands. When, therefore, he heard this, since he could neither be broken nor terrified by adversity, Giraldus followed his warning with cheerful countenance and head erect, recalling to mind the saying, 'If they persecute you in one city, flee into another'.[1]

So he proceeded to Oxford and there found his two advocates, who had supported him through the whole summer in every suit and had been well paid for their services; but now both had been turned against him by the Archbishop and refused to accompany him to St. Albans, nor could he obtain others, save one only who had lately come from abroad and was utterly unknown; and even he, fearing the threats of the public power, was most unwilling to support him and only consented on hard terms. So hastening towards St. Albans, the Archdeacon, bringing with him a large number of witnesses, both clerks and lay, boldly appeared before the Judges, who were then all present in person, on the day after[2] the Nativity of the Blessed Virgin. But the Archbishop lay, as it were in ambush, not far off at Dunstable, about twelve miles away, that he might be able to receive and send back frequent messengers to St. Albans, whither he had sent all his clerks and advocates.

First of all, then, the clerks of the Archbishop, knowing the saying of the comic poet, 'Try all things ere you take to arms',[3] on behalf of their Lord offered the Archdeacon, through the Judges, the most ample Church revenues, if he

[1] Matthew x. 23. [2] Sept. 9th, 1202. [3] *Ter. Eun.* 789.

DE IURE ET STATU

would abandon both suits and cease from troubling the Archbishop. But Giraldus, seeking in all things the profit not of himself, but of his Church, and striving with all his might to restore its ancient dignity, placed the following document in the hands of the Judges, in which he set forth the terms on which he would accept peace and concord.

'Since it is well established that our Church of Mynyw was for a long time Metropolitan and remained in enjoyment of full Metropolitan power, save for the use of the pallium, down to the days of Henry I, by whose power and violence it began with other Churches of Wales to be brought under the rule of the Church of Canterbury (as may be gathered from the 'Divisions' of Pope Anacletus, the *Register of Gregory* and the *Ecclesiastical History of Bede*), let it again, if it please you, become a Metropolitan See, but subject to that of Canterbury, for one Metropolitan Church is often subject to another; for example, the Metropolitan Church of Bordeaux is subject to that of Bourges as being the seat of the Primacy. For a Church cannot, as you know, hold the Primacy unless it has an Archbishop subject to it. But though the Church of Mynyw at the time of the Blessed David and his twenty-five successors down to Sampson of Dol, who took away our pallium with him (as may be gathered from ancient chronicles and the truthful assertions of the men of old), had within the space of Wales, as it now is, and the five English Bishoprics (to wit, Chester or Coventry, Hereford, Worcester, Bath, and Exeter) a total of twelve suffragans, it would now be content only to possess those three which are within the borders of Wales. For thus the original seizure by Canterbury, invalid because violent, might in part be purged, since with its consent the Church of Mynyw would rejoice in its pristine, though

INTERIOR OF ST. DAVID'S CATHEDRAL

PROPOSES COMPROMISE AT ST. ALBANS

not its full, honour. And because now for some time, namely during the time of our last three Bishops, who alone of all our Bishops received consecration at the hands of the Archbishop of Canterbury, it has (though unjustly) been subject to Canterbury, so would it thus remain; and so the Archbishop of Canterbury would have the greater honour, since in lieu of a mere suffragan, he would have an Archbishop subject to him, and would ease both his conscience and his shoulders of much of their burden, because he would govern a remote country, some fifteen days' journey distant, and a race divided from England by difference of language, laws and customs, through a Vicar, who would not be ignorant of the ways and manners of the people and would reside among them and be diligent in their office. But that I may not seem either to have claimed or now to claim this dignity for myself in person let any man be made Archbishop of our Church provided he be a fit person, according as the Lord Pope, the King and the Archbishop may direct. Thus this great quarrel would be put to rest forever.

'Another means of securing peace, if perchance this should not please the Lord Pope, to whose direction we commit everything, or even the Archbishop, might be secured if the Judges would accept the evidence of the old and feeble witnesses whom we produce and if their testimonies were sent under their seals to the Lord Pope and kept under seal in his records, that the right of our Church might not perish through lapse of time; while a second sealed copy were kept at Canterbury, and a third at Mynyw. Thus throughout the life of the present Archbishop (whom may God long preserve for the honour of his Church) this controversy would be at rest, unless it should be revived by will of the Lord Pope or even by order of the King. And that it may be clear to all that I have not undertaken such labours that I might

DE IURE ET STATU

obtain the See of Mynyw for myself, I will resign my election into the hands of the Lord Pope, and by his wisdom let a strong and vigorous Shepherd be provided for our Church, poor, pillaged and almost reduced to ruin as it is, to reassemble and repair what has been dispersed asunder. But if the Lord Pope disapprove or the Lord Archbishop refuse either settlement, nothing remains but to let these suits run their full course.'

This document was at once sent to the Archbishop by his folk. And when he had read it and reread it, most of his counsellors and the more prudent among them approved this offer of peace and compromise; above all the Bishop of Ely, who was so prudent and well skilled in law, asserted that, if he were Archbishop of Canterbury, he would prefer to have an Archbishop with his suffragans in Wales, subject to himself on terms that would ensure a firm and lasting peace, rather than by provincial right to possess four Cathedrals there under simple Bishops, always hovering in their allegiance and litigiously inclined. But the Archbishop put his trust in three things; the power of the King whom he held at his beck and call, either through affection or more often through fear on account of the troubles of the war by which he was beset; the Chapter of Mynyw, which he had utterly corrupted; and the Roman Court, which he thought could be corrupted, which God forbid! And therefore he refused the proffered peace, but put off replying till he had consulted all his suffragans on the matter. Wherefore I have thought it not beside the mark, here to insert the letters sent to the Archdeacon by Mauger, Lord Bishop of Worcester, who, like the Bishop of Ely, was eager for peace.

'Master Mauger to Master Giraldus, greeting! I set forth with all diligence and sedulous care both the ways to peace and concord between yourself and the Archbishop, which were propounded in your letters; and I openly expressed my opinion concerning the two English Canons, because they would have no peace, but desired war. But the Archbishop, after taking counsel in secret and debating the matter with persons of knowledge, replied that he could give no certain answer for the present, since the matter concerned not himself alone, but all his suffragans. But he bade me, as his surety, to tell you that he would do it, if his suffragans agreed and if the Lord Pope should approve and be ready to confirm the conditions set forth by you.'

And so since there was no way left save litigation and the prosecution of the suits, the Canons and clerks of Mynyw came forward together with the old and decrepit, whose wont it was to sit for ever idly at home, almost all of them having been driven to come by violence and being ready, from the fright they were in, to say anything against Giraldus. And when the Bishop of Ely saw this and noted the most outrageous slanders proceeding from the lips of the oldest, he said, as if in jest, before them all, 'Behold how your nation and priests have delivered you into our hands!' looking at the clergy of Mynyw as he spoke. And amid the general laughter that followed, the Archdeacon replied: 'For it is written, "They are a very froward generation, children in whom there is no faith".[1] And this saying may now be with truth applied to them, who on the most serious occasion take arms against their mother, and like red-handed matricides should, according to the penalty prescribed for such a crime, be sewed up in a sack with a cock, a serpent and a monkey, and thrown into running water.[2] For they come forward in three degrees in this their condemnation. Some are cowed by threats, which is bad enough; others are enticed by gifts, and this is

[1] Deuternomy xxxii. 20.   [2] The ancient Roman penalty for parricide.

worse; and some are blinded by the desire for the promotion either of themselves or of their friends in that same Church which they assail, and this is the worst of all; while all alike swerve from the way of truth and, though they may perchance have power to escape the vengeance of man, shall assuredly not escape the vengeance of God.'

Meanwhile the suit concerning the election being laxly conducted, large numbers of witnesses were brought forward on both sides. But of the opposing party the Clerks of Mynyw, departing not from their corruption, all vied with one another in attacking Giraldus. For those who were not old and decrepit said they were poor; and though perchance in comparison with the wealth of England, they were poor, they were yet not so poor that they could not have gone to Rome at their own expense; and moreover the Archbishop was ready to provide sufficient journey-money from his own purse to all who would go to Rome to bear witness on his behalf against Giraldus, as will be abundantly clear in the sequel. But by the cunning of the opposing party it had been said, and the same was published, with threats, by the public officers, that any man who did not give evidence against Giraldus on behalf of the King and the Archbishop here in England, should assuredly go to Rome to bear witness against him there. And so forthwith these wretches, panic-stricken by this empty terror, leapt forward here, there and everywhere to perjure themselves. For some, that they might be admitted to perjure themselves among the old men, said that they were sixty, though they were not; others again, that they might commit perjury among the poor, falsely swore that they had not so much as forty shillings income. And so they were doubly perjured, since wittingly and of their own accord they swore falsely that straightway they might swear more falsely still; as was afterwards clear

THE WITNESSES ARE TERRORIZED

from their evidence when it was made public at Rome; for they asserted that they had never elected Giraldus and never done anything in regard to him that could be called an election.

But when the Abbot of St. Dogmael, who then made his first appearance before the judges, had to be examined as to his literacy, first of all the Judges offered him the letters of the Lord Pope to read, wherein was contained the Commission to inquire concerning himself. But those who spoke on his behalf, being clerks and accomplices of the Archbishop, replied that he ought not to be tested by writing of this kind, to which he was not accustomed, but rather by some Church books. A missal was brought, written in a large and legible hand; and when it was offered him by the Judges to read and expound, by their leave he withdrew aside to consult with the clerks of the Archbishop, and after a long and tedious delay refused either to read or to expound, retiring after his answer had been inserted in the Judges' report.

Further, when the Canons of Mynyw said that they did not wish either to support or give their assent to Giraldus in the suit concerning the standing of their Church, the Archdeacon replied that they had first given their assent, but had later been turned away from him by violence and the spoliation of their property at the hands of his opponents. And when he was ready to prove this forthwith by means of suitable witnesses, namely priests and clerks, and said that the Lord Pope would admit these proofs, if the case were being tried before him, the Judges, none the less, either out of their own presumption, or desiring to propitiate the Archbishop, to whom they were provincially subject, at length formally declared that they would not accept the proofs submitted in this matter by the Archdeacon (wherein the Pope afterwards said that they were wrong) and that they would proceed no further in the suit concerning the

DE IURE ET STATU

standing of the Church, since none of the Canons supported him; as was afterwards inserted in the Judges' report.

This done, since many adversaries came forward in great numbers, all at the direction of the crafty schemer his Arch-Adversary, to lay their complaint concerning the wrongs and grievances put upon them by the Archdeacon, in accordance with the injunction contained in the last letters obtained against the Archdeacon, the latter complained that he had lately been despoiled by the devising of the Archbishop and of other adversaries who now brought false charges against himself; and he produced his chaplains who had suffered spoliation and said that he would make no answer to these charges, unless he were first put into possession of all that had been taken from himself. He also declared that he could procure neither advocates nor any other helpers owing to the malice of his adversaries and the league into which secular justice and the power of the Church had entered against him, but that he and his were denounced in the market-place and the streets as public enemies of the King and of his realm. On account of these grievances he appealed to the Lord Pope, and finally before his Judges in public audience, in virtue of the powers and authority committed to him by the Supreme Pontiff, he pronounced sentence of excommunication against his said despoilers, Nicholas Avenel and William FitzMartin, who had plundered his Prebend of Mathry, and further he placed their lands under an interdict. Finally ... he sent his clerks and messengers to the March of Wales on the day appointed by the aforesaid Judges,[1] from whom he had appealed, and took care to renew his lawfully made appeal not only through the voices of his messengers, but by a precise statement in writing as a last farewell to his Judges. None the less the latter, to

[1] See p. 237.

GIRALDUS SETS OUT FOR ROME

oblige the Archbishop, continued to harass the Archdeacon and, daily accepting proofs from his opponents concerning the losses they had suffered, condemned him, absent as he was and on the point of setting out to go to the Court of Rome, to pay his adversaries damages to the amount of one hundred and seventy marks, and with ingenious precaution they deferred the execution of this unjust sentence to the Easter of Pentecost following, that the news of it might not reach him while he was at the Court. Now all this was done at the prompting of the Archbishop and his creatures, that the condemnation of Giraldus by such judges might be a makeweight to the Archbishop's condemnation by the Roman Court, commanding him to pay the Archdeacon's expenses.

But the Archdeacon, loftily disdaining all the machinations and malice of his adversaries and turning his back upon them, set forth without delay on his journey to the Roman Court, whence he hoped to secure remedies for all his troubles; and first of all he went to London to make his preparations, and thence to Canterbury to take ship for foreign parts. But all this he did secretly, avoiding the public causeway and travelling stealthily by side paths. So coming to St. Augustine's at Canterbury and being warmly welcomed and faithfully concealed by the monks, who like himself regarded the Archbishop as their adversary in many things, or rather in all, he caused a ship to be made ready secretly for him at Sandwich . . . But when he had stayed there for nearly eight days (for the east wind blew contrary), behold suddenly there came messengers from the Justiciar and the Archbishop who, having heard that Giraldus had set out toward those parts, issued a proclamation that no man, clerk or lay, should cross without letters from themselves. And the same orders were given at every port and all along the coast, while a special proclamation was issued concerning Giraldus himself, forbidding him to cross, nay even commanding that he should be searched for in every house at Sandwich and seized if he could be found. Wherefore he sent the following letters to his Judges, who on the day after the Feast of St. Luke[1] were to deliver their report to the parties in London before the Archbishop and as many of his suffragans as could be assembled; and these letters were read in public audience.

'To the venerable and beloved in Christ, Eustace, by the grace of God, Bishop of Ely, and to the Dean of London and to the Archdeacon of Buckingham, Giraldus, Archdeacon of Brecon, greeting in the Lord! I make known to your discretion that at Sandwich, where there is a public crossing for every man, I was prevented from crossing the sea, and on the Friday next after the Feast of St. Denys[2] a search was made for me in every house of the said town, which belongs to the Church of Canterbury, by servants of that Church that they might seize me; and when they could not find me — for so it pleased the Lord — yet since I was hidden not far from there because I feared the malice of man, it was there and in the Isle of Thanet publicly proclaimed by the heralds of the Archbishop and the Justiciar, that no man should take me or folk of mine across the sea. Behold how well they have obeyed the commands of the Lord Pope, who ordered the Archbishop in no wise to hinder me or mine or suffer any other to hinder us from pursuing either suit without fear. But the Canons of Mynyw who were willing to support me have been despoiled, as also have the clerks of my Prebend, while its laymen have been carried away and bound in chains. I have been deprived of my revenues of the Prebend of Hereford and the Church of Chesterton. Nor is there any man to remedy these wrongs. For he that should have done so, despite my

[1] Oct. 19th, 1202.　　[2] Oct. 9th, 1202.

FORBIDDEN TO CROSS THE CHANNEL

frequent entreaty, has become my oppressor and the author of all these things, as by the grace of God shall be set forth at the proper time and place. But do you do your duty and delay not to add to your report this the last and bitter crown of all my wrongs and to set forth the violence and fear that I have been made to suffer. May your paternity fare well in the Lord!'

Therefore Giraldus, neither terrified nor dismayed by these things, undaunted as ever, with new counsels and remedies meeting each new stroke of fortune, sent forward to Flanders a certain clerk of his, who crossed the sea with part of his money under the disguise of a poor man. Then turning rein back towards Feversham and crossing the Thames to Tilbury, he passed through Essex to the coast near St. Osyth, seeking a ship. But since in that place there are not often to be found ships big enough to carry horses, he resolved to enter a small vessel and, skirting the shore to the right with his clerks and more valuable possessions, to transfer himself to the Flanders ships which lay in the outer harbour of Sandwich awaiting only the help of a west wind, and, leaving his horses behind him in England, to buy others for himself in Flanders. So with this resolve he entered the boat and when for three nights and days he had lain hid therein with his folk, waiting for a favourable wind from the north-west, being forewarned of the snares already laid for his capture, he escaped with difficulty to the place where his horses were hidden and, crossing the Thames at another point and proceeding by unwonted ways which none the less caused him much peril and loss, once more presumed to enter the boundaries of Kent where he was most hated and insecure, being everywhere watched and sought for. And since it was impossible for Englishmen to land on the sea-coast of Boulogne by reason of the war between the Kings, and therefore there was no direct crossing from Dover, he went with elaborate caution to those parts where it was thought less likely that he would attempt to cross; and so, following hard on fortune and ever pressing forward, 'thinking naught done, while aught remained to do',[1] he disguised himself as best he could and, keeping his folk apart from him, lay hid in a small cottage near Dover for eight days and more; there he received his messengers who brought him the report of the Judges which was most necessary for the whole conduct of his affairs, whereupon he hired a ship at an exorbitant price and on the day after[2] All Saints, sailed secretly and following an indirect course, with great difficulty he got to Gravelines. But since at the same hour there arrived there persons who had sailed direct from Sandwich ... even there he feared the power of his adversary which was not small in those parts and in the sea-ports of Flanders, and lay hid till nightfall in the bottom of the ship beneath the oars and benches. But in the morning, when he made haste to go to St. Omer, whither he had sent part of his money ... he learned from pilgrims and others whom he met, that all English who were found there were seized, despoiled and cast into the public prison. Hearing this, therefore, he changed his plans and path, and betook himself to the castle of Challi about six miles distant to the north. But on the morrow a Canon of St. Omer, named Alexander, who knew and loved him, came to him and conducted him safely thither, where after he had spent the night in secret with his friend, he found his clerk whom he had sent before him with his money; and on the morrow he pursued his journeys toward Douai and Cambrai, since the road was safer for travellers in those parts, leaving Artois far on his right; for there Englishmen were being seized and cast into prison.

When, therefore, he had lain two nights at Douai and

---

[1] See p. 64.   [2] Nov. 2nd, 1202.

found none of the comrades whom he had hoped to meet there, on the third day he took the road to Cambrai and had proceeded about two miles in that direction, when, behold, a servant of Nevelon, that most wicked Warden of Artois, who was despoiling all Englishmen and sparing none, having been sent on in advance by his Lord to the Countess of Flanders at Valenciennes (whither the Count himself was going), met the Archdeacon, not directly, but coming across his path from the right, as evil chance would have it; and as soon as he saw the servants clad in new clothes who followed Giraldus, thinking from their dress and bearing that they were English, he quickly overtook him, and those who went before him. But how the Archdeacon, finding no safety in flight nor any security in the refuge offered by the Church,[1] was constrained to pay a heavy ransom, and how he came to Paris and there found the Elect of Bangor, who had crossed to Normandy, and how proceeding thence to Troyes and Clairvaux, he came to Cîteaux, where he procured the not unmerited deposition of the Abbot of Whitland and, as being the chosen minister of vengeance for the wrongs of St. David, delayed not to fulfil his appointed task; and so by long stages, passing through Burgundy, and crossing the Alps, he entered Italy, and, being forewarned, escaped the snares laid for him by his enemy by avoiding Parma and unexpectedly going straight to Bologna, where he lost the two Canons of Llandaff whom he had brought with him (for secretly and by guile they clove to his enemies); and how coming to Faenza on the third day before Christmas, he hardly and with much difficulty recovered the twenty gold marks which he bought in obols[2] of Modena from citizens of Bologna at the market of Troyes; and how while he was there in great necessity he

[1] Table of Contents, *De Rebus*, III, 161, which shows that he actually took sanctuary and was there besieged until he paid.
[2] See Appendix VII.

DE IURE ET STATU

found greater generosity in a foreigner than in his fellow countryman and comrade the Elect of Bangor, to whom he had often proved so good a friend; and how on the third day of Christmas[1] he hastened on his way through Bagno di S. Maria beneath the Alps of those parts,[2] and trusting himself and his comrades to the care of fortune, passed those steep and sheer mountains, so dreadful and perilous, no less on account of their snows than by reason of the robbers that haunt them, and at last reached the vale of Spoleto, where the inhabitants were amazed that he should have crossed those Alps, so full of dangers and despoilers, with all his folk and with so little loss — all these things are full set forth in the *De Gestis*[3].

And so proceeding through those parts, several days being given to the journey, he came to Rome two days before[4] Epiphany. Now the Elect of Bangor by reason of the sentence whereby he had been cast out from his order, of which sentence the Abbot of Cîteaux had informed the Lord Pope, did not venture to enter the city forthwith, but had resolved to lie hid not far from the city or rather in its suburbs, until the Archdeacon had first sounded the mind of the Pope; but the Archdeacon, though it was with difficulty that he succeeded in inspiring him with courage and confidence, took him along with him to the Court. Now the Pope, as was his wont, welcomed the Archdeacon honourably and with a kiss, but to the Elect of Bangor he said, 'Brother, I am told that you have been excommunicated'. Whereat the Archdeacon interposed, 'My lord, if it please you, no credence should be given to the words of adversaries till both sides have been heard and the truth is known'. And forthwith the Pope greeted him also with a kiss, saying, 'Such is their assertion, but do you see to it'. For his

---
[1] Dec. 28th, 1202.   [2] The Apennines.
[3] Table of Contents, *De Rebus*, III, 162-6.   [4] Jan. 4th, 1203.

HE REACHES ROME

adversaries had been before him and had defamed him thus by means of letters from the Abbot of Cîteaux, testifying to the fact.[1]

When, therefore, the Archdeacon had found a lodging in the Lateran not far from the Court, the Elect of Bangor, who had plenty of money, would not any longer lodge with him as had been his wont, but dwelt by himself. For he knew that the Archdeacon had been robbed in Flanders and that the money left him would soon be exhausted, and he feared that, if he lived with him, he might have to lend him money. Yet that his own suit, now almost despaired of, might not be brought to nought, he did not cease to seek help and counsel from him. But the Archdeacon, though all these things were clear to him, none the less feigned not to observe them and did his best to further his suit no less than his own, thinking that the latter might profit thereby.

So in the first Great Consistory after Epiphany, coming forward with a crowd of supporters, he thus began: 'I beseech your Highness, pious Father and Lord, to be pleased with patience and diligence to hear a long story full of our wrongs and loss. Oft-times a man with foreboding mind will anticipate the evils that he fears; and thus it was that in the year which is done, when your Holiness was pleased thus to write to our Judges in respect of the inquiry to be made concerning the assent of our Chapter in the matter of the standing of our Church, I was at once filled with forebodings of what should be, and said in public audience that this would merely provide my adversaries with a clear opportunity to malign me and corrupt our Chapter. For they had already found that it could easily be corrupted by soft words and benefits and promises; and when they could make no headway thus, they did so by threats and terror

---

[1] cp. Table of Contents, *De Rebus*, III, 163 (following Giraldus's visit to Cîteaux: *Indulgentia Domini Papae Bangorensi electo concessa*.

and the spoliation of their goods. Yet your prudence conceived that it had provided a remedy for such evil by writing to the Archbishop as follows:[1] "You, my brother, know well how long and how much our beloved son, the Archdeacon of Mynyw, has thought it his duty to labour on behalf of his suit, and how he has spared neither his person nor his purse, shrinking neither from the inclemency of the weather, the distemperature of the air, nor the perils of the road, etc. Wherefore we charge you, my brother... neither... to prevent or suffer others to prevent the fulfilment of our command both in the matter of the standing of the Church and in that of his election. Also we charge you not to inflict loss upon the clergy or laity of Mynyw who may assist him in either suit, nor frighten them by threats, nor win them over by soft words from bearing witness to the truth and presenting themselves before those to whom we have written on these matters." But he has clearly shown how obedient he is to your commands; for in their despite he has with benefits and blandishments enticed to himself the clerks of Mynyw who were ready to support me in both my suits, and has frighted them from me by threats and terror and the spoliation of their goods. And yet in all these letters to your Highness he presumes to call himself your devoted son. But of a truth, sincere devotion consists in deeds rather than in words or even writings, in action rather than in talk or lip-service. For the proof both of devotion and love is found in the testimony of works. Now that these things are true and that he has thus in all things despised your command, we were prepared to prove before our Judges in England, and we are prepared to prove it here in your presence by unexceptionable witnesses. Wherefore since he ceases not thus to rage against us and ours, but against almost the whole clergy of England, employing against us the public power which

[1] *Invect.* III, 12.

HE DENOUNCES THE ARCHBISHOP

he has at his beck and call, therefore let your apostolic severity make it its care so to curb such insolence and pride, that the punishment of one may strike fear into the hearts of many, and that other Prelates may learn from the example of his chastisement to refrain from such deeds of reckless audacity. For, as Ambrose says, "He that indulges one unworthy man, provokes all to be infected with the contagion of his sin. For the ease with which pardon is won is but a spur to transgression".'

And when he had made an end, the Archdeacon delivered to the Pope letters from the Princes of Wales with their seals attached, which they had written in common on behalf of the Church of Wales; and these he caused to be read not in the Consistory, but in his own chamber.

These letters (from Llewelyn ap Iorwerth, Prince of North Wales, Gwenwynwyn and Madog, Princes of Powys, Griffith and Maelgwn, Rhys and Maredudd, Princes of South Wales) reiterate the grievances of the Welsh against the Archbishop. They add nothing to what has already been told us by Giraldus, and their style suggests that they come from his pen. The report of the Judges was also produced by both parties, together with the arguments concerning the evidence given at St. Albans; also fresh evidence now given in the Consistory, and refutations of criminal charges; but all these are omitted by Giraldus because already in the De Rebus *(See Table of Contents,* III, *170 ff.).*

The following seems to belong to this portion of his third visit to Rome since it deals with the report of the Judges before whom he appeared at St. Albans. But there can be no certainty. The title given in Invectiones I, 10, *is merely*: 'His reply delivered during his third visit to Rome. It is an attack upon the Archbishop who "is guilty of all the charges made against him at St. Albans".' *It adds little to our knowledge of the case, but it is interesting by reason of the charges brought against the Archbishop. The latter has accused him of his unscrupulous*

INVECTIONES

use of the seal of the Chapter of St. David's. This is his answer (much abbreviated):

He has on divers occasions sent letters, purporting to proceed from the King, to various quarters; but therein he acted falsely, since he sent them to the enemy without the King's knowledge against the interests of the crown and the security of the realm. Wherefore, his dishonesty being detected, he was during the past year deprived of the royal seal to his great confusion and pecuniary loss.[1] Moreover, it is known that he is now engaged upon a similar attempt, having once more written similar letters, on account of which he has laid himself open to grave accusation, as he has also on account of certain other scandalous proceedings, being charged with having sent food-supplies into France in defiance of the royal prohibition; and on this account he was twice or thrice before my departure summoned to Normandy by letters and messengers from the King there to answer for his conduct. This is dishonesty of the gravest kind. But none the less you shall hear of a yet greater crime... Through all the lands of Canterbury which are wide and fertile, he issued a public proclamation that no man should sell or buy corn save to or from himself. Therefor he sells to widows and orphans in small measure amid their tears, and when times have changed buys from them in large measure amid their lamentations... In every barren year he sends merchant ships crammed with corn for sale to distant parts, where he hears there is famine, selling not like Joseph for the saving of the people, but at twice, nay, ten times the just price, indulging his greed and cruelty to the height of his desire... Moreover, knowing as well he might, since it was done by his advice, that owing to the increasing violence of the war between the Kings an order had been issued that a search

---

[1] This appears to allude to the same incident as that related in the speech against Andrew in 1201. See note on App. v.

THE CRIMES OF THE ARCHBISHOP

for arms should be made in England, he caused all arms that were anywhere for sale to be purchased, and collected a vast number in a very short time. Then as soon as a further order was made that arms should be procured throughout the realm, he forthwith offered his store of arms for sale... and made a vast profit... This is his religion, his theology, his philosophy of life, on which he spends all his efforts, that by commerce, by sending merchant vessels (as we have said) to distant parts for sake of gain, by purchase and sale, one as foul as the other, and, worst of all, by putting out his gold and silver at interest by the agency of the Jews to the great scandal of all England, he may heap up boundless treasure, by means of which, being so often accused and most worthy of condemnation, he may placate even the secular courts and escape scot-free... His wickedness is past compare and there is no iniquity on earth, nor has there thus far been such iniquity as his among the clergy, nay, not even the iniquity of the priest Palumbes,[1] of whom in his days it was said, 'O Almighty God, how long shall the iniquity of Palumbes the priest endure?' The Convent of Holy Trinity felt his wickedness and, but for your saving help, would have felt it even to its destruction The Church of St. Mary in London felt it; for he burnt it. The Innocent Longbeard felt it; for him he hanged;[2] and a little later[3] Wales felt it; for he slew three thousand of them. The Elect of Bangor also felt it: for after his canonical election and the interposition of his appeal, he thrust an Englishman into his place and, that this act might be effective, caused him to be expelled from his order by the Abbots of England and the Chapter of Cîteaux. And now last of all the Abbot of Saint Augustine, the special son of the Roman Church,

[1] See Appendix VIII.
[2] St. Mary-le-Bow was burnt during the suppression of the rising of William FitzOsbert (Longbeard) in 1196.
[3] The battle of Pains Castle (1198). See p. 131.

INVECTIONES

defended by so many and authoritative privileges, has felt that iniquity: for, at the order of the Archbishop, he was dragged from the altar where he was celebrating, in the very canon of the Mass at the moment of turning, and cast to earth with the body of Christ which he held in his hands, and trampled underfoot by impious men, beaten, wounded and dragged from his own Church of Faversham together with his assistant monks who were mangled like himself by the madness of their assailants. Since the martyrdom of the Blessed Thomas no such atrocious crime has been perpetrated in England. But this is so much the more atrocious than that crime and the more horrible in as much as the outrage thus offered to Christ himself, Christ the Head, and the very body of Christ is far more grievous than any outrage offered to His members.[1] And I too have felt his wickedness and feel it to-day; for in defiance of the Pope's prohibition and protection, I was, with our Canons and clerks, despoiled of my goods and my revenues, was proclaimed as a public enemy at every crossways in the realm, and finding no safety in the island forbidden to cross the sea; I have been hounded from place to place by persecution ever growing yet more fierce, and last of all taken prisoner in Flanders, dragged from the church itself in which I had taken sanctuary, and forced to pay ransom for my liberty ... It is a wonder that he should have ventured to accuse me of simony, seeing that his every promotion, nay his whole life stinks of simony. For he is not merely a Simoniac and a Gehazite; nay in him Simon Magus and Gehazi are believed to have risen again. It is a wonder also that he should have ventured to speak of any man's continence or incontinence or

[1] The incident is recorded in *Thorne's Chronicle* (Twisden, p. 1843). The writer like Giraldus is no friend to the Archbishop, but he clearly states that though the outrage was done in the Archbishop's name, it was done without his knowledge; and adds that the Archbishop excommunicated all concerned, since 'so horrible a deed had not been done in England since the murder of Thomas à Becket', using almost the same words as Giraldus. The date is 1201.

THE CRIMES OF THE ARCHBISHOP

to tell lies about it, when his own lasciviousness... spares neither nuns nor married women... Witness a certain Abbess who shall be nameless but not blameless, whom he has now for the second time got with child and that quite recently to the great and grievous scandal of the country. Witness also a certain veiled damsel, of high and noble birth, who with an Abbess, her sister, visited the court of the Archbishop more frequently and on more familiar terms than was seemly, and has now returned thence, being with child for the third time, unless perchance rumour lies concerning him in this and other matters... Let him then learn from this and perceive how foolish it is, how unprofitable and how much exposed to retaliation, to provoke men of letters either by deeds or by writing. Let him learn that the pen can wound more sharply than the sword. For the wounds of the latter heal, but those of the former endure to all eternity.[1]

We now return to the De iure et statu Meneuensis Ecclesiae.

Now since his adversaries knew the character of their witnesses, all of them worthless creatures who could easily be refuted, they proceeded with elaborate precaution to accuse him, among other things, of simony, a charge wherewith all persons of whatever reputation, character or guilt (and without exception all such men as themselves), are indiscriminately discredited. But the Archdeacon, as soon as these witnesses were produced before the Judges to take the oath, said that he would speak[2] against the character of each, against the Canons of Mynyw as foresworn and excommunicate, against the monks as gadabouts and deserters of their houses, and, against the ribalds as utterly worthless and, like the rest,

[1] See the *Retractationes* of Giraldus (R.S., I, p. 426) where he apologizes for the charges made against Hubert Walter in the *Invectiones*, admitting that they were based on hearsay only.
[2] The speech may be found in *Invect.* I, 12.

DE IURE ET STATU

hired for the purpose. Moreover he proceeded to deal with three of the witnesses, Foliot, Philip (who pretended to be a deacon and was not), and Golwen, a monk nicknamed the Fool, saying, 'Such are the witnesses they have produced against us, False, Fools and Foliots'. And also concerning Osbert the Archdeacon, whom with Foliot he had condemned as excommunicated by himself and foresworn, he added the following words, since Osbert by his outpouring of empty and frivolous words and by speaking merely on hearsay, had in the presence of Pope and Cardinals in the Consistory, kept the Judges examining him for three days: 'To borrow a rhetorical argument from his name, Osbert may be taken as equivalent to Ospert, i.e. *os apertum* or "Open mouth". Nor is it wonderful therefore if he vomited forth much from his open mouth.' And again he said of him: 'The *gurgulio* is a worm dwelling entirely within the throat, bursting at a light touch with a sound and also a stench. It is easy therefore to apply this comparison to the worm that is before us.'

I have thought fit also to add this from the *De Gestis*.[1] On a certain night there came to the Archdeacon out of the multitude of his adversaries two brothers, a priest and a clerk, who had been brought by Foliot and bought[2] by the Archbishop; and these on account of a quarrel that had chanced to arise among their number revealed to him many things concerning their secrets and their machinations. And among other things they revealed this, that when they departed from the Archbishop in Kent, at a certain manor of his named Otford,[3] the Archbishop in his chamber gave to the whole body of witnesses, whom he had collected against Giraldus out of England and Wales, the sum of forty-five pounds sterling as expenses and pay; but first he made each of

[1] Reference uncertain.   [2] *ducti ... conducti*.
[3] Remains of the Palace are still to be seen near the Railway Station at Otford.

them take a solemn oath upon the Cross, that they would faithfully oppose Giraldus according to the counsel of the clerks who were to go with them; and that five or six of them were prepared to bear witness concerning the election both of himself and the Abbot and to assert that they had been present at both elections, although they had never seen Mynyw, while some of them had never set foot in Wales — of whose number the priest said he was one. The Archdeacon, therefore, thus forewarned, in the notes for the examination of witnesses which were to be given to the Judges wrote also that they should be examined concerning the pay given and the oath taken at Otford, and concerning the position of the Church of Mynyw, the latter question to be put to those who had never been there, their names having been given by the informants. So when Osbert the Archdeacon was the first among the witnesses of the opposing party to be questioned concerning the pay that was given and the oath that was taken at Otford, he replied that the Archbishop had in truth caused forty-five pounds sterling to be paid in his chamber to those who were to go to Rome on his behalf, because they were poor; but that he did not know whether it was a loan or a gift. He said also that they swore faithfully to support the Archbishop's clerks with whom they were going and to give like support to the proctor of the Church of Mynyw. Now Ifor, the traitor of Llandaff,[1] was the first to be examined of those who were not of Mynyw, and being asked concerning the position of the Church of Mynyw, replied that it was on a hill, far from the sea,[2] and had only one tower, and that its bells were bad. So it was clear that this witness was a liar and suborned. But these two who had been examined first (one being from Mynyw, the other from

---

[1] He had been convicted of theft and perjury at Troyes; see Table of Contents, *De Rebus*, III, 162. He may have been one of the two Canons of Llandaff whom Giraldus lost on the journey.

[2] Whereas it is in a valley not far from the sea.

DE IURE ET STATU

without) at once forewarned all their witnesses against these questions which had been made and were like to be made again. Wherefore none of them afterwards was willing to say anything about the pay given at Otford. But they said, as they were schooled to say, that they had there sworn to render faithful support to the proctor of the Chapter of Mynyw. Also those who came from without were fully instructed concerning the position of the Church of Mynyw and all its circumstances. But examiners who use all care and caution do not permit those who have been examined to have access to those who are about to be examined, until the proceedings are ended.

Now since ' He wins all votes who mixes grave with gay',[1] let it not be deemed beside the mark, if here I insert the tale how Giraldus by his care and elaborate caution kept his horse despite the false claims of a gadabout monk. A false monk named Golwen came from Wales, whom the Archdeacon had excommunicated because he had deserted his house of St. Dogmael and had gone through Wales under false pretences preaching without authority, that he might fill his purse; after this he had been enticed by the opposing party to come to Rome to support them against Giraldus, and he was already there with a crowd of creatures like himself. Almost every afternoon he bitterly denounced the Archdeacon in the presence of the Chamberlain of the Lord Pope, claiming a certain horse belonging to the Archdeacon, which he said Giraldus had stolen from him. Now the Archdeacon did not deny that a small and feeble horse, scarce capable of carrying the gadabout on his rounds, had been taken by one of his Deans together with his false relics and other spoils, because he went about without leave and was also excommunicate; but this wretched beast had nothing save its colour in common with the Archdeacon's horse,

[1] Hor., *A.P.* 343.

GIRALDUS ACCUSED OF HORSE-STEALING

which was big, strong and of no small value. Such was the truth of the matter; but the gadabout on the contrary, being ashamed of nothing, persistently asserted that this horse was his; and a multitude of witnesses from the serving-men and ribalds of the opposing party were all ready to swear that this horse was the same that they had seen in possession of the gadabout, even when it was a colt. For it was at the instigation of the clerks of the Archbishop, who desired to put the Archdeacon to confusion in the Court, that this most worthless gadabout did all this, and they sent all their ribalds to help him to prove his case. But Golwen was fired to do this by three considerations: firstly, that he might win the favour of the opposing party whose hireling he was; secondly, that he might even thus be revenged upon the Archdeacon; and thirdly, that he might acquire a most excellent horse and make no small profit thereby. And forthwith he wallowed every day before all the world, weeping and sobbing at the feet of the Chamberlain who was a simple fellow, ignorant of law and without the least experience of the ways of such gadabouts. Indeed the foolish fellow was so much moved as to give all too ready credence to his complaint, and actually caused the horse to be taken to his own stable, as though to hold it in trust. The Archdeacon, therefore, seeing that those ribalds were prepared to prove anything at a nod from their masters, and being far more anxious at the thought of the disgrace that would fall upon himself and of the insults that his enemies would use, if they should win the day, than he was about the loss and expense, was so distracted by all this that he was naturally less able to give his full attention to each one of the several affairs that he had in hand. For he was most of all intent on his own suits concerning his election and the standing of his Church, above all the latter, and was scarcely less concerned about the suit of the Elect of Bangor than about

DE IURE ET STATU

his own, and was now much distracted and hampered by this frivolous dispute which had cropped up by chance, being harassed almost every day by pleading in the morning before the Pope in the Consistory and in the evening before the Chamberlain. Wherefore knowing that if the ribalds' evidence went any farther he would without doubt fail in that suit with confusion to himself, he put forth all his strength and energy to expose their fraud and falsehood and to outwit guile with guile. So when one evening the parties were brought before the Chamberlain and the host of ribalds were coming forward to give evidence for the gadabout, a certain person, instructed therein by the Archdeacon, addressed the chamberlain as follows: 'It is strange that a man, than whom there lives none more worthless in all the world nor one more given to gadding about, a man who has deserted virtue no less than his Order, should be allowed in this Court to lift up his voice to trouble a good and honourable man. For that horse, which was taken from him in Wales and which he falsely asserts to be this horse, was a gelding, whereas this horse is entire.' And at once the gadabout leapt forth into the midst and, being both hasty and shameless and itching to affirm or deny anything whatsoever, if thus he might be the gainer, turned to the speaker and said 'You lie without a doubt and I will prove it. For my horse had everything that a good horse ought to have, and has them still, as my Lord the Chamberlain may perceive and, if it so please him, may cause to be seen and proved without delay'. This said, the Archdeacon and his friends at once demanded that this evidence should be taken down word for word; and so it was done, as is the custom in those parts ... And the Chamberlain at once sent certain of his servants together with ours to inspect the horse in the stable, and the gadabout went also that he might show them the more surely how things stood. But in a

GIRALDUS OUTWITS HIM

short time they returned, and one of the Chamberlain's servants said: 'My Lord, we have done what you commanded of us, and could find no such thing there; and the monk himself who came with us, although he inspected the horse more carefully than we did, making a careful examination both with eyes and hands, could not find anything there except a useless rod and an empty bag.' This jest was hailed with universal laughter, and the Chamberlain postponed the case to the following afternoon. And when that same night he repeated the matter to the Lord Pope, the Holy Father was dissolved in laughter and ordered that the horse should be restored to the Archdeacon and the gadabout bidden to hold his peace. And on the morrow this was done to the great confusion of the opposing party and the huge joy and exultation of the whole Court when they heard of it. For almost all of them drew an omen from this event and foretold that this victory was beyond a doubt the herald of other victories in great matters that should follow.

> And it truth it is clear,
> If the Court were severe
> And Justice sincere,
>   If truth did not fail,
>   But held equal the scale,
> Though empty the bag,

assuredly the hopes and prophecies of many would have been fulfilled.

Now it happened that at this time the Pope went to the Maidens' Fountain (*Fons Virginum*), whither he delighted oft to go to walk, when occasion offered. Now this was a most beautiful fountain not far from the south side of the Lateran, pouring forth cold clear water and enclosed by man's art in Parian marble, whence it sent forth a pleasant and ample stream to water the fields. And when the bell of the Palace heralded his going forth ... the Archdeacon with the Elect of Bangor and his comrades followed the Pope; and when he had come to the fountain and had sat down with his comrades at a little distance in the field which was there, the Pope who was sitting by the bubbling waters of the fountain, a little apart from the rest with the more intimate of his household, as it were in a room beside a narrow path and shut in on all sides by waves and waters, ordered the Archdeacon to be called to him and to come alone and unaccompanied. And being thus made one of those who sat together there, when the Pope asked him how matters had gone in the suit between himself and the monk concerning the possession of a horse, he repeated briefly and frankly what the Pope had already heard from the Chamberlain, and told how he had outwitted guile with guile, and how by the sharpness of his cunning the bladder of all those falsehoods had been pricked, as by a little needle, and had burst with a report.

He then proceeded to make and also to repeat sundry ribald jests about the monk. The puns cannot be adequately reproduced and are somewhat broad; but they amused the Pope.

At this the Pope burst out laughing and said to the Archdeacon: 'Are these the sort of witnesses they produce against you?' And the Archdeacon made answer: 'They are indeed, for never were such worthless witnesses produced in this Court nor so many bribed in one business. I would that your wisdom knew them as thoroughly as we have come to know them.' And the Pope rejoined: 'If ever you have known how to write and handle a theme, you will need all your diligence to handle the treatises which they are going to produce against you and all your prudence to answer their charges.' To which the Archdeacon made answer: 'My Lord, if we are suffered to find grace in your eyes and just examination from your

THE POPE AT THE MAIDENS' FOUNTAIN

Judges, we shall, God helping us, bring all their falsehoods and frivolous fabrications to nought by telling the truth. But if all else fail them, they derive confidence and strength from the money of their Lord and from the inexhaustible well[1] of the treasures of Canterbury, their sole refuge and solace on which all their hopes of victory are stayed. Wherefore they boast that, if need be, they will at last boldly and effectively (which God forbid!) bring this one sole conclusive argument, an irresistible hammer-stroke to demolish all the proofs on which we[2] rely. But he who tramples underfoot the gold that is offered him, nay, who counts and values all gold as worth no more than sea-weed, he shall never be induced by English bronze or silver to deviate from the straight line of equity or swerve from the way of truth.' To this the Pope made answer: 'Care nothing for their boastfulness or vain speaking, but watch diligently over your suit, as we have told you. For the inflexible justice of the Roman Court will always in the end shine forth in accordance with the deserts of the case and not of the persons concerned therein. But now let us talk about the grammar of your Archbishop, and do you tell me how he began a sermon before the Synod, and how on Palm Sunday he discoursed on the Three Persons.'

And so after the Pope had for a long space indulged now in serious talk and now in merry, while all wondered and the rivals and adversaries of the Archdeacon grew sick with envy because the Pope held so long a conversation with him, they all returned to Rome.

Giraldus refers the reader who desires to hear the stories about the Archbishop to the Libellus Invectionum *(i.e. Book* I, 5*). They are also found in the* Gemma Ecclesiastica *(which the Pope had read; see p.* 165*)* II, 36. *They are too good to lose*

[1] See p. 228.
[2] MS. has *uestra*, which may be right—*sc.*, all the support you give us.

INVECTIONES

and are here appended with a few unimportant omissions. The passage forms part of a reply to his butt, Andrew (see p. 203). The occasion of its delivery is uncertain.

'Andrew also presumed to say that if his Lord were present and opened his sacred lips to address us, he would set forth his argument far better and far more elegantly. Would that we could make such trial of him so that you might hear the monster utter forth his own eloquence! ... You would hear more tropes and figures of speech than Donatus ever noted in his *Barbarisms* or than even Priscian has recorded ... For once when he was about to speak in a Synod, he began as follows: "Hear and understand, all you who are present in this holy Synod (*in isto sacro sinodo*)", and then when someone murmured "A! A!" he corrected himself and said "*in ista sacra sinoda*". And then when the same person or another murmured "O!" and "A!" he accepted the correction and said "*in isto sacro sinoda*". And again at Oxford, when a great number of learned lawyers were gathered together and he was seated as it were on the tribunal before them, he said, "*Vultis stare isto compromisso?*" And when someone murmured "*isti*", again he accepted the correction and said, "*Vultis stare isti compromissi?*" And when there was a murmur among the clerks, one who was sitting among the rest of the lawyers, a certain Martin, broke silence and cried aloud before them all, "Why do you murmur thus among yourselves? It is the grammar of the ancients that he uses". And thereat all of them burst out openly into the laughter which they had repressed within them out of reverence for the speaker, and ever since Martin has been an object of hatred to the Archbishop. I will add a third excellent utterance for which he was responsible. It happened once that when King Richard used the following Latin formula, "*Volumus quod istud fiat coram nobis*", the Archbishop, who was present with many other great personages, desiring to correct the King, said "*coram nos, Domine, coram nos*". And when he heard this the King looked round at Hugh, Bishop of Coventry, a learned and eloquent man, who at once replied, "Stick to your own grammar, my Lord, for it is much better", and his words were followed by loud laughter from all who were present.

'But to pass from his words . . . to his opinions, we may be content with a single example for the present. On the Palm Sunday following the death of King Richard, when the procession was over and he stood in the pulpit of Rouen Cathedral, mitred and crowned, between two learned and discreet Archbishops, Walter of Rouen and John of Dublin, presuming to preach to the people in the hearing of such distinguished men, he said: "Now that she-ass on which Jesus rode into Jerusalem on this day, what did she carry? Merely the man? God forbid! Nay, she carried Father, Son and Holy Ghost." He then proceeded to speak so boldly of the Three Persons and Their properties, in words that were inconsistent both with Their equality and with sound doctrine, so that I think it safer and more decent to pass them by in silence. It is true then, as Jerome says, that knowledge breeds fear, while ignorance breeds boldness and presumption. Wherefore this man, who was almost illiterate and utterly uninstructed in the Holy Scriptures . . . presumed on such a solemn occasion and before such a vast audience, when almost the whole city had gathered together, out of the depths of his ignorance to distinguish between the properties of the Three Persons, to the leading astray of the ignorant, the horror of the learned, and to his own confusion and damnation. Moreover, on the Feast of the Holy Trinity it once happened that he commanded Master Peter of Blois, Archdeacon of London, to undertake the duty of preaching. And when the sermon had been delivered, full of sound Catholic doctrine, the

DE IURE ET STATU

Bishop as if applauding his efforts and commending the sermon, said to him, "Whence, Master, came that store of wisdom with which to-day you have refreshed us, discoursing so admirably concerning the properties of the Three Persons and teaching us so well and clearly that our Lord Jesus Christ is Father, Son and Holy Ghost?" And he, with downcast face and full of shame, answered never a word. But this utterance of the Archbishop, spoken in the hearing of many, made some to blush for shame, while in others it wakened unrestrainable laughter and gave occasion for mockery. See what a man sits at England's helm of state!'

He proceeds on the strength of these utterances to accuse the Archbishop of being an adherent of the Arian heresy, and concludes with a long denunciation of Andrew, which is scarcely worth quoting. The De iure *continues:*

But meanwhile, there being sharp debate in the Consistory over the evidence which was now published, Tynemouth began to bubble with words and overflowed with eloquence; and since much-speaking often goes hand-in-hand with error, among other arguments with which he sought to prove that the Archdeacon had shown great cruelty towards his subjects in the administration of the Church of Mynyw and was therefore unfit to be its Bishop, he stated that he had in the presence of the Judges at St. Albans excommunicated all the Canons of Mynyw because they would not support him or consent with him either concerning the standing of their Church or concerning his election. But the Pope, having a sharp and subtle mind, at once asked the Canons if this were true; whereupon Osbert and Foliot and the rest all proclaimed that this was in truth so, thinking that the Archdeacon would be condemned upon the spot. But the Pope made answer to them, 'Since he had authority from us and the power so to do, on what ground do you claim to appear or bear witness against him?' And when they were dumb like men confounded, the Pope said in a lower voice to the Cardinals, his assessors, in the hearing of his Chaplains also who sat at his feet, as though he desired that his words should be revealed to the Archdeacon, that the latter could not have a better plea on which to defeat all the Canons. Then turning to the Archdeacon, he asked if it were true that he had thus excommunicated all the Canons. But Giraldus, seizing the opportunity offered by the Pope's argument and the confusion of his opponents, with increased confidence set forth the true story of the whole affair. 'In truth, Holy Father, I did excommunicate by name those two Archpirates of the Archbishop, Osbert the Archdeacon and Reginald Foliot, by whom he corrupted the whole of our Church; for they had from the beginning rebelled against your command and had utterly refused to obey me in my custodianship of the Church of Mynyw which by your gracious kindness was committed to my charge; and they also despoiled me. And when others of their accomplices, both Canons and others who were thought to be Canons, and Vicars also, promiscuously and irreverently made common ground with them, despite my prohibition oft repeated under threat of my anathema, I excommunicated them for rebellion and contumacy. But I did not, as my opponents assert, excommunicate any of them at St. Albans; but when they were brought forward to bear witness against us and our Church at the command of the King and the Archbishop, I proclaimed to the Judges that they had all been excommunicated by me.' To this the Pope replied: 'All then were excommunicated both according to your declaration and their own confession.' So, the Consistory being dissolved, the Pope retired to his chamber; and while the crowds of those departing and descending were still jostling in the Palace, one of the Chaplains of the Pope who had heard the aforesaid words from his lips as he sat at his feet, came to the Archdeacon, who with his companions had not yet risen from the bench, and advised him to stick to that plea, than which he could have no better against his adversaries, to wit, the plea of excommunication.

Thus, on account both of the conversation at the Maidens' Fountain and of this Consistory, his adversaries were filled with confusion and despair, while on the other side almost the whole Court was exultant and rejoiced because all believed that the Archdeacon's suit was like to be victorious. Wherefore a certain Spaniard, a most excellent advocate in the Court, was wont to say, as though applauding the Archdeacon and his comrades, 'Be of good courage and act with confidence, since Justice and the Lord Pope are on your side'. But the opposing party, trusting in its purse rather than in justice, on that same night, as a sort of salutation to the Pope, paid the Chamberlain two hundred pounds, the first instalment of a propitiatory offering. And to each of the Cardinals and the seniors of the Court they gave separate gifts and promised much greater, if their Lord were enabled to win the day against the Archdeacon.

Now in course of time Giraldus, perceiving, from the scandalously false evidence that was put forward, that his opponents would strive by hook or by crook to make out that the election of the Abbot of St. Dogmael preceded his own, though in fact it was much later, spoke as follows, in the presence of the Pope, employing rhetorical presumptions and adducing proofs as well to counter their false proofs.[1]

'Holy Father, that the election of the Abbot was not first to be made, as my opponents falsely maintain, I prove as follows by accurate statements and true presumptions, and also by certain positive proofs and

---

[1] A slightly different and longer version of these arguments is given in *Invect*, IV, 3.

sure inferences I puff away the scandalously false fabrications which they produce against me.

'Immediately on my first coming hither the Archbishop of Canterbury sent after me certain letters of invective addressed to you, whereto we made answer in obedience to your commands, and we still have these letters ready to our hand. In them he heaped together everything he could devise that might hinder my promotion; but he made no mention of any election being made before mine. But if indeed such an election had been made, he would neither have forgotten it nor have passed it by in silence, more especially if that election had been made by himself.

'Again in the following Lent a little before Easter there came to the Court a certain Buongiovanni, a clerk of the Archbishop of Canterbury, who being asked by you whether he had any special charge from his Lord against myself, ... replied that he had not, but that his Lord had bidden him tell you, if perchance he should find me in the Court, that four were nominated of whom one was the Archdeacon, but when he was at once rejected by the King, the Canons of Mynyw, a little before the Christmas preceding, elected a certain Abbot at London with the King's assent and in his presence and that of the Archbishop as well. And when you asked whether his Lord had confirmed that election, he was silent because I was at that time in the Court. And when you pressed for a reply, he only said that he was not bidden to answer this, but thought that the election was not unpleasing to his Lord. But you on the spot annulled all that had been done against my election from the time when I made my appeal and set forth to come to you. Wherefore, if the Archbishop had forgotten the election, made by himself and made before my own, at the time when he sent his courier, he would assuredly not have forgotten it when he sent his clerk.

DE IURE ET STATU

'Again on my second coming to the Court, when both parties, by order of the Lord Suffredo and Peter of Capua and in their presence, had made their statement of fact, it was clear to all from the statement of Foliot, who acted as proctor for the Abbot of St. Dogmael, that the election of that Abbot was made half a year or more after my own ... Moreover in Easter-week following the death of King Richard, the Archbishop returned to England, where he crowned Count John upon Ascension Day and afterwards, the King having forthwith returned to Normandy and, the whole realm being pacified, the Archbishop remained in England throughout the summer into the autumn. But why, during this interval, did he not confirm or even consecrate his Abbot, if he had been the first to be elected, there being no obstacle, since no other election had so far gone forward?[1] But he never even summoned that Abbot to him during all that time, as he might easily have done by courier, nor did he ever set eyes upon him.

'Again it is a custom in England, though not a commendable custom, that as soon as anyone is elected with the assent of the King, he forthwith assumes the administration of all temporalities, even before his confirmation. Wherefore if the Abbot had been elected at Epiphany with the King's assent, he would without doubt have taken over the administration as soon as a messenger could return from the King. But he did not take it over before Christmas, because up to that time the Prior of Llantony held it. Therefore he was not elected before.

'Again about the Feast of St. Michael next after the election of Giraldus the Archdeacon, the Archbishop again returned from Normandy to England and at once ordered the Canons of Mynyw to come to him with letters of ratification, as Archdeacon Osbert says, that

---

[1] The MS. of *Invect.* IV, 3 reads *praecessisset*. But *adhuc* is in favour of *processisset*, the reading of D.

they might receive consolation from the appointment of a new Shepherd; and they sent three Canons, but without letters of ratification. For they were ashamed of these things and afraid thus openly to contradict what they had done so recently. For Osbert says that because they had no letters of ratification, they did not sing *Te Deum Laudamus* at the election of the Abbot at Lambeth, nor did the Archbishop counsel them to do so. Now it is clear that if the Archbishop, acting in lieu of the Chapter, had already elected the Abbot, he would not have asked for letters of ratification, since he did not need them, nor would he have dissuaded them from singing the *Te Deum*.

'Again from the letters of our Chapter which were sent to the Archbishop at Gloucester, on the occasion of that presumptuous examination,[1] to seek confirmation of the Abbot, it is quite clear that they had not given the Archbishop their votes for the election, but had merely besought him to inform them of the assent of the King to one of the four nominees after inquiry had been made into their fitness. Wherefore they say that when it was understood at length from letters of the Archbishop and the Justiciar that the King gave his assent to the appointment of the Abbot of St. Dogmael, they then elected him as their Shepherd. So on that occasion they lied less shamefully than afterwards. For they had not yet thought out the ingenious device of making the first last and the last first.

'Again on the actual election of Giraldus and also afterwards the Archbishop, by letters and messengers from himself and the Justiciar, ordered the Canons of Mynyw to elect the Prior of Llantony. But if he had previously elected the Abbot, he would never have been so lost to shame on that occasion as to have thrust the Prior upon

[1] There is no evidence as to the exact nature of the proceedings at Gloucester, though there are other references to them.

them. Wherefore since the Archbishop is wont to be precipitate in such matters (as is clear from the case of the Elect of Bangor), our Chapter, fearing that he would send them the Prior already consecrated without any previous election or even nomination, sent you letters protesting against the Prior. So, if they had believed that they would then meet with any obstacle with regard to the Abbot or any other, they would without doubt have written against him on behalf of their Elect and the liberty of their Church.

'Again, that the whole story of their having delegated their powers to the Archbishop was false and fictitious, is quite clear from the following consideration, namely that the Canons of Mynyw would never have been so mad as to confer the power of electing a Bishop upon the Arch-Adversary of their Church who had never any desire that they should enjoy the ministrations of a good and vigorous Shepherd. And this may also be gathered from another fact, that the Abbot, whom he is said to have elected, is very like himself in all matters of learning. Nor is that wonderful since, as Plautus[1] says: "From that which has no sense, no sense can come."

'Again if the Archbishop, in lieu of the Chapter, had elected the Abbot on the Epiphany next after the death of Bishop Peter, as my opponents falsely allege, it is certain that he would have confirmed his own election, since there was no impediment to such a course. For the election of the Archdeacon was not made till half a year and more had past, to wit, on the Feast of the Apostles Peter and Paul. But neither before nor after the election of the Archdeacon did he confirm the election of the Abbot. Therefore he never elected him.

'These arguments, Holy Father, as you know, are of a rhetorical character, based on inference and probability, but presumptions rather than proofs. None the less they

---

[1] The quotation is actually from *Lucretius* (II, 888)!

deserve far greater credence than do the assertions of the most worthless of witnesses.

'But in addition to these numerous, strong and important presumptions, I have proofs provided by three witnesses, two being produced by myself and one by my opponents. For, as six of our Canons were sent to make the election on the Feast of St. Michael next after the Bishop's death, so by the command of the Justiciar, acting on orders from the King and the Archbishop, four of our Canons were sent to the Justiciar in London about the beginning of Lent either to make an election or to go abroad to the King and the Archbishop. To these the Justiciar persistently offered the Prior of Llantony for their choice and, because they were unwilling to accept him, with the Justiciar's assent they dispatched one of their number to go to King Richard to request his assent to the election of Giraldus the Archdeacon, a fact which is proved by two of our witnesses, Nicholas the elder[1] and Hugh a serving man, and also by Osbert the Archdeacon, a witness for our opponents. For Nicholas says that he was in the company of the clerks of Mynyw who were sent to King Richard to request his assent, and that they went first to Normandy and then followed the King to Poitou. He himself, when he went to France proceeded to the Schools, where a little later he heard that, King Richard having been slain, the clerks of Mynyw had returned to his brother Count John. And Hugh, the serving man, says that he then went with the clerks of Mynyw and was with them when they turned back on hearing of King Richard's death and came to Count John at the castle of Chinon. But Osbert, who says almost everything on hearsay, asserts that he heard that four Canons were again sent to the Justiciar in England to make the election and that thence they sent two clerks

---

[1] *Maior*. The sense is uncertain. It might mean 'major domo', or 'chamberlain', or 'a senior'.

DE IURE ET STATU

to King Richard a little before his death. And though the time of that mission is not mentioned (perhaps because through some oversight the question was not asked), still it may be inferred from the words of each of these witnesses that it was about Lent. For they all say that, finding King Richard slain, they turned to his brother and successor, Count John. Now King Richard was killed about fifteen days before Easter. Whence it is clear that, if the Archbishop had elected the Abbot on the Epiphany preceding, or even if he was empowered by the Canons to elect him, he would not have caused the Canons to be troubled to go from Wales into England and from England into Normandy or Poitou for the purpose of electing a Bishop, nor would he have sent them across the sea to distant regions on such a fruitless and laborious errand. Now these direct proofs, like the logical presumptions previously put forward, are both strong and clear. Whatever therefore may befall me hereafter when judgment is given . . . let the whole Court know that I shall endure it with tranquillity, now that I have convincingly set forth the true sequence of events.'

When, therefore, his opponents perceived that the Archdeacon's suit was daily becoming more acceptable to the Court and that their fraudulent fiction was now almost unmasked, Palm Sunday and Easter now being near at hand, they had recourse to a most efficacious remedy, a salve that blinds the eyes and makes some purses[1] heavier and others lighter, a last refuge and a bow that never misses its mark in the Court of Rome, and strove with the vastness of their bribes to corrupt, first the Chamberlains and the Counsellors, and next the Pope and the Cardinals, that so the election of the Archdeacon might be annulled. Yet when the Cardinals considered the matter they were not agreed among them-

---
[1] The play on *oculos* (eyes) and *loculos* (purses) cannot be reproduced.

selves. For the sounder part thought that the election of the Archdeacon should be confirmed, both because it seemed to be supported by truth and reason, and because they knew that his promotion would be most useful and profitable, as long as he lived, on account of the suit concerning the standing of his Church which he brought against the Church of Canterbury. Others, however, being hand in glove with the Archbishop and corrupted by him, felt that the money offered them in such abundance ought under no circumstances to be rejected, and said that the Archdeacon was a man of such courage that, even in the position in which he then was, he would never cease to trouble the Church of Canterbury concerning the dignity of his Church.

For the Archbishop, after peace was made between himself and the Archdeacon,[1] was wont to assert that the controversy had cost him eleven thousand marks, not to mention the loss of his good clerks and servants who died at Rome. For he had given this huge sum of money to the clerks whom he sent to the Court, that if they saw that the promotion of the Archdeacon was likely to go forward, they should not stint money to prevent it and to purchase peace and quiet for himself and the Church of Canterbury so long as Giraldus was in the land of the living. Therefore seeing that his suit was like to grow in favour from day to day, in obedience to the commands they had received, they poured forth vast sums of money in all directions that so they might corrupt the Court and turn it from the way of truth.

But the Archdeacon, since the mind of man cannot look into the future, being ignorant of all these things until after judgment was given, was eager that Judges should be appointed before whom he might speak against the character of the witnesses. And when he had repeatedly spoken of this to the Pope and the latter had

[1] See p. 347.

always dissuaded him from so doing, saying that it would be a slow business and might, with the summer heats so near at hand, even be dangerous to health, the Archdeacon replied that he had rather that the business was slow and that he himself would await the hot weather even to the prejudice of his health rather than that suits whose justice was so manifest should risk the loss of their due reward through the lies of the most worthless of witnesses. For his adversaries were aware of the character of their witnesses, and, because they knew that they could one and all be refuted, more especially since the plea of excommunication would puff all the Canons out of the Court, they toiled with all their might to remove this peril, by heaping gifts upon the Pope and Cardinals and increasing their promises of gifts to come. For they knew, as the whole Court knew, that if the evidence of the witnesses who brought criminal charges against Giraldus were rejected on account of the charges which in turn were brought against them, no penalty could be imposed upon the Archdeacon beyond canonical purgation. So almost all the secretaries of the Pope and the members of his household strove to dissuade him from this course, since this remedy could not legally be refused him if he persisted. For some of them, and others speaking through them, said that it was a wonder that a discreet man, who had won the favour of the Pope and of the whole Court, should desire to postpone his own promotion and defer the judgment which must be given in his favour. Cardinal Ugolino also, who was the Pope's cousin and had hitherto been the Archdeacon's principal champion and friend in the Court, but had now been utterly corrupted like the others, was stronger than all the rest in dissuading him. And since an enemy who is trusted has all the greater power for harm, he advised the Archdeacon to consult the Pope, who loved him, in secret and to obey his counsel. And the Archdeacon, alas! too credulous,

POPE DECIDES TO EXPEDITE MATTERS

knowing nought as yet of the great corruption that had been wrought, straightway approached the Pope, who was wont to show him such great honour and almost to be his advocate in all his suits, and spoke to him on the matter with all confidence. And the Pope, prone and prompt to dissuade him, made answer thus: 'If you speak against their witnesses and they likewise speak against you, there will never be an end to your litigation, and the hot weather will come on, which, as you know, is dangerous to persons of your country. But if you will consent to renounce the production of witnesses on both sides and to deliver the evidence in writing, then by the grace of God, we will quickly dispatch the business. Nor should you have any fear that we shall ever consent to fail you in your legal rights.'

Now on the morrow the Pope having summoned the Archdeacon to his chamber and with him Tynemouth, who had managed not only the dissuasion of Giraldus, but also the whole business of corruption, set before them in the same terms the alternatives of a speedy settlement or a dangerous delay; whereupon Giraldus who had thus unhappily been persuaded and had been induced to place excessive faith in the honesty of the perfidious Court, said that he would at once entirely renounce the production of his witnesses and all other supports on which his case rested; while Tynemouth renounced the like on his part with joy, provided always that the Archdeacon would renounce his plea in respect of the excommunication of the Canons; for he feared it as an effective weapon against them. He also feared his Lord since it was an utterance of his own, made in full Consistory, which had given Giraldus the opportunity for putting forward that same plea. But the Pope, because, as has been said, he had given authority for putting forward this plea and also because he desired thus to conceal as far as possible the fact of corruption, at once put

DE IURE ET STATU

in his word, saying, 'He will do this, provided you are ready to renounce your pleas, whereby you sought to prove him guilty of crime'. This said, both parties made the renouncement plainly and absolutely, and then proceeded to renounce the production of witnesses. But afterwards when both parties were brought before the Pope and Cardinals on account of the criminal charges brought against the Archdeacon, the latter said that he desired to speak a few words in defence of his reputation and asked that he should be heard. And when the Pope said that there was no need for him so to do, the Archdeacon replied, 'Nay, my Lord, I love my reputation far more than I love that Bishoprick'. But the Pope, that he might make an end of the business the more speedily, said, 'Brother, from the beginning of our acquaintance we have commended your honesty and commend it still, nor have we ever heard aught that was not good concerning you save from the mouth of your adversaries; and they do not deserve credence. Wherefore he whom we defend needs, we believe, no other defence'.

So, Holy Week and Easter being hard at hand, the suits were adjourned for the time being, and a vacation was granted for discussion and deliberation, and also for drawing up the judgments to be delivered. And if any man desires to see the Archdeacon's defence of his reputation let him turn to the close of the *Libellus Invectionum*.[1]

So during the days of Easter, when the Archdeacon visited the Pope, among other things the Pope said to him, laying bare in part what he had conceived in his mind, that he should not be in any wise afraid on account of the Kings or Princes or magnates that opposed him, since nothing could stand in the way of his promotion save it were some plea put forward by his opponents. For he had received during those same days letters directed

---
[1] I, 13. A good specimen of his eloquence, though never delivered. It adds little to our knowledge of the case.

ACCEPTANCE OF IMMEDIATE JUDGMENT

against the Archdeacon at the instigation of the Archbishop of Canterbury, both from the King of England and from his nephew Otho, King of the Germans, for whom the Pope at that time had a special affection. Now these two among the Princes of the Earth were regarded with much favour in the Court, the latter because of his hope of the Empire, the former because of his lavish gifts of gold and silver, and hopes of more to come. To this the Archdeacon replied that, if such witnesses were believed, whose like for vileness had never been brought forward in the Court, not one Archdeacon only or one Bishop Elect, but even seven Archbishops more firmly and strongly established then the Archbishop of Canterbury might be deposed and degraded. Yet (he said) if he had not been dissuaded from denouncing such witnesses, their allegations might easily have been proved worthless and brought to nought. But the Pope, when he heard him, shook his head and smiled, with a glance at Cardinal Ugolino who was sitting at his side.

So a few days later on the third day[1] after the Close of Easter the Pope sitting in the Consistory in the presence of the Cardinals and of the parties to the suit, either that he might receive the fulfilment of their promises without delay or that he might gratify the great men aforesaid by expediting judgment, made haste thus to pronounce his judgment: 'Two Bishops Elect of the Church of Mynyw are put forward, the Abbot of St. Dogmael and Giraldus the Archdeacon. On behalf of the Abbot it is propounded that after the death of Bishop Peter six Canons of Mynyw were sent to the Archbishop of Canterbury with letters of ratification from their Chapter for the election of a Shepherd of their See. But since the assent of the King, being at that time abroad, was not known, they gave their votes for the election into the hands of the Archbishop of Canterbury who was about to go abroad to the King.

[1] The tenth day after Easter, i.e. April 16th, 1203.

DE IURE ET STATU

And he with the assent of the King elected the Abbot on the following Epiphany in the Isle[1] of Andelys in Normandy. But since in the letters of ratification it was set down that these six might elect, but not that they might delegate their powers to another, the election thus made by the Archbishop was null and void. For they conferred on him that which they had no authority to confer. Therefore we cancel this election as null and void.

'Again on behalf of the Archdeacon it is propounded that on the Feast of the Apostles Peter and Paul[2] after the death of their Bishop almost all the Canons of Mynyw met together at Mynyw for the purpose of making an election and that there by common and unanimous assent they all elected Giraldus the Archdeacon and straightway appealed to our hearing. But since it might still be doubtful whether the election of the Abbot made by the Archbishop ought to be regarded as valid — for they might well have doubts[3] about the act of the Archbishop — ' (the Pope employed these words to gloss over his own acts) 'and since they proceeded to another election before that doubt was resolved, we cancel that election also.'

See how he framed and founded the whole of this judgment on a lie contrived by the cunning of the opposing party; as though it were certain that the election of the Abbot in the Isle was the first to be made, as was alleged by perjured witnesses whom we had excommunicated and had also refuted by true and irrefragable arguments; whereas in their testimony there was not a word of truth, but all was fiction and falsehood.

It is clear from this how dubious are the chances of suits, wherein blind and uncertain, wandering and erroneous hazard brings forth results, many of them undeserved and many past all expectation, above all when a suit seems to concern great Princes and men clothed in

[1] See p. 207.   [2] June 29th, 1199.   [3] Reading *dubitari* for *dubitara*.

THE POPE ANNULS BOTH ELECTIONS

great power, and favourites also of the Roman Court who strive against their adversary with all their might, and by letters and messengers supplicate for his overthrow, most of all, if it be lawful to say so, when perchance masses of metal, gleaming red and tinkling loud and casting an evil spell on eyes and ears, do not suffer the scales of justice to be balanced true. Wherefore we have thought it worth our while here to cite the words that Hildebert, Bishop of Le Mans, wrote in his *Letters*,[1] among other things to the discredit of the Court: 'Many things were against us when we set out to Rome, the weather with its storms, the Alps with their snows, the waters with their floods, the Emperor with his fetters, the state with its disorders and the Palace with its exactions. But in truth we believe that all these perils may be brought to nought by prayer, save only the exactions of the Court of Rome, which neither prayer nor fasting can assuage.'

Great was the exulting and great also the insulting of the opposing party, even as they that conquer exult when they have taken their booty and divided the spoil.[2] For they cared nothing for the annulment of the Abbot's election; for their joy at the annulment of the election of Giraldus, whose promotion they had so greatly feared, swallowed up all their other anxieties. Nor had it ever been the Archbishop's purpose that the Abbot nor any other from that Church or even from that country should be promoted there; his sole aim was to stir up schism among them by divers promises and deceptions, and by creating confusion between several elections; and because, 'if a kingdom be divided against itself, it cannot stand',[3] by all these means he sought solely to hinder the promotion of the Archdeacon who alone had been lawfully and canonically elected, and whom alone he feared, as was made clear by that which was afterwards done, and shall be revealed in what follows.

[1] *Ep.* III, 4. [2] Isaiah ix. 3. [3] Mark iii. 24.

DE IURE ET STATU

Now on the morrow the Archdeacon, coming forward in full Consistory, thus addressed the Pope: 'Father and Lord, the cause of my long labour is as you know twofold. Wherefore, one of my two suits being extinguished by the judgment which it has pleased you to give, I entreat your Holiness that the other, on behalf of which above all else we so oft have toiled in this Court, namely the suit concerning the dignity of our Church, may proceed in due course and on its own merits.' 'And who', said the Pope, 'would champion this suit?' And the Archdeacon made answer: 'I myself, Father, if it so please your wisdom. For if I am not the Elect of that Church, I am none the less its Archdeacon and Canon, its lawful son and no bastard, ready, so far as in me lies, to snatch my mother and my brethren from the unmerited servitude which they endure.' Then the Bishop of Ostia, the generous and courteous Octavian, first Cardinal, whose place was ever at the Pope's right hand, made answer 'Now in truth it is clearly shown that he sought and seeks the profit of his Church rather than his own, and that it was love rather than ambition that made him labour thus'. So said he, and a murmur of approval followed from the multitude as the whole Court gave Giraldus their applause, if not with their voice, at least in their desires.

Thereupon the Pope rose at once from the Consistory and retired to take counsel with the Cardinals on this matter; and after a brief delay the Archdeacon was summoned before them, and it was decided that a Commission should be granted to him according to his desire. For the very fact of his petition pleased them no less than its evident justice; moreover, if the suit proceeded, it would bring no small profit to the Court. Now the form and substance of the Commission was as follows: the Pope, as often before, in accordance with the Archdeacon's desire and his demand so often made, declared

GIRALDUS CHAMPIONS HIS CHURCH

that if he could prove that the Canons of Mynyw had ever given him their assent in respect of the suit concerning the standing of their Church, and afterwards had been caused to desert him by violence or spoliation of their goods, he should be admitted to plead and the suit should proceed in conformity with the Commission of the preceding year. The Pope also, at his request and in his favour, granted that the judges should be chosen, not as before from the suffragans of Canterbury, but from the province of York, doing this to console him for his previous defeat and also because the whole Court was attracted by the prospect of a controversy that would bring them such profit.

Now when his adversaries heard this, they were not as they had been the day before, but departed sad and full of consternation, with downcast faces and drooping heads. For they had hoped (and it was for this they had given such vast sums of money) that, once the suit concerning the election was extinguished, the other concerning the standing of the Church which they dreaded so much and on account of which they had made such efforts to prevent the Archdeacon's promotion, would suffer the same fate. But since they saw themselves baulked of their hope and cheated of their desire, they feared the heavy anger of their Lord, whom they knew to be an austere man and whose money they had lavished in such profusion without obtaining peace for him; and their hearts were sick with grief. Such is the working of the just judgment of God, that those whose hearts are set on deceit should themselves be filled with grief, finding themselves deceived; for

> There is no juster law than this, that all
> Who use such craft by their own craft should fall.[1]

But when the Court and the foreign clerks that

[1] *Ovid. A. A.* I, 655.

DE IURE ET STATU

attended the Court from all parts of the world heard this, they said that this Archdeacon was truly worthy of honour and of an honourable Bishopric, and that the Church to which so great a man had been called and for whose dignity he had toiled so nobly and devotedly and was still resolved to toil, was unhappy in that it had not prevailed to have him for its Prelate.

This done, when the Archdeacon came to the Pope in private, the latter, flattering him and desiring to console him after his failure as best he might, said to him: 'Brother, your toil and courage are much to be commended; for you have fought so manfully against Kings and Princes and a Pontiff of such power and wealth, on behalf of your own right and that of your Church. And it must needs be that God will reward you for what you have done, if your intent was in truth such as we believe it to have been. And we have sustained you in all your efforts without stint of our good will by giving you custody of the Church of Mynyw and by writing on your behalf, now sharply and now lovingly, as the occasion demanded.' To which the Archdeacon made answer: 'Let Him who is the searcher out of men's hearts and who knoweth the secrets of their minds, judge concerning my intent. But that I have undertaken this labour solely out of my zeal for God and for our Church is clear from this that, though I have been robbed of my hope of the Bishopric, I have still continued in my endeavour. And since man has no remuneration for my toil, it must needs be that God, who leaves no good work without its recompense, will give me my reward. Moreover the custody of the See which was committed to me was more burdensome than profitable, since the Archbishop threw all things into confusion.' But the Pope, striving that in some one thing at least he might please or seem to please the Archdeacon, rejoined by pointing out how he had, by the form in which his judgment was cast, trampled

THE POPE TRIES TO CONSOLE HIM

under foot all the criminal charges brought against him, had made no mention of them in pronouncing his decision, and had thereby crushed them as nothing worth, deserving neither repetition nor remembrance, so that they could at no time do him any injury. To which the Archdeacon, while thanking him and being grateful[1] for his kindness, replied that those charges had been sufficiently extinguished by the answers of himself and his supporters and that, if he had been allowed to speak against those abandoned witnesses and had not been dissuaded, they would without more ado have been more fully and completely crushed and discredited....

Now how the Cardinals wrote on Giraldus's behalf and sought cautiously and secretly to bring it about that he should be re-elected; how Octavian, Cardinal Bishop of Ostia, caused a loan to be made to him and sent him after the Pope to Palestrina; how he came thither and obtained a loan through the Pope as well; how the Pope absolved him from his vow to take the Cross, from which he had already been absolved by the Cardinal,[2] but had been forced to take it again by the shameless impudence of the Archbishop; how the great successes won after his misfortunes, and the seeming favours shown him by the Pope caused the envy and vexation of his opponents to increase, and how he was given his costs by sentence of the Court — all these things have been clearly set forth both in the *Invectiones*[3] and in the *De Gestis*.[4] But I have thought it not beside the mark here to relate how his costs were given him and how a dispute took place concerning this between Tynemouth and the Cardinal appointed to hear the matter.

---

[1] *et in bene gestis gratus existens* (omitted by Brewer).
[2] See pp. 116 and 220 *n.*
[3] III, 17, 18; IV, 6, 7, 8.
[4] Table of Contents, III, 187, 188, 193.

BOOK V

BUT meanwhile there was frequent debate before Cardinal Ugolino, who had been appointed to hear the matter between the Archdeacon and Tynemouth (whose name seems in English to sound like *Os claudens* (mouth-shutter)) concerning the condemnation in costs, since the former claimed the costs as due to him by law, while the latter did not close his mouth, but on the contrary opened it most fiercely.

A statement of the arguments on both sides follows, which is of minor importance.

After hearing the arguments of both parties the Pope adjudged half the costs to the Archdeacon; and though he demanded a hundred marks as his due and was prepared to prove it, the Pope assessed the amount at sixty marks, ordered this sum to be restored to him, and wrote to this effect to the judges appointed to enforce his decree ... At this his adversaries were beset by manifold perplexities. For over and above this condemnation in costs at which they were grieved, being in great fear of the anger of their Lord, it was necessary to pay the bribes which they had promised to the Court without delay, and they could only get the money on very hard terms, whereas they had hoped to borrow from the markets in France. And above all Tynemouth was tormented by still greater terror of his Lord on account of the suit concerning the standing of the Church which was still in being. Wherefore by much entreaty and not without difficulty he secured letters from the Pope and from individual Cardinals, excusing him to the Archbishop, praising his work and saying that it was not his fault that the latter suit had not been extinguished. Moreover just at this time when the opposing party paid them the

THE COURT HOPE FOR MORE BRIBES

greater part of the money promised, the nostrils of the Court were filled with a whiff of prospective profit, and the form of the Commission granted in respect of this suit which was already in draft, was, at the instance of Tynemouth, thus vitiated and varied from its original form. For in lieu of the words, 'If the Archdeacon shall be able to prove that the Canons of Mynyw had ever given him their assent in respect of the suit concerning the standing of their Church and had afterwards been caused to desert him by violence and spoliation of their goods, [*then let him be admitted to plead*]', there were substituted the following: 'Unless he can be debarred from pleading by the interposition of some lawful plea, then let the Archdeacon be admitted etc.' For because the Chapter of Mynyw was to their knowledge so easy to corrupt, his adversaries hoped that he could be debarred by the plea put forward in the past year, to the effect that he alone could not plead in a case of such importance without the support of the Chapter. Yet they were disappointed in this and the additional sum which they had paid for this alteration was wasted. For if the suit should chance to proceed, it could be proved by many arguments (which the Archdeacon had diligently and anxiously collected both at Rome and Bologna) that one of the Chapter alone could act in this suit without the support of the Chapter, nay even if they opposed him.

The arguments drawn from Canon and Civil Law which follow, but are not here translated, are given also in Invect. v. 20 *where they are spoken of as 'arguments which either were introduced or could be introduced in the Roman Court'. Some may have been used when the 'plea' just mentioned was first put forward. But in the preceding paragraph, while the first sentence suggests that these arguments were used, what follows seems against this view. So the first sentence may mean no more than that their money was wasted because the occasion for urging the plea never arose, while it could easily have been refuted if it had been put forward. In any case the story proceeds without further reference to this problem, as the suit clearly did not proceed any further for the time being and was, as we shall see, ultimately dropped.*

Moreover Tynemouth (thanks to the aforesaid propitious whiff)[1] secretly obtained letters concerning the making of a new election by the Chapter of Mynyw and concerning the annulment of the former elections, and these he sent in haste by courier to his Lord, that the election might be made under his control, while the Archdeacon was still absent. But the Archdeacon, catching wind of this beforehand, immediately spoke to the Pope concerning the matter and got other letters entrusted to himself in the same form. Further the Pope, that he might do something to console him, granted him such judges as he desired to choose and at his instance added the last clause but one[2] in favour of the Church of Mynyw. Now the letters were as follows:

An abstract of these will suffice:

I. *Innocent III to the Bishops of Ely and Worcester.*

The elections of Giraldus and the Abbot of St. Dogmael are both annulled. The Canons of Mynyw are to elect a Bishop within two months of receipt of this, and the election, which must be unanimous, is to be confirmed by the Archbishop. If they fail to elect, you are to choose a Bishop and have him consecrated by the Archbishop. But the latter is not to make him take oath not to support the suit concerning the standing of his Church. Given at Ferentino, May 26th (1203).[3]

II. *The same to the Bishop of Durham and the Dean and Prior of Holy Trinity at York.* We ordered the Archbishop to appear in person or by his proctors in

---
[1] Reading *fauorabilis*. MS.
[2] i.e. the clause about the oath; see close of abstract of Letter I.
[3] See *Invect.* IV, 4.

INSTRUCTIONS FOR A NEW ELECTION

the suit concerning the standing of the Church of Mynyw. As he did not appear, we appointed the Bishop of Ely the Dean of London and the Archdeacon of Buckingham to investigate the case. Nothing was done by them, wherefore, 'unless the opponents of Giraldus can debar him from pleading by the interposition of a lawful plea', do you now summon the parties and witnesses. If the Archbishop refuse to appear, do you none the less hear the witnesses (*sc.* old and decrepit men) produced by Giraldus. Given at Ferentino, June 18th (1203).[1]

III. *The same to the same.* Letter dealing with the condemnation of the Archbishop in costs to the amount of sixty marks. Given at Ferentino, June 20th (1203).[2]

IV. *The same to the Bishops of Ely and Worcester and the Archdeacon of Buckingham.* Giraldus is absolved from his vow to take the Cross. Given at Ferentino, June 4th (1203).[3]

V. Letters of revocation directed to the 'Judges of the March' who had so harassed Giraldus.[4]

VI. Letters against his despoilers whom he excommunicated (*sc.* Avenel and FitzMartin).[5]

VII. Letters against the Clerks who despoiled him (*sc.* Pontius and Osbert).[6]

VIII-X. Letters confirming gifts of two Canonrics and one Parish Church.[7]

Now in addition to securing these letters from the Chancery, which could not be done without the usual trouble, paying his debts to the Pope and the Bishop of Ostia, and further providing sustenance and journey

[1] Only found here. Was also in *Invect.* II, 7, which is lost.
[2] *Invect.* III, 17.   [3] Ibid., 18.
[4] This and the remaining letters are not given here in full, but merely mentioned. This letter is in *Invect.* III, 19.
[5] *Invect.* III, 20.   [6] Ibid., 3.   [7] Ibid., 21-3.

money for his return, there remained the necessity of settling with his creditors in the Court, who were many; and this was not the least among his difficulties. He had approached money-lenders from Bologna on the matter and had hoped that they had come to an agreement about the contract, so that nothing remained to be done save to write and give securities. But they with malicious ingenuity put off the matter from day to day, until all the money-changers, whether of Rome or from elsewhere had gone away; and then because they now alone were left, since necessity knows no law, he entered into a contract with them on hard and most grievous terms, being forced to pay interest almost equal in amount to the capital; and in addition to his other vexations, the term which had been granted him, namely until he reached the market of Troyes in France, was now abbreviated to the time when he should reach Bologna, while the payment of the interest was increased, and both the sum borrowed and the interest thereon would have to be paid within fifteen days of entering that city. Further they seized all his letters as security, including the testimonials given him by the Pope, and finally they took his solemn oath that he would not depart from them save by their leave or when he had paid both the capital sum and its 'penalty'. For in those parts the money-lenders call the interest the penalty, a metaphor which is only too expressive of the truth.

Moreover that monk, who claimed to be the Elect of Bangor, had meanwhile completed his business as best he could, and had gone off with a Commission granted him by the Pope. But although he was wealthy and had been so strongly supported and helped by the Archdeacon, he had no regard for him now, but left him in the Court afflicted with anxieties and in sore straits with none to help him. Thus he found that man like almost all the clergy of Wales; for he used to say that among the laity he found much good faith, but among the clergy in whose cause he was fighting, he found none.

But God oft takes vengeance in respect of things for which men take none, and even as he sometimes rewards virtuous actions in his own good time, so likewise he brings retribution upon the wicked even while still they live. Thus it came to pass that this monk, entering a wood incautiously and alone, fell among thieves and was robbed not only of his money whereof he carried no small sum (as he afterwards himself confessed), but also of his letters and all his goods; and so within two days he returned to the Court and entering the lodgings of the Archdeacon he told him of the misfortune that had befallen him, saying that it was no more than he deserved because he had refused a loan to a good friend and comrade and also to St. David the patron of Wales; and therefore divine vengeance had by the hands of robbers taken from him all that he possessed. But by the aid of a monk of the same Order, a Penitentiary of the Lord Pope, whom he himself had often enticed by trifling gifts, he got fresh letters and payment of his expenses till he should reach France.

Further, that trouble and difficulty might beset Giraldus on every side, his good palfrey, which he had kept for himself, alone out of the five or six which he had brought with him, was found dead in its stall. And this mischance was rendered all the more vexatious by the fact that he was on the point of setting out homewards at once with the money lent him and the men who lent it, whom he was compelled to follow. But courageously spurning all the outrages of fortune and omitting nought that required to be done, but watchfully intent through all adversities upon the interests of his Church, both present and to come, he caused the letters of Commission in respect of the suit concerning the standing of the Church, which were granted to him on each of his three visits to

Rome, to be inscribed in the Register of the Pope, that for all time they might be found therein. For the tenor of the letters granted during his last visit, while included in that of the letters granted during his second visit, contains also some additions.

Having thus come to the end of his business and having purchased such a horse as he could get, he went to the Pope and took leave of him in some such wise as follows: 'The time is now come, Father, that I should return to my own country for the rest of my life. For now I do not take leave of you in the hope of returning, as was my wont before, but I am come to bid a last farewell to your Court and shall never more return.' To which the Pope rejoined: 'God forbid! What will happen then to the dignity of the Church of Mynyw? I feel sure that you will not thus abandon the suit concerning its standing.' And the Archdeacon made answer: 'He who brought to nought the suit concerning my election and altered for the worse the original form of the Commission concerning the dignity of my Church, once and for all extinguished that suit also. Thus far I have considered the convenience of the Court; henceforth I shall consider my own convenience and my own peace. For never, had not the Court first deserted me, would I have deserted the suit concerning the dignity of my Church. But now that my defences are down and all that supported me is shattered, I cannot cling to empty clouds. God knows that in regard to my promotion, if it had gone forward, I sought above all things the profit of my Church, poor and pillaged as it is and rich only in the rumour and remembrance of its former wealth and dignity. But in seeking to repair such ruin I have got nothing for myself but boundless and immeasurable toil and torment that shall be with me while life endures.' But the Pope, who seemed to be somewhat moved by his words, made answer: 'Brother, God, methinks, has provided better for you in

HE BIDS FAREWELL TO THE POPE

this matter than you hope; for in his mercy he has snatched you from great disquietude and has perchance reserved you for greater things.' To which the Archdeacon replied: 'I know and am sure that so pure and pious an intent as mine has been in my desire to profit our Church, will have its reward from God, if not in time, at least in eternity.'

So having taken his leave, he came from Ferentino to Rome in one day's journey, and from Rome to Bologna in six, with his creditors to go before him as his guides; and there they pressed for the repayment of their money with greater urgency every day. Now to add to his troubles it happened that certain Spanish clerks, who had at that time given security there for their comrades, since the latter did not pay and they themselves could not were seized by their creditors and cast into prison. Wherefore all the scholars of Bologna had made a compact together and taken oath that they would not stand as security or as sponsors for anybody. And so there seemed nothing left for the Archdeacon to do save to surrender himself to his creditors, since owing to this mischance he could not find any among his companions and acquaintances who would go bail for him. This was one of the greatest of all the troubles that beset him during the whole of his journey. For he knew how much money his messengers ought to bring for him at Troyes, and he knew also that this sum would scarce suffice to pay what he owed. Wherefore, if the interest, heavy already and certain to be increased, were allowed to grow while he awaited their arrival from distant lands, and since moreover his own revenues had been almost exhausted by so many misfortunes, he reflected anxiously that, being unable to pay so large a sum, he had not only failed in the business he had undertaken, but would be a ruined man and a prisoner for the rest of his life.

But since God is ever near in time of trouble and never

abandons those that hope in Him, the chief among his creditors came to him secretly and finding him in extreme despair, said to him: 'Good Sir, do not be thus cast down. For last night God blest thee in my dreams; and I beheld you exalted to place and power. Wherefore I am assured by that which it has been vouchsafed to me to see, that, these troubles overpast, you will grow old in perfect peace and happiness. This being so, we will send you to the market of Troyes. But since contrary to our whole design, we shall deal so liberally with you and set you free, do you see to it that you delay not to repay that which you have already borrowed or yet shall borrow from us.' And when the Archdeacon had thanked him from his very heart, his creditors sent a boy to fetch his partners and scriveners, and after they had computed the previous interest that was due and had fixed further exorbitant interest to be paid thereafter, a contract was made with all the formalities and securities that are customary in those parts.

Now the Archdeacon, filled with joy at the restoration of his liberty no less than if life itself had been restored to him, did not at such a moment trouble himself at all about the anxieties arising from this burden of debt, but hastened on his way toward Troyes with the companions to whom they had assigned him after making him swear that he would not depart from them without leave. And so after passing through Lombardy and crossing the Alps, when we were drawing near to the boundaries of France by long and rough marches through Burgundy, since neither stumbling-blocks nor misfortunes ever come single, a mishap befell him more perilous than all the rest. For when we were drawing near Châtillon-sur-Seine and had it already in sight, the Castellan, coming forth with his followers from the castle on his way to the Seneschal of the Duke of Burgundy, by mere chance met us and the palmers in whose company we were travelling.

HE IS TAKEN PRISONER IN BURGUNDY

And when they had already passed by the pilgrims who were in front of us, the last of them, a youth and the brother of the Castellan's wife, espying the Archdeacon (who after his custom was the last of the company) gazed at him attentively beneath the felt hood that he wore against the rain and forthwith asked his name. And when this was given him, he bade him stay where he was for a while. And the Castellan, calling back his followers, hastened to the spot and asked who he was. And when he heard that he came from Wales, he ordered him and all the others (merely because they were with him) to be seized and taken to Châtillon, as coming from the land of the King of England, who was then at war with the King of France. The Archdeacon was deeply afflicted not only by his own arrest, but still more because his comrades, who being pilgrims should have privilege of peace, were seized and hindered on his account. Now they were almost all of them Normans and from the neighbourhood of Rouen. But they said that they all came from Gisors and its neighbourhood, which was at that time occupied by the King of France. For if they came from the realm of the King of England, neither pilgrims nor clerks nor monks of any Order save the Cistercian were allowed peaceful passage in France because of the war between the two Kings. Now there was among the palmers a priest who was actually French and not Norman; and he boldly approached the Castellan and, telling a virtuous lie to win his comrades' freedom, asserted that they came from the neighbourhood of Gisors and that they were all palmers and pilgrims of the Holy Sepulchre, except only the Archdeacon, whom they had first met at Pavia as he came from Rome. This last statement was true, but without the lie, would have availed them nothing towards their release; the Castellan, however, believed them and set all free save the Archdeacon and his comrades.

But when all were going, save the Archdeacon and a boy who was his foot-servant, the robbers were filled with wonder; for they said it was not possible that a man of such importance as the Archdeacon, who had been elected Shepherd of a Metropolitan Church, should travel without any retinue. Wherefore they would have detained certain of the pilgrims as being his servants. But when the truth was made known by the priest, they let them all go and committed the Archdeacon and his boy to public custody in the house of the Castellan. And when they asked him who had been his adversary in the Roman Court, he replied that it was a great man, the Archbishop of Canterbury, who had sent his clerks against him; and when they asked who those clerks were, he replied that they were Robert Balbus and John of Tynemouth. And when they heard John's name, they said: 'We have caught that same John, and you may thank him for your own captivity.' And when he asked their meaning, they made answer that when John was seized by them he said that he had such an Archdeacon and Elect for his adversary and told us his name, describing also his appearance and stature and saying that he would follow within eight days. And the young man, the brother of the Castellan, said that he recognized him from the description given to him, namely that he was tall of stature and had large and shaggy eyebrows, and it was above all by his eyebrows that he had known him. Whereat the Archdeacon rejoined that it should have been enough for John that he had opposed him in the Roman Court both with his tongue and with his Lord's money and had got his election annulled; he might at least have refrained from having him seized on his journey now that he was poor and plundered on all sides; and he added, moving them all to laughter, that if he had known that the shagginess of his eyebrows was to bring him to such hurt, he would have removed that huge forest growth either by fire or steel. After this they made him open his bag and turn out his letters and all else that was therein. But they found none of the letters concerning his last visit to Rome and the urgent business on which he was engaged; for the merchants of Bologna, who held them as security, had taken them to the market by another way, nor did they find any coins therein save eight *deniers* of Dijon,[1] not worth two pence sterling. But they handed over the bag padlocked with all that it contained to the wife of the Castellan, while they left his lean and puny horse to the care of the stableman and delivered the Archdeacon himself into the custody of a servant. Now this happened on the sixth day of the week, and on the morrow they expected the arrival of the Seneschal whom the Castellan had gone to meet.

So the Archdeacon spent all that day without tasting food and all the following night without sleep, being in the depths of despair when he considered the peril of his present plight, which seemed past all cure, and thought of his captivity and misery beyond all human solace or support. For he knew that his high birth and his descent from the Princes of his country were, thanks to his adversary, not unknown to his plunderers, that no mention had been made of his own poverty or that of his native land, and that his enemy, though a liar, would win more credence than himself who spoke the truth. His only consolations were the counsel given him by the best of brothers and that saying of Gregory so oft repeated and so oft to be repeated: 'The adversity which thwarts good intent is a probation of our virtue and not a sign of reprobation'[2] . . . And he called to mind also the saying of Philo the divine: 'When the help of man fails us, we must have recourse to the help of God.'[3] Therefore his purpose was firmly fixed that if on the morrow he should be permitted to go to church to receive the Holy Sacra-

[1] See Appendix IX.   [2] See p. 162.   [3] See p. 69.

DE IURE ET STATU

ment, he would take sanctuary there by clinging to the altar and its relics.

So when it was morning and the sun was newly risen, by leave of his warder he went to the house of the Canons, which was in the town, and there with great devoutness he received the Holy Sacrament, humbly and with tears seeking counsel and succour from God and from St. David in this his sore necessity. Moreover since the Seneschal was to come about nightfall, he resolved that when the bells rang for Vespers he would seek the church and there take sanctuary. So he returned to his lodging, not to say his prison, and there took food and his noonday sleep. But in the afternoon there came to him the lady of the house, a good woman with much compassion for his sorrows; and with her came a knight of the Seneschal's who told him that the Seneschal would bring his adversary with him and that he was much pleased now to know that he was a clerk of the Archbishop of Canterbury; for hitherto John had kept this from their knowledge; wherefore although he was to be left at Châtillon to await his liberty having lost his horses and the money that was found upon him, no inconsiderable sum, he did not think he would be set free before the coming of the Duke, who was in Normandy on an expedition with the King of France; or more likely he would be kept there until a ransom had been obtained in proportion to his means or (to be more precise) to those of his Lord. But he said that he thought his Lord the Seneschal desired to deal mercifully with the Archdeacon. On hearing this Giraldus gradually took heart and courage again and determined that he would await the mercy of God where he was and would seek no other refuge. In the evening the Seneschal arrived and brought Tynemouth with him; but leaving him in another house, he came forthwith to the Archdeacon and questioned him first in public concerning his standing, his nation and

HE IS ALLOWED TO GO FREE

his country, and how it came that he was found so poor, when he had been a Bishop elect and a great man. And when the Archdeacon replied that he came from a poor country and had failed in his suits at Rome through the wealth of his adversary, the Seneschal a little after called him apart and questioned him more diligently concerning Tynemouth, asking who he was and whether he was rich or poor and if he were a clerk of the Archbishop of Canterbury, entreating and adjuring him to tell the whole truth. And the Archdeacon testified that he was in truth a clerk of the Archbishop and one of his dearest, and that he had revenues of a hundred marks or more in churches and prebends. So, when their talk was ended, the Seneschal retired, saying that he would take counsel on the morrow as to what he should do with them. And on the morrow which was Sunday, the Archdeacon, after he had received the Holy Sacrament and broken his fast, was told that he should go free; but Tynemouth was told that, since he was the clerk of one who was the Counsellor of the King of England, the enemy of the King of France, he should remain in their power until the Duke returned from his expedition All his property, to wit, his horse and bag, was at once restored to the Archdeacon, nothing being kept back. But Tynemouth was taken to the keep of the Castle. And when the Archdeacon, passing freely through, beheld him weeping and lamenting, he said to him: 'There is a proverb that he takes a sorry vengeance on his grief, who adding grief to grief thereby increases it. By describing my appearance you laid a snare for me that I might be taken; and this my capture which you procured has become the cause of your own detention and has proved worse for you than for me. For it is written in the Psalms,[1] "he hath made a pit and digged it and is fallen to the ditch that he has made". None the less you should refrain from tears,

---

[1] Psalm vii. 15.

DE IURE ET STATU

because your Lord is so rich and so powerful that he will easily set you free.' But John replied: 'Nay, if I have ever known my Lord, he will care little about setting me free, thanks to the suit about the dignity of your Church, which you have revived.' And the Archdeacon continuing to jest and rail against him, thus taking such vengeance as he could, made answer: 'My counsel is that you should patiently endure all these things, regarding them as a penance for the perjuries which, by your advice your Lord caused to be committed against me, first at Gloucester, next at St. Albans and lastly at Rome' ... So therefore the Archdeacon, so often shaken, but never forsaken, so often tried but never denied, so often taught, but never outfought[1], was lost in thanksgiving to God and to St. David. For as the Apostle says:[2] 'We are troubled on every side, yet not distressed; we are perplexed but not in despair, persecuted but not forsaken, cast down but not destroyed, always bearing about in the body the dying of Jesus, that the life also of Jesus might be made manifest in our body.'

Thus after these adventures he came cheerful and full of joy to the market of Troyes which was but a little way off, as though to harbour after shipwreck. And there it chanced that the clouds passed from the face of Fortune, and she smiled more brightly upon him; for having found his messengers and paid his debts to the Bolognese, he came to Paris, where he found that venerable man, John, Archbishop of Dublin, who loved him and was at that time sojourning there, an exile for the sake of his Church. And since at Troyes he had spent all the money brought him in paying his creditors, he accepted a loan from the Archbishop, who also took him with him, and thus by God's grace he crossed the March of Normandy, which the war had rendered most insecure

---

[1] An attempt to reproduce the deliberate assonance of *toties afflictus et non derelictus, toties expertus et non desertus, toties instructus et non destructus.*
[2] 2 Corinthians iv. 8.

and perilous, and came unhurt to Rouen. Now hearing that the Bishop of Ely was come thither, he went to him that same evening and was joyfully welcomed by him with a kiss. And after listening to stories of the Roman Court and conversing on a diversity of things, the Bishop told him that two Canons of Mynyw had come with letters of ratification from their Chapter to elect a Bishop and that they had already spoken on the matter to the King, who had sent them to him as being one of the Judges appointed by the Pope in the matter of the election, with orders that he should come to him as soon as he might, to choose one of the three nominees. Wherefore on the morrow he was going to the King at the Castle of Elbœuf.

But to make clear the train of events during the Archdeacon's absence, you must know that the Archbishop of Canterbury having received the letters of the Pope which Tynemouth had sent him by courier, had at once summoned the Canons of Mynyw before himself and the Justiciar at Northampton, that a fresh election might be made, and having shown them the letters annulling the former elections, he proposed to them that, according to the custom of the English Church, they should nominate a certain number of persons and then with the assent of the King or his Justiciar take one of them for their Elect. But they after deliberation on the matter said that they would not go back on their former nomination of the two Abbots and Giraldus the Archdeacon. But when Reginald Foliot who was present heard this, he leapt forward in their midst, saying that he had been nominated with those others on the former occasion and, that since they now nominated those three, he ought not to be left out. But the Canons replied that this was a wholly different occasion and a fresh nomination had now to be made whether of those same persons or of others, and that his name had only been added to the list to increase the number of nominees. But the Archbishop and the Justiciar, though in all other respects he was most unworthy to be nominated with the others, yet since he was an Englishman while the others were Welsh, used all their efforts to secure that Foliot should be one of those nominated; and when they had got their way, they further proposed that the name of Giraldus should be removed from the list, because he was hated by the King and the Archbishop and was a disturber of the peace and quiet of the Church of Canterbury. So the Canons, to secure the promotion of their own folk, which they desired far more than the advantage of their Church, being eager above all for the election of the Abbot of Whitland, with whom they were almost all connected by ties either of blood or affinity, were easily induced to do as they were bid. Having therefore nominated the two Abbots and Foliot, two clerks of the Church of Mynyw, whom they regarded as Canons, one a Welshman named Samuel, the other an Englishman, namely William, priest of Carmarthen, were chosen to go with letters of ratification from the Chapter that they might elect that one of the three to whom the King should give his assent; and for that purpose they crossed the sea to Normandy. For the Archbishop had taken every care to secure this, in order that the election might take place in the absence of the Archdeacon, and had caused these clerks to be sent, not knowing what they carried, with letters from himself stating no more than the fact of the nomination, and others from the Justiciar advising that Foliot should be elected in preference to the Welsh Abbots; for he was an Englishman without a drop of Welsh blood in him, and had twice gone to Rome and had laboured there (so he asserted) for the honour of the Archbishop and for the security of the Church of Canterbury. But on account of the judges, who had been put in charge of the election and were now across the sea, they were sent to the King,

FOLIOT IS TO BE ELECTED BISHOP

that the election might take place in his presence and that of the judges, before the arrival of Giraldus the Archdeacon. The Archbishop, however, before they started on their journey, being now sure of having his way, said publicly, when talk arose concerning the three nominees, that all might rest assured that neither of the Abbots could be elected, since one was illiterate and the other born out of lawful wedlock. Now on hearing this the Welsh Canons were filled with consternation, and Samuel rejoined that he would, if need be, swear with forty men of proved reputation to support him, that the Abbot of Whitland was born in lawful wedlock. To which one Master Simon, a clerk of the Archbishop, knowing well what his Lord desired, retorted, 'Of what use are such words, when common talk through all the country says the contrary?' From which it may be gathered how readily men of that nation will perjure themselves if profit may be won thereby. But Martin, the brother of the Abbot, was much incensed by these words of the Archbishop and, taking apart Master Simon and other clerks of the Archbishop, he said, 'Is it thus your Lord has deceived us? Where are now his promises, where all those assurances upon oath, where all his outstretching of his hands to his Crozier to confirm his pledges? It may be that Giraldus still lives. If our opportunity be not gone for ever, the memory of his words will make us less credulous and less easy to deceive.' Alas! this Martin and the Abbot his brother, in virtue both of their talents and their learning, would, considering their time and country, have been most useful instruments of their Church, had they been firm-set upon the sure foundations of faith and had they not been corrupted and deceived by empty promises. But enough of this.

Now in the morning the Archdeacon came to the Bishop's Mass and there he found the clerks of Mynyw;

DE IURE RT STATU

and immediately after the celebration, when they had come down from the Presbytery, the Bishop withdrew to the nave of the Church that they might sit down there together, as had been arranged in their talk of the evening before; and there Giraldus thus addressed the Bishop before them all: 'I have heard that the Canons of Mynyw have taken counsel concerning the election of a Bishop and, without awaiting my return, nay, seizing the opportunity of my absence, have proceeded to make their nomination with unseemly haste and great indiscretion; for it was their duty to have waited till they were informed by letters from the Lord Pope (or at least by letters of the Judges directed to them), that the former elections had been annulled, before proceeding to make a new election. Wherefore since it is clear that they have acted indiscreetly and unlawfully, I here interpose my appeal that they may not proceed to an election in accordance with a nomination made in such a manner. Again these clerks whom we see here, prepared, as they tell us, to make an election on behalf of the Chapter of Mynyw, are not Canons. For one of them gave his prebend to his son, and the other unlawfully by means of the secular power laid violent hands on a prebend which had been conferred by me in virtue of the apostolic authority committed to me by the Pope. Again both of them have been excommunicated by myself. Wherefore, even if in all else they were qualified, they could not make an election. Again only one of the Judges is present, though the other[1] has not given any excuse for his absence or appointed a deputy. Further none of the three nominees are fit persons to elect, since one of them is illiterate, another born out of lawful wedlock, and the third deserves rejection for the many enormities he has committed. Thus that neither these may elect nor any of those be elected, for the aforesaid reasons, I appeal.'

---

[1] The Bishop of Worcester. See below and p. 306, Letter I.

HE APPEALS AND STOPS PROCEEDINGS

To this the Bishop of Ely made answer: 'Your most fortunate arrival has been our salvation and has saved us from much trouble. For the King had determined that the election of Foliot should be made on that very day in the presence of himself and of the Bishop, the latter in his capacity as Judge invested with authority for the purpose.'

So horses were brought and the Archdeacon and the two clerks of Mynyw accompanied the Bishop on his way to the King at the rock of Elbœuf. And when they came thither, the Bishop, taking Giraldus with him, went to the King who was hearing mass. Now when the King saw the Archdeacon, he said to the Bishop: 'See how pale the Archdeacon is, who has come back from the Roman Court after losing all his labour there!' To which the Bishop replied: 'It is no wonder that he is pale after all the toil he has endured on this his third visit to Rome. And as for his labour he does not count it wasted; for he has come back with his suit concerning the dignity of his Church in excellent trim, having, moreover, got judges appointed from the province of York, a privilege which before he was unable to obtain.' And the King made answer: 'In this suit I ought to help the Archdeacon, seeing that it is for the honour and increase of my royal power, since it seeks to re-establish a third Archbishopric within my kingdom.' To which the Bishop made answer with a smile which, though but slight, was yet full of meaning: 'In this suit all of us who are suffragans of the Church of Canterbury would be against you.' And the King rejoined: 'Ah, if he had my help, how he would prosper, who, alone and helpless, causes such trouble to the Archbishop and all the rest of you!' But when Mass was over, the King sent all the rest away, keeping only the Bishops of Ely and Norwich and some few of his secretaries with him in the Chapel; and he began to consult the Bishop of Ely more closely concerning the immediate election of a Shepherd for the Church of Mynyw from among the three nominees, but more especially concerning the promotion of Foliot in accordance with the counsel of the Archbishop, at whose nod all things at that time were done, through fear of him rather than through love. But the Bishop related how the Archdeacon had interposed his appeal on grounds that were most just and proved to him that for definite reasons the election could not be made for the present. Wherefore it was then and there decided that the King should write to the Archbishop and the Justiciar, giving orders that since, owing to an impediment which had arisen, the business could not then be completed, it should be carried through, in England and in their presence, by the election of that one of the three nominees who seemed most fit, or of any other good man whom the Canons of Mynyw might wish to add to their nomination; and further that the Bishop of Ely should inform them that on the arrival of his colleague the Bishop of Worcester a joint letter would be sent from them both to the Chapter of Mynyw, bidding them proceed to a new election in accordance with the tenor of the Pope's command. Such was the decision. But when the Bishop of Ely had returned, the clerks of the Chapel, who favoured the Archbishop, and the keeper of the King's seal, who fought under the Archbishop's standard, so altered the form of the letters as to bid them elect one of the three nominees or any other fit person whose name might be added to the nomination, always excepting Giraldus the Archdeacon or any other Welshman. But on that same night the clerks of Mynyw came to the lodgings of the Bishop of Ely and, finding the Archdeacon there, they told the Bishop how the form had been changed after his departure. But the Bishop replied that, while he was present, no exception of any kind had been made. He added that he had often heard of letters being lost by

A REGULAR ELECTION IN ENGLAND

land or sea, hinting that these letters might be lost or that it might be pretended that they had been lost. This he said on account of the Archdeacon, whose promotion he greatly desired.

Now at Rouen the Archdeacon found a youth, Cadwallon ab Ifor, his kinsman, then serving the King as a soldier in his wars, who entertained him generously at his own expense so long as he was in those parts, lent him money to pay his debts and even provided for his expenses as far as Wales. The Archbishop of Rouen, Walter of Coutances, a most excellent man, also received him with great honour and made him a suitable present, which he further enhanced by the following words: 'This Archdeacon would not suffer aught of his own right or that of his Church to be lost by cowardice or sloth, but scarce can honesty however great it be, nay, scarce can Justice herself defend herself against violence and great power and abundance of money.'

BOOK VII

HAVING therefore done all that could then be done in those parts, and hearing that on the Sunday after the Assumption of the Blessed Mary[1] the Bishop Elect of Lincoln was to be consecrated at Canterbury, and that the Archbishop had purposed on the same day to confirm Reginald Foliot as Bishop Elect of Mynyw, if the affair had proceeded before the King as he designed it should, the Archdeacon hastened to the sea and was at pains to cross as soon as possible and to come to Canterbury on the appointed day. So when a great number of suffragans had assembled, since the Archbishop lay grievously sick at Maidstone and had entrusted the performance of his duties to his suffragans, after a long dispute between William, Bishop of London and Dean of the Bishops, Gilbert, Bishop of Rochester and Chaplain to the Archbishop, and Godfrey, Bishop of Winchester and Sub-Dean of the Suffragans, at length they came to a friendly settlement, and William of Blois, the Elect of Lincoln, was consecrated by the Bishop of London. Now during this consecration, when the Bishops were seated by the High Altar in their Episcopal robes, letters were read aloud in public audience from two Welsh Bishops, Henry of Llandaff and Reiner of Llanelwy, in which they excused their absence, while giving their assent to the consecration. Whereupon the Bishop of Rochester said to Giraldus who was sitting there with the rest, 'Now you may clearly see what the Bishops of Wales do and how they recognize that they are subject to the Church of Canterbury'. To which the Archdeacon made answer: 'I am not displeased that they should do what it is their duty to do. Nevertheless they do it by compulsion; and

[1] Aug. 17th, 1203.

GIRALDUS RETURNS TO ENGLAND

I am striving to discover not what is done, but what ought to be done.'

Moreover, before they departed from the Church, Giraldus, in the presence of all the Bishops, the officers of the Archbishop and all the clergy, renewed the appeal which he had made in Normandy before the Bishop of Ely, repeating the same reasons and rejecting the three nominees on the ground of the charges severally brought against them. Then leaving Kent behind him, he set out for Oxford and the Midlands and by dint of much labour and expense, having sent messengers thither and having left others beyond the sea, succeeded in obtaining letters of citation from the Judges, that is from the Judges of the Province of York in respect of his costs and of the standing of his Church, and from the Bishops of Ely and Worcester in respect of the election and other matters.

Meanwhile, hearing that the Archbishop, being now recovered, had summoned his suffragans to London, he sent his clerks thither with letters, that the appeal, which he had made for the first time in Normandy before the Bishop of Ely and secondly, at Canterbury, in the presence of the Suffragans, might now for the third time be repeated in the presence of the Archbishop himself, and then at last, having left undone naught that should be done and yet having lost[1] his labour, he hastened toward Wales. Now the letters ran as follows:

'To the venerable Lord and Father, Hubert by the grace of God Archbishop of Canterbury, Giraldus, Archdeacon of Brecon, greeting! We make known to your Paternity that now, openly and publicly and in your presence, by these letters present and by the voices of our clerks, we renew that same appeal which we made in Normandy in the presence of the Lord Bishop of Ely, and afterwards in the presence of the Bishops and Suffragans and your officers

[1] *omittens . . . amittens.*

DE IURE ET STATU

who were present at the consecration of the Lord Bishop of Lincoln, and that appealing persistently to the power of the Lord Pope, we forbid you to proceed to any nomination or election, until such time as the letters of the Judges, charged to make provision for the election in accordance with the Apostolic mandate, have been sent to the Chapter of Mynyw; we forbid you also to do this without our presence or assent, since I am Canon and Archdeacon of that Church and moreover appointed its custodian by the Lord Pope. Above all we appeal against the election of any of the three persons now nominated, since they are such as may not lawfully be elected. For the Abbot of St. Dogmael is wholly illiterate, as has been proved by the report of the Judges and again at Rome by five or six witnesses of his own party; and he is also an ambitious man who, after my election, knowing well that it had not yet been cancelled, suffered himself to be elected and thrust in over my head; also he undertook the administration of the temporalities of the Bishopric, although his election had not been confirmed (as a number of witnesses even of his own party have proved) and despoiled thereof the man to whom the administration had been committed by authority of the Lord Pope. As for the Abbot of Whitland, he was born out of lawful wedlock and is most ambitious, and further has brought his own house to ruin and destruction. As for Reginald Foliot, but a short time ago he was an unchaste boy, and now that he has come to manhood, is a slave to every lust, witness the children of either sex that have recently been born to him and are still squalling in their cradles. Moreover he has committed perjury against his own Church and is a public enemy. Wherefore he ought in no wise to be promoted therein nor to be allowed any share in any benefice thereof; for he has not blushed of late to assail its liberty and dignity with all his might. These several charges we shall be prepared to prove at the proper time and place. Wherefore we appeal against the election of any of these, and against your confirmation of any whom you may presume to elect.'

Now Tynemouth by the aid of the Archbishop of Lyons had meanwhile (though not without difficulty and the payment of a heavy ransom) escaped from his captivity. And when he came to England, he incurred the indignation of his Lord on account of the vast sums of money which he had squandered at Rome without securing the extinction of the suit concerning the standing of our Church; so that for fifteen days or more he was not suffered to appear before him. But at length by the intercession of important persons he succeeded, though with difficulty, in securing his forgiveness and his place.

Meanwhile, the Archdeacon came to Wales where, that he might nowhere be free from trouble and persecution, he found that his Archdeaconry of Brecon had been thrown into great disorder by the aforesaid Judges of the March[1] who had shown themselves so hasty against him that thus they might win the favour of the Archbishop. For they had appointed the Priors of Llantony[2] and Aberhonddu[3] to give effect to their sentence, and these Priors had, at the instigation of the Arch-adversary, so harried the Archdeacon's proctors by frequent summons and peremptory orders, that they could find no remedy for the future nor any defence, save by the delivery of all the revenues of the Archdeacon in those parts into the hands of his enemies in quittance of the aforesaid sum of one hundred and seventy marks. But the Archdeacon, whose interests were thus jeopardized, was not a little anxious both because of the great loss thus incurred and on account of the shame and insult put

[1] See p. 237.
[2] Apparently Llantony of Gloucester, though he testifies later (see p. 346) that the Prior of the latter place had never done him any harm.
[3] Brecon.

upon him by his enemies, and used all his wit and diligence to meet guile with guile. And so on the first day after his arrival, there being no room for an appeal, since no appeal can be made from an execution unless the executors have exceeded their duty, he tricked them by deposing his former proctors and by appointing others whom they had not summoned. But on the second day, when they summoned the Archdeacon himself and had hoped to conclude the whole business as the Archbishop had commanded, he outwitted them in the following manner. For with great ingenuity he alleged that, using the privilege of a crusader (since before his journey to the Court of Rome, he had once more taken the Cross),[1] he had sold all the corn of the Church of Llandduw and all the produce of the Archdeaconry for three years in advance to two burghers of Aberhonddu, and that he had spent all the money thus received upon the business of his Church. But meanwhile the merchants had carried away all the corn, so that the executors, when they came on the next day, found nought save empty barns. Now the letters of citation were as follows:

'To the venerable Giraldus, Archdeacon of Brecon, Geoffrey of Llantony and John of Brecon, Priors, greeting in the Lord! Although we might have proceeded with the execution, because you neglected to present yourself on the appointed day in the Chapel of St. Mary at Crickhowell, that execution might be made by us, to whom this charge was committed by the venerable Abbot of Wigmore, the Prior of Wenlock and Master Adam of Bromefield, in respect of a hundred marks which by Apostolic authority they sentenced you to pay to the Abbot of St. Dogmael, and of forty marks due to Osbert, Archdeacon of Carmarthen, and of thirty marks due to Master Reginald Foliot, yet none the less

[1] See p. 220.

HE OUTWITS THE JUDGES OF THE MARCH

out of our kindness we have thought fit to warn you that you should with all speed satisfy the aforesaid creditors, and do you to wit that, if you fail to do so, we by the authority of the aforesaid Judges, on the eve of St. Matthew the Apostle,[1] in the Church of Llandduw, shall execute more fully that which we have been enjoined to perform. Farewell.'

But the merchants showing the documents and charters relating to the three-years agreement, with which they had been armed in advance, and with the help of discreet and well-skilled men who had been sent with them (since in contracts of this kind he who is first in time is first in right), sent both executors and adversaries confounded and empty-handed away. And a little later those over-hasty judges received letters from the principal judges of the Archdeacon, revoking their authority and annulling all their wrongful acts. Moreover, the chief adversaries of the Archdeacon, both those whom he had excommunicated and those who had despoiled him, each received letters of summons which he had not without much labour secured.

Now in the meantime Giraldus, going toward Mynyw through the mountains of Builth and Cardigan, met Osbert, Archdeacon of Carmarthen, who had been sent in advance by the Archbishop to hinder him with letters from himself and the Justiciar to Nicholas Avenel, Bailiff of Pembroke. And having received these, he made haste and came to Mynyw before him on the Friday. For the Canons of Mynyw had received a command to appear before the Archdeacon at Mynyw on the following Sunday. And on the Saturday night preceding, when he was lodged at Haverford, it seemed to William, Chaplain of Laurenni, a good and honest man to whom the Archdeacon had committed the charge

[1] Sept. 20th, 1203.

of his affairs in those parts, that as he lay asleep a little before dawn, a boy outside the house began to repeat these words, as it were a stave from a song, 'Marvels you see, yet greater would you see (*uideatis*)'. And when the priest sought to correct him by crying 'yet greater shall you see (*uidebitis*)', the boy, impatient of correction, continued as before to repeat 'Yet greater would you see'. And at length he also uttered this prayer, chanting it aloud: 'O Lord, let thy pity cleanse and fortify thy Church and seeing that without thee it cannot stand secure, let it ever be guided by thy grace.' Now on the morrow, while the Archdeacon was going towards Mynyw, the priest told his dream in the hearing of all that were with them. And straightway the Archdeacon expounded the dream saying: 'We shall perchance find matters in some confusion at Mynyw because the Bailiff has got there before us; wherefore we shall marvel. Moreover, before we leave the country, it may be that some greater marvel shall befall us. And as for his using the subjunctive "You would see" instead of the future "You shall see", it was as though he should say, "Seeing this, you would meet with your reward". And as for the prayer which he added at the end of his refrain, it seems to suit the present case of the Church of Mynyw, exceeding well; for in truth it greatly needeth to be cleansed and fortified.'

When therefore they had passed through the province of Rhos, which is far from 'rosy', the Archdeacon and his folk came to the rocky land of Pebidiog, beguiling the journey with talk on divers matters; and behold, the son of Samuel, of whom we spoke earlier,[1] came at his father's bidding and asked the Archdeacon to send back his brother whom he had brought with him from France, where he had been studying in the Schools; for he said that if he brought him in his company to Mynyw, his

---

[1] See p. 321.

ALL AT MYNYW ARE AGAINST HIM

father and all his kin would forthwith be despoiled by the public officers. And he told how on the day before the Bailiff of Pembroke had on behalf of the King and the Justiciar ordered that not one of the Canons should wait for the Archdeacon at Mynyw; and these commands they obeyed with all the greater readiness because, as it seemed, a former grievance had been wiped out by a later benefit. For when their messengers returned from the King bringing letters, in which, as has been related,[1] they were ordered to make a new nomination and election, provided that no Welshman was among the names presented, they had been sad and very anxious, so that then they all longed for Giraldus and his coming thither, and openly asserted that they would elect him again if he came quickly; for they declared that he was worthy of honour and promotion beyond all others, above all in that Church, for whose dignity he had toiled in such peril, and which, in defiance of the King and the Archbishop, he had of late in Normandy so valiantly preserved from such a calamity and plague in the shape of Foliot. But this they did not say because they desired the advantage of their Church or the promotion of the Archdeacon, but in order that these words of theirs might be reported to the Archbishop by his accomplices, to the end that, if perchance he might be prevailed upon to temper or change his commands, they might be able even thus to secure the promotion of one of their own folk and so gratify their carnal affections, by which alone they were moved. But the Archbishop, having been forewarned concerning their words and intentions, sent letters to them from himself (through the Bailiff of Pembroke) and from the Justiciar (through Osbert the Archdeacon) ordering them to proceed without fear to the election of any suitable person of any nation, Welsh, Irish or whatever best pleased them, so long as they did

[1] See p. 320.

DE IURE ET STATU

not choose Giraldus. Now the Canons were rejoiced at this for the sake of promoting one of their own folk, for which they longed so eagerly, and devoutly obeying these commands, left the town and the Church at once, that they might not appear before the Archdeacon at the Chapter. But he, having heard this from the son of Samuel, sent back the other son to his father lest he might incur further loss on account of himself; and forthwith all his companions from those parts (save only William of Laurenni), to wit, Masters Walter and Geoffrey of Haverford and others took their leave and departed from him; for they feared the public power and the fierce persecution with which they were threatened. But the Archdeacon said to them on their departure, 'Behold the dream of our comrade; for we have seen marvels and shall soon see greater'; and approaching Mynyw, accompanied by his one sole Achates[1] from those parts, he found in the Church none save their vicars and Samuel the ex-Canon, who had been left by the others to hear what the Archdeacon would say and to answer him. For all of them had conspired against him even more grievously than was their wont.

And now indeed the Church of Mynyw was divided in respect of the Welsh; for there were two very different parties[2] whose enmity was of long standing, the one consisting of the descendants of Jonas, the other of the descendants of John. Now of these the latter opposed the Archdeacon with all their might for the sake of the Abbot of Whitland, whose promotion they sought at the promptings of the flesh, as being one of themselves; while the others had hitherto favoured the Archdeacon. But after receiving the aforesaid letters, which were full of guile and deceit, instructing them to elect any save only

[1] Achates, the faithful friend of Aeneas; cp. *Aen.* I, 312, *uno graditur comitatus Achate*.

[2] The MS. wherever it speaks of these parties uses the word *paries* ('party-wall') perhaps 'sections'.

HE FORBIDS THE CHAPTER TO PROCEED

Giraldus, the two parties were reconciled and became friends, on the understanding that the name of Robert the son of Jonas should be added to the other three already nominated, and that they should elect either Peter, Abbot of Whitland (who had already been deposed by the Abbot of Cîteaux at the instance of Giraldus), or Robert, despite his age, now verging on decrepitude, and that they should seal this solemn agreement with an oath. For this reason then all the Canons there residing unanimously and from their heart resisted the Archdeacon and because they feared that he might coerce them in virtue of the power and authority committed to him, they interposed their appeal through Samuel and their vicars. But the Archdeacon gave orders that, in his absence and until they received letters on this matter from the Judges, they should make no nomination or election, since in the position in which they then were no appeal could protect them. For all those whom he had excommunicated were by that very fact disqualified from making either an election or nomination. But on that night he found none save a poor widow, emboldened thereto by her lack of possessions, who would harbour him in their house or even speak with him outside the Church, on account of the prohibition to this effect which had been made by the public power. Wherefore at the entrance to the town, when he was descending on foot towards the Church, a married woman said to him, 'There are many folk at Mynyw to-day' (she spoke of the laity) 'who are sad because they cannot give lodging as is fitting and as they desire'.

This, then might be regarded as a fulfilment of the vision; for it might well seem marvellous that neither citizens would harbour nor Canons hold converse with such a pillar of the Church of Mynyw, who was fighting so nobly on behalf of its dignity and for the honour of the whole country.

DE IURE ET STATU

So on the morrow the Archdeacon withdrew to the country of Pembroke and when he had stayed there for a few days, he called together the clergy of those parts and on the Thursday before Michaelmas he held a general Chapter of the province in the Church of Caereu. And there at the very outset of the proceedings a certain priest revealed a dream which had appeared to him the night before. It seemed to him that, when the Archdeacon was holding the Chapter in that very place, a man came with the news that a wolf was throttling his horses in the churchyard; and straightway he saw the wolf entering the Church and assailing the Archdeacon with open jaws; but the latter went at once to meet the wolf, put a halter over his head and a bit in his mouth and last of all, clapping a saddle on his back and girthing it well, leapt upon his back and, urging him on with sharp spurs, rode him all the way to Mynyw, the whole Chapter following at his heels. And behold, straightway, at that same hour there came a man of no mean place among the great men of the country, one Robert FitzRichard, who alone among all the magnates of those parts was not kin to the Archdeacon either by blood or affinity; and he presumed without more ado to enter the Church like a mad dog and with sacrilegious mouth to insult and abuse the Archdeacon, calling him a traitor to the King and his realm, and uttering the most violent threats against him. And as though he were raving mad, he broke open the door of the house in the churchyard and took away by force two horses of the Archdeacon (for he found no more) together with all else belonging to him that he could discover. But the Archdeacon instantly, by the authority of the Lord Pope which had been committed to him, publicly before all the Chapter bound him with the chain of his anathema. But see how quickly the vision of the wolf was brought to fulfilment! For in the burden of excommunication that was put upon him might be seen the halter, the bit and the saddle. Again that other vision of marvels seen and greater yet to be seen was also fulfilled therein, since the Archdeacon was insulted and despoiled in his own country, for whose honour he was exposing himself to such toil and peril; aye, and this happened in those parts of the country whence he was sprung and where it was scarce credible that such a thing should befall him. But it was the accidental absence of his friends and kinsmen, all of them great men in those parts, and also the requests and promises of the Archbishop and the Justiciar that gave occasion for this outrage.

For the Archbishop was unspeakably annoyed and anxious on account of the vast sums of money which he had spent without profit at the Court of Rome, seeing that the suit concerning the standing of the Church of Mynyw was still in being and like to prosper. He therefore made the hand of the public power, which was at his beck and call, to be heavier than ever upon Giraldus and his supporters, so that, wherever he might be within the realm, he should be despoiled of everything, of his horses and more especially of his letters, as though he were a public enemy, and that all his following, both mounted and on foot, clergy and serving men alike, should be delivered into public custody, the body of Giraldus alone being left scatheless and unhurt, though not immune from loss. Now when all this had been contrived and determined in England, chance had brought this wicked man to those parts and he had straightway promised that he would do this thing in Wales, being one who never shrank from any outrage or disgraceful deed. So when he took the Archdeacon's horses from the churchyard, he sought most eagerly for his men and for his letters. But Fortune, whose way it is to thwart Giraldus's business and yet not to bring it utterly to naught, had, while his clerks stayed with him in the Church, sent on all his servants, with pack-horses, baggage and letters, some miles ahead to a place toward Mynyw, where he had resolved to lie that night; but of this the robber knew nothing. Further this malicious fellow brought the Bailiff a number of instructions directed against Giraldus and his folk; of which one was to the effect that all the friends of Giraldus, his household and his kin, should be vexed by divers annoyances and afflicted by the spoliation of their goods. And this was carried out in respect of the lesser persons of either sort, but the greater and more powerful, as is the way of the world, were left wholly unharmed. Nor was it wonderful. 'For censure sparing crows pursues the dove'.[1] About the same time a knight of witty speech, who was lately come thither from Devon, presumed publicly to utter the following words in disparagement of St. David, but in praise of the Archdeacon. 'This Archdeacon would be a good and valiant knight, if he served a good Lord. He would be a peerless fighter and a doughty champion, if he had a strong patron and protector.' In truth he spoke with more folly than wisdom, as if he knew not that He who saith, 'Vengeance is mine! I will repay', is long-suffering and tarries ere He strikes; but when He strikes, His vengeance is most heavy and oft vexes those whom He receives for His own and whose works and deeds are acceptable to Him, now to prove them, and now to purge them so that their understanding may be increased.

But meanwhile by messengers of the Archdeacon from abroad and also by those of the Archbishop, who was eager to bring the matter to a speedy conclusion, there came letters from the Judges, namely the Bishops of Ely and Worcester, addressed to the Chapter and ordering that a new election should be made within two months after receipt of these instructions by that same Chapter,

---

[1] *Juv.* II, 63.

ORDERS RECEIVED FOR THE ELECTION

whom the Archbishop had utterly corrupted and deceived. And knowing that if they did not do so, according to the form of the Apostolic mandate a Shepherd for the Church of Mynyw must be appointed by the Judges, as they might think fit, he sent letters both from the Justiciar and himself, fixing an early date whereon the Chapter should elect a Bishop in England and in their presence; and that he might encourage them to come, he took care by means of deceitful letters from the Justiciar, in addition to the promises which he had made before, to renew his former statement that they should elect any man they pleased from the bosom of their own Church or elsewhere, excepting only Giraldus the Archdeacon. Also that he might the more effectively turn away the hearts of the whole Chapter from Giraldus, he had given his plighted word and sure security to five or six persons whether from the members or from the body of the Church, all of them men by whom he knew that he could best create parties and schisms in the Church, that he would give them the See of Mynyw, if he was able to keep Giraldus from it.[1] Wherefore since each one of them was moved by the flesh to seek his own advantage, it was brought about that they should not turn the eye of their intent to the common advantage of their Church and the whole country.

Yet we make an exception in the case of one man and one only, who is worthy of praise not only in the present but in days to come, to wit, Henry FitzRobert. Would he had been as sound and strong in body as he was in heart and mind! For alone among the residents he, in his zeal for his Church, clove to Giraldus staunchly and inseparably from beginning to end; nor could he be won away from him by flattery or promises,

---

[1] Such must be the sense, but *clero* must be eliminated to secure it. The Archbishop had promised the See at one time or another to the Abbot of St. Dogmael, the Abbot of Whitland, Geoffrey Prior of Llantony of Gloucester, and Foliot. Who the others were is not clear.

DE IURE ET STATU

by threats or fear, or even by the spoliation of his goods.

Giraldus, therefore, seeing that his Chapter had been utterly corrupted and led astray by the cunning of the Archbishop, this man alone excepted, and perceiving also that, unless he barred the way, some useless Shepherd would be set over the Church of Mynyw, in his zeal for his Church and the honour of his country, for which rather than for himself he believed he had been born, resolved, at whatever risk, still to toil on and struggle manfully on its behalf. He went therefore to his nephew William de Barri, a youth of excellent character, the son of that best of brothers, of virtuous father virtuous son, and borrowed horses from him together with all that was necessary for his journey. Then making no delay he hastened toward England, with his wonted vigour passing through the forests of Dyfed, crossing the hills of Cardigan and descending thence through Builth as far as Brecknock. And there, although daily he heard rumours of yet more grievous persecution and conspiracy awaiting himself and his followers, yet since no adversity could daunt him, he steeled his heart to meet all difficulties and ordered his journey into and through England after the following manner. He sent his letters and original documents every morning about two or three miles ahead of himself in the hands of a faithful messenger who was known but to few, while he had another following him at about the same distance and carrying his money, in order that if he himself were seized, the robbers might not find his silver and lead.[1] Also as far as might be, he avoided public roads and populous cities. Again such was his care and forethought that he had a clerk ready who, the moment he should hear of his capture and detention, should hasten to the Roman Court to secure his liberation, being provided with the money for the journey and with letters from the Archdeacon already

---

[1] i.e. his money and his documents with their leaden seals.

GIRALDUS GOES TO LONDON

written to meet such an emergency. He took care also to protect himself by frequent and devout repetition of the following prayer: 'Almighty and merciful God, hear our prayer and keep us from all adversity, that unhindered both in mind and body we may have freedom to perform all that thou wouldest have us do.'

So Giraldus, thus forearmed against all mischance, hastened by long and continuous marches into England as far as London and Essex, where finding the Archbishop and the Canons of Mynyw at Waltham, whither they had been summoned, he boldly entered among them and in public audience renewed the appeal which he had already so often made by messengers and letters, forbidding them to elect any of the three nominees or to make any election at all without his assent. He also asked the Archbishop to confirm the sentence of excommunication which he had passed on Robert FitzRichard who had despoiled him. But the Archbishop, who knew that the crime had been committed to win his favour and almost by his instigation, began to quibble and to put forward defences, so that he should not do what he was both asked and bound to do; and he caused to be read aloud certain letters from a miserable adversary of the Archdeacon, to wit, Fulk, Prior of Pembroke, testifying that the robber had in the presence of himself and others interposed his appeal before sentence was passed. But the truth was that the evil man, who was never ashamed of any deed that outraged morality or even the laws of nature, had abused the privilege of appeal by employing it the instant he entered the Church and had forthwith proceeded to commit sacrilege, as though he had thus secured immunity. The Archdeacon, however, replied to the Archbishop that public robbers could not be protected by any appeal, as was laid down by the law and as the Archbishop ought very well to know; and further that a sentence passed with authority

DE IURE ET STATU

from the Lord Pope ought to have full effect, even though it lacked confirmation by any lesser person.

Meanwhile, when the Canons assembled in London eight days later to make the election, the Archdeacon omitting naught that should be done, although at great peril to himself and his supporters, took care to be present in person, committing all things to God and to St. David, for whose honour he was labouring. Also on the Wednesday[1] before the Feast of St. Martin he came in the morning to the Archbishop at Lambeth and first of all renewed his appeal against the making of any election without his presence and assent, and then crossed the river to the Justiciar at Westminster. But he, as soon as he saw the Archdeacon, began to thunder forth threats, which, however, being a man of moderation, he kept within decent bounds. And since, as Solomon says, 'a soft answer turneth away wrath,'[2] his anger was assuaged by prudent speech, and taking the Archdeacon with him, he proceeded to the Chapel of St. Catherine,[3] where the Canons of Mynyw and the clerks of the Archbishop were gathered together to make the election. For since, according to the custom of the English tyrants, elections are wont to be made in the presence either of the King or of his Chief Justice, the Archbishop, while sending both the Canons and his own clerks thither, absented himself of set purpose, so that the thing which they were preparing to do contrary to all order might not be ascribed to himself, though everything was in fact being done by his devising. For out of all his rich store of guile this was pre-eminent, that (though everything was done by him) none the less by his wonderful power both of simulation and of dissimulation he made it seem that he was doing nothing at all.

First of all then the Justiciar called the Archdeacon

[1] Nov. 5th, 1203.   [2] Proverbs xv. 1.
[3] The scanty remains of this Chapel may still be seen in the Infirmary of the Abbey.

apart and spoke to him in secret, urging him to refuse his assent to the election of anyone of his own Church or country; for it was they who had betrayed him and foresworn themselves against him; and since they had broken faith with their Church and failed their country he counselled him to revenge himself upon them by excluding them from election even as they had excluded him, and since both his own Church and the Court of Rome had failed him, he urged him to nominate some good man from without who was in no way opposed to him. And the Archdeacon, who had this very thing in his mind, readily lent an ear to his advice and, that he might not seem to be more eager for his own advantage than for that of his Church, nominated two priests of Normandy, who had for the most part been on our side, namely Richard, Dean of Rouen, and Philip of Eu, Archdeacon of the same Church, both of them honest men and discreet and both, like our own people, of Trojan descent.[1] But the Justiciar, saying that he knew neither of them, begged him to think of other persons in England whom he might be willing to nominate as suitable and known to himself.

After this, when he had taken leave of the Justiciar, the five or six Canons of Mynyw, who had been sent thither, took the Archdeacon aside and sought to persuade him to agree with them on someone from the body of their Church or at any rate from one of its members.[2] And when they had mentioned a number of persons, Canons first, then Abbots, and lastly Priors, the Archdeacon, remembering the nomination which they had made at Northampton (from which they had with such readiness excluded himself), and how they had never given loyal support either to himself or to their Church, rejected them all, giving irrefragable arguments against each one.

---

[1] i.e. Bretons of the blood of Brut, like the Welsh.
[2] i.e. either members of the Chapter or from the clergy of the diocese.

DE IURE ET STATU

And at length they offered him Geoffrey, Prior of Llantony, as being a member of the Church of Mynyw, But none the less he refused him also for two reasons: that he had sought the Bishopric from the beginning and that he had shared the Archbishop's board and was almost a member of his household; wherefore it was clear that the question of the standing and dignity of the Church of Mynyw could never be raised by him against the Archbishop.

So on the morrow, which was a Sunday,[1] when they assembled in the same place in the presence of the Justiciar, the latter made trial of the Archdeacon's mind yet once again, advising him secretly to nominate some good men from England and none from Wales, saying that they had betrayed and deceived him. Whereupon he nominated two, Roger, Dean of Lincoln and Walter Map, Archdeacon of Oxford, saying that they were good and honourable men. But the Justiciar urged him to nominate some who, while being Englishmen, were more intimate with Wales and acquainted with the customs of both nations. Giraldus then named two others, Master Hugh of Mapnor, Dean of Hereford, and William Foliot, Precentor of the same Church. Then the Justiciar, while commending these, asked him why he refused the Prior of Llantony, who was an honest and honourable man. To which Giraldus replied by alleging the causes mentioned above ... And so when the Justiciar had urged him with many words to nominate the Prior, but had failed to persuade him, the whole business was put off till the morrow.

But on the Monday[2] morning, which was the Vigil of St. Martin, when they had assembled at the appointed place, the Justiciar began once more with all his might to press for the nomination of the Prior of Llantony; for

[1] Nov. 9th, 1203. The last date mentioned was Wednesday; the intervening days must have been taken up with negotiations.
[2] Nov. 10th, 1203.

the Archbishop and the Justiciar were then of one mind in desiring his promotion, since the former desired to promote his physician, while the latter was eager to confer the Priory of Llantony, when vacant, on his son-in-law Henry de Bohun. Moreover since the Archdeacon could not be induced to give his assent, the remaining Canons of Mynyw, cheated of their hopes, were enticed by bribes and entreaties, by presents and promises, to nominate the Prior. This being done and allowed by the Justiciar (as is the custom in England), although the Archdeacon protested and appealed, the rest with voices raised aloud burst into a hymn of praise. Yet there were few or none there of the body of the Church of Mynyw whose minds were in unison with their voices. But the Archdeacon, when the hymn was finished and the tumult abated, burst forth as follows: 'A strain has been sung here either by men's voices or in their hearts, which shall soon beyond a doubt be as though it were unsung. For we have appealed against this person, assigning causes for so doing, and we maintain that appeal.'

When therefore the Justiciar with a great crowd at his heels went through the Chapel and the Cloister of the Monks towards the Chapter where the Archbishop was awaiting him, Giraldus who was following with the rest, firmly resolved to protest even in the presence of the Archbishop and to interpose his appeal, forbidding him to confirm such an election or to presume to consecrate one thus elected, began, as he went, to reflect on all the vices and vicissitudes of the Roman Court, on whose justice no man can rely when he is opposed by money, to remember the detestable immorality of that most wretched Chapter of Mynyw, their fickleness and unchastity, their falseness and their fraud, and to consider that a prudent man who had so oft faced such perils on behalf of such a college or rather such a gang, would be most unwise to embark on such an adventure again.

DE IURE ET STATU

And when he considered the character of the Elect and reflected that he, unlike others had never presumed to oppose him[1] and that he was actually a member of his Church, then thinking it victory enough to have cheated all his adversaries of their desire, and suddenly changing his purpose he said openly in the Chapter (or, if he did not say it in so many words, might have said), 'I have struggled enough, I have toiled sufficiently and not without advantage. For I have, before such an audience, revived the claim of our Church, which slumbered or rather was buried for so long, and neither slothfully nor like a coward have championed my own claims in the face of such great obstacles. Wherefore that I may not be found obstinate and unceasing in opposition, I give my assent to this election which certain of our Church have made, since the Elect is believed to be a good man — but only on one condition, that my allies, to wit Maurice of Cardigan and three or four of our Canons, now in Ireland, shall also give their assent'.

Thereupon the Archbishop and the Justiciar and the whole assembly were filled with wonder and joy that he so suddenly and beyond all hope bowed to their will, and all thanked him and besought him to lend his aid to win over the aforesaid persons and to perfect the work so well begun. So leaving this assembly and the city as well, without delay he set forth towards Oxford. But almost at once, when he was scarce a mile from London, he was overtaken by two messengers from the Archbishop, Honorius, Archdeacon of Richmond and John Tynemouth, who faithfully labouring for peace and a full and perfect reconciliation between the Archdeacon and their Lord, at length reached this agreement, that the whole quarrel should be entrusted for settlement within a certain date to two arbitrators, Eustace, Bishop of Ely, chosen by

---

[1] He had resigned custody of the *See* on hearing of Giraldus's election; see p. 189.

GIRALDUS UNEXPECTEDLY ASSENTS

Giraldus, and William, Bishop of London, chosen by the Archbishop, the settlement to include on the one hand the quarrel concerning the standing of the Church of Mynyw and its costs (for both of which the Archbishop had already received a summons), and on the other hand a pledge on the part of Giraldus that he would do nothing to hinder the confirmation or consecration of the Archbishop's favourite, now Bishop elect. When therefore they met in London on the day after the Feast of St. Nicholas,[1] which had been appointed for the purpose, on which day not only the two Bishops, but almost all the suffragans had been summoned for the consecration of the Elect of Mynyw, the aforesaid Bishops first of all directed themselves toward the making of peace between the Archdeacon and the Archbishop. So after divers deliberations and much taking of counsel, at last, because Giraldus was alone and unsupported by his Church in the question of that Church's standing, and because he had learned from experience that he could place no reliance on the Roman Court, they induced him to abandon his suit, during the lifetime of this wealthy and powerful Archbishop. On the other hand they compelled the Archbishop to pay the sum which the Pope had awarded the Archdeacon by way of costs. Moreover that the Archdeacon might be under greater obligation to the Archbishop, and that the latter might himself be more secure concerning him, they advised him to confer upon him ecclesiastical revenues amounting to sixty marks. And he in deference to their counsel faithfully performed a part of this compact, but dying not long after was unable to make payment in full.

This done, when the Archbishop was going to consecrate his Elect, the Judges appointed by the Pope, namely Eustace, Bishop of Ely, and Mauger, Bishop of Worcester, after first summoning the suffragans and Giraldus the

[1] Dec. 7th, 1203.

Archdeacon, produced the letters last obtained from the Pope...[1] Now in the last clause but one, added at the instance of Giraldus, the Pope charged the Judges to see to it that no security should be given by the Elect of Mynyw, binding him not to champion the claims of his Church. So when the letters were read aloud, the Judges charged the Archbishop that he should not exact such security, and the Elect that he should not give it.[2] The consecration was then celebrated duly and without impediment.

Therefore taught by long experience that there was scarce any good faith and very little honour to be found among his brethren and fellow-Canons, since he thought it would be unseemly any longer to consort with such men who beside their many other transgressions had so often foresworn themselves to their Church and to himself, Giraldus went to the Archbishop and revealed to him the purpose long conceived and now ripened in his heart, asking him to prevail upon the Bishop of Mynyw, who would refuse him nothing while he was so new in office, to confer his Archdeaconry and prebend upon his nephew, then a stripling, whom he had brought with him for this purpose. He added also, that the Archbishop might be more favourably disposed to do this, that since he himself would have ceased to belong to the body of the Church of Mynyw, he might by granting this request be the more assured that he would not in future raise the question of the standing of the Church against him. And the Archbishop, though at first he hesitated and feared some trick, at last after taking counsel with his folk, said that he would do it, provided he might be assured that his nephew also would never raise that question during his life-time. So, after Giraldus had resigned his Archdeaconry, the Bishop of Mynyw at the request of the

---
[1] See p. 306.
[2] It was, however, suspected that the oath was administered in private. See *De iure et statu*, VII, p. 345.

GIRALDUS RESIGNS ARCHDEACONRY

Archbishop made the nephew Canon of the prebend of Mathry and instituted him Archdeacon of Brecknock. And after this, at the nephew's presentation and petition, the Bishop granted Master Giraldus free and perpetual administration of the revenues from both benefices, all this being secured for him by the Archbishop who used his influence to that end.

Now the reasons for this resignation were many. The first has already been given. The second was that it had never been Giraldus's intent to await the final stroke of death in the tenure of so exacting an office which presented so many occasions for transgression. The third was that this dignity had been acquired, not undeservedly, yet none the less by force (seeing that it was taken in virtue of his powers as legate) from the old Archdeacon who was his predecessor. The fourth was this, that at the general taking of the Cross, before he took the sign upon his shoulder at the instance of the King, the Archbishop and the Justiciar, he had resigned into the hands of Archbishop Baldwin all his Churches and prebends, both in England and in Wales, which he had acquired, not without pangs of conscience, by the help of friends or by his following of the Court; and the Archbishop . . . graciously assigned the custody of the same to the Archdeacon until such time as they should return from Jerusalem; so that in truth he was thereafter merely the custodian and not the rector of these benefices . . . The fifth was that the best of brothers, so often mentioned in these pages, even as he escorted him on his way and at his very departure on his first journey to Rome, besought him with tears to make it his care in due time and place to promote this his youngest son, to whom in baptism he had given his uncle's[1] name, and since he was given to the study of letters, had him brought up to be a clerk, and to advance him to ecclesiastical revenues and more especially to his

[1] *Patrui* which is the reading of the MS., and not *patrinum*.

Archdeaconry and prebend, repaying him the love with which he, Philip, had loved his brother from childhood. Often therefore Giraldus used to address this nephew, whom he made (as it were) and beneficed with ample revenues, quoting these lines of Virgil, in which Aeneas is introduced as saying to his son:

> O boy, learn virtue and true toil from me,
> Fortune from others![1]

---

[1] *Aen.* XII, 435.

THE CLOSING YEARS

With the close of the sixth book of De Iure et statu Meneuensis Ecclesiae *the autobiography of Giraldus comes to an end. Though he lived for some twenty years longer, the veil that covers his retirement is rarely lifted. That he continued his literary labours we know; for the* De Iure *itself, the* Speculum Ecclesiae *and the* De Principis Instructione *were all completed about 1215. His life was not free from trouble, as we shall see, but despite flashes of the old fiery temper, he had weathered the worst of the storm and his heart was set on peace. In 1207 he went once more to Rome, but in a very different temper and for a very different purpose. He shall tell his own story.*[1]

Moreover, though Master Giraldus had thrice gone abroad to Rome on account of the aforesaid suits, yet after only two years had elapsed, he firmly resolved to seek the thresholds of the Apostles for a fourth time, but solely by way of pilgrimage and devotion, in order that by the labours of the journey, by the giving of alms ... and by true confession and absolution, all the stains contracted in his past life and that also which he had incurred by the security which, with some loss of honour, he had been forced both by Church and State to give, when he was reconciled with the Archbishop, might be wiped away past all doubt. And ... between Epiphany and Lent and through all the season of Lent he obtained ninety-two years of indulgence, and to make that number up to one hundred and more, he had himself made a brother of the Hospital of the Holy Spirit, known also as the English School, which had been established by Pope Innocent III. And there he obtained indulgence of a seventh part of the penance enjoined upon him and also

[1] *Invect.* v, 12 and 13 (abbreviated).

merited to receive the privilege of participating in all the masses, prayers and spiritual benefits of all the Churches and Abbeys of all Rome ... Moreover, he resigned into the Pope's hand all the churches and ecclesiastical benefices, of which some had been given him in his boyhood while he was unworthy to hold them, and others had been conferred upon him by his parents and kinsmen, who were moved thereto by the bonds of the flesh, and had perhaps been taken from more worthy persons by force, or acquired through the court or in some other unlawful manner; and he committed himself wholly to the Pope's wisdom for the guidance of all the days of his life that might be yet to come and for the salvation of his soul at the last. And the Pope of pure grace and by his free gift restored all these to him before his departure and gave him salutary instruction for their use and governance and showed him how he should live henceforth and how provide for his final departing. Let the careful reader therefore consider whether the labours of Master Giraldus should be regarded as spent wholly in vain.'

Temptation awaited him on his return. For

while Master Giraldus had gone abroad to seek the thresholds of the Apostles, John, King of England, hearing that Master Stephen Langton had meanwhile been elected Archbishop of Canterbury at Rome,[1] for this reason summoned a Council at Oxford, where ... he began to complain of the troubles and wrongs that had been put upon himself and his father by the Archbishops of Canterbury and by the monks of the same place, adding in the hearing both of Bishops and Barons of the realm, that he had followed the worst advice in ever hindering Master Giraldus, who had raised such a controversy with the Church of Canterbury; and with an oath he swore that, if Giraldus raised that suit again and reawakened the controversy, he

[1] 1207.

JOHN TEMPTS HIM TO RENEW STRUGGLE

would not only not hinder him, but would help him with all his might. And when Master Giraldus returned from Rome, he spoke secretly with him on this very matter and with words of persuasion encouraged him once more to return thither, promising him great assistance therein. But when Giraldus replied that, since he had a good, learned and discreet man as Bishop of Mynyw, he should enjoin this task upon him, the King replied that for such a struggle he would have no champion or fighter other than Master Giraldus.'[1]

Where he took up his dwelling on his return we cannot tell. That he had his troubles is clear from the seventh and last book of the De Iure et statu Meneuensis Ecclesiae, *which is largely concerned with the reasons for his failure to fulfil the ambitions which he cherished for himself and for his Church — a process which consists to a great extent in the denunciation of his adversaries and an exposition of the motives which led the Canons of Mynyw to reject him. A prophet has no honour in his own country; and his moral and religious standards, more especially in regard to concubinage, were too severe for them. Of the new Bishop he has little good to say, save that he did of old resign his custody of the See on hearing of Giraldus's election. But he is quite clear that Geoffrey's motives in seeking the Bishopric were purely worldly. For seeing the interminable delays that attended Giraldus's prosecution of his claims at Rome,*[2]

he revived the hope that he had cherished of being able, some day, to walk mitre-horned, and strove with all his might to win his desire ... And when a monk from 'the regions of Mynyw' came to him and said, 'I wonder that you should desire so poor a See ... in a wild land and in the midst of enemies, while you are Prior of so noble a house, in so fair and peaceful a place, equipped with fine buildings and planted so pleasantly with vines and gardens and orchards. And above all I marvel, seeing that in the

[1] *Invect.* v, 22. [2] *De iure et statu*, VII (R.S. p. 392).

whole Bishopric there is scarce a single house worthy of a Bishop'. To which the Prior made answer, revealing his ambition and his worldliness, 'Say what you will about the lack of houses, and seek to fright me as you please by talking of the wildness of the land and the hostility of its inhabitants! For none the less I would have you know that "mine" is a much more precious word than "ours".'

That he was hand in glove with the Archbishop, he says, is clear from the fact that he rewarded the 'archpirates' of the Church of Mynyw, sc. Osbert, Foliot and others, by conferring upon them the richest revenues that his Church could provide.[1] At first, it is true, he feigned extreme strictness and showed himself inexorable to barons and knights holding lands of the Church.[2] But this was merely to extract money from them and his whole administration of the See showed his greed for money, and his avarice grew from day to day. Worst, perhaps, of all,

being unable any longer to conceal his longstanding hatred of Giraldus, by vile suggestions pouring an old man's poison into a young man's ears, he estranged, from him his nephew, the Archdeacon of Brecon, whom he had so amply enriched with the goods of the Church. And filling him with unnatural enmity and ingratitude, he inflicted grievous loss upon the youth ... not only inflicting on him a stain which shall stick fast for ever, but depriving him utterly of that sound foundation in letters, so necessary to all liberal learning, which he would abundantly have obtained, if he had cleaved to his uncle as it was fitting he should do....'[3]

Further,

emboldened by the fact that the censure of the Church was lulled to slumber for a while by the cloud of the Interdict, for three or four years he kept Giraldus

---

[1] *De iure et statu*, VII (*R.S.* p. 346).
[2] Ibid., p. 348.   [3] Ibid., p. 352.

from effective possession of the Church of Tenby, which the latter had canonically acquired, and to gratify his avarice appropriated all the fruits and revenues of the church.¹

However at last²,

as a result of his gluttony and the avenging anger of God, which from time to time inflicts temporal punishment on those who are given to wine and vice, he was suddenly seized with the palsy, which deprived him not merely of the use of half his body, but of all. Wherefore it is all the more a matter for wonder and pity that the more grievous and prolonged his bodily affliction became, the more immoderate and burning became his ambition, and that as his weakness grew, so his greed seemed daily to increase.'

Moreover,

he was so maddened and afflicted by the disease that before his death, in defiance of all law and order he excommunicated sundry persons of high authority, all of whom by the intervention of Giraldus were immediately absolved to the great confusion of the Bishop who was rebuked by his Superior.³

After a pathetic but unavailing attempt to secure permission to retire to his old home at Gloucester, that he might end his life among the monks whom once he ruled, he died towards the close of 1214⁴.

Once more Giraldus was offered the vacant throne by a party among the Canons.⁵

Some of the Canons, who seemed to be most influential in the Chapter, sent letters and messengers to

¹ *De iure et statu,* VII (R.S. p. 353). He was specially attracted by its fish-tithes!
² Ibid., p. 354.   ³ Stephen Langton.
⁴ Custody of the See was assumed by the Earl Marshal on Jan. 11th, 1215. Iorwerth, the new Bishop was consecrated June 21st, 1215 (see Lloyd, p. 688 notes; also *De iure,* I, p. 132-3.
⁵ *De iure,* I, p. 132.

Giraldus, who was then in England, urging him and advising him to prepare himself with all speed to receive the governance of the Church of Mynyw; and they promised him the support of themselves and their followers, provided he would consent to be guided by wisdom and prudence. They sent also one of themselves who was his friend and kinsman, to discover if he could be induced to give promises or some security as to his future policy. But on both occasions they found him firm and inflexible; for he said that he would refuse to be chosen to a good English Bishopric, not to speak of that poor and pillaged See which they now offered him, if his election was accompanied with the least taint of damnable sin or simony. And so being unable to get any other answer from him, they betook themselves to fresh designs ... But if he had been called unanimously by all of them and had been able to secure the assent of both King and Archbishop, which ... would have been a miracle, then he would not have refused the burden and the poverty proffered him; for he recalled to his mind the saying of the Holy Scripture, 'What God wills, do thou will; else art thou not straight'.[1]

He was after all on the verge of seventy and may well have been purged of his old ambition.
Under these circumstances the Canons,[2]

since they saw that the public power was much weakened and the liberties of the Church by grace of God increased, came to an agreement that they would elect one who was wholly Welsh, to wit, the Abbot of a certain poor monastery in the diocese of Mynyw;[3] and this they did although the King had asked them ... to elect a certain Englishman, and the Archbishop had written to them urging them to grant the King's request. And indeed they knew the

---

[1] See p. 157.   [2] *De iure et statu*, p. 361.
[3] The Premonstratensian house of Tally near Llandeilo.

THE ELECTION OF IORWERTH

Abbot to be a good and simple man and of their own race, with no foreign tincture either in his character or his upbringing, and further that he was like to do everything according to their desire, indulging his native land and acquiescing in the practices whereby clergy succeeded to their fathers' benefices and had concubines dwelling with them in their houses... and they thought also that owing to his innate simplicity and easy-going liberality they had no cause to fear that he would chide or correct them for their sins.

Of Iorwerth's rule Giraldus is silent. It is clear that he was scarce enthroned when Giraldus wrote. He contents himself with exhorting him to be a good Bishop[1] *and with warning him against the sin of simony.*

I hope he was not guilty of simony in respect of his election, but he did give a richly-embroidered cope of pure silk, which he had bought in London, to the Church of Mynyw, when Bishop Geoffrey was dying or just deceased.[2]

Still whatever his fears for the future may have been, it must have been a real satisfaction to him that at last St. David's had a true Welshman for its Bishop. And he had one other great cause for satisfaction; for, in Stephen Langton, Canterbury had a great Archbishop, a churchman and a scholar after his own heart. He had not improbably been present when Langton was made Archbishop at Rome in 1207.[3] *And now Langton had at last returned*[4] *to his native land to be the effective ruler of the Church of which he had so long been Primate merely in name. Giraldus had already presented him with his* Description of Wales,[5] *an*

---

[1] His exhortations, found in the main in MS. 400, Corpus Christi, Cambridge, which was not collated by the editor of the *Rolls Series*, are almost wholly concerned with the suppression of the abuses which Giraldus has so long denounced; in other words, if he was to be a good Bishop, he must be another Giraldus. For the text of these passages see *Medium Aevum*, 1935, 145 ff.
[2] *De iure et statu*, p. 364.   [3] See p. 351.   [4] 1213.
[5] *De iure et statu*, Pref., *ad init.*

LETTER TO STEPHEN LANGTON

appropriate gift to the Archbishhop who almost immediately after his return had played an active part in procuring a truce between the Welsh Princes and the King.[1] *And in 1215 he gave him his* De Iure et Statu Meneuensis Ecclesiae *prefaced with a highly laudatory dedication. He may even have presented the book with his own hands. For just before Langton's departure for Rome in the autumn of 1215 he writes:*[2]

After I had been so greatly refreshed by the delight of your conversation at Guildford, a rumour reached my ears, as I was on my way to Canterbury, which much disturbed and saddened me. For a number of persons told me that you purposed about the Feast of St. Michael next to journey to the Court of Rome and to visit the thresholds of the Apostles that there you might (which God forbid!) resign the high office in which you show such eminence ... and by the incomparable vigilance of your pastoral care provide for the advantage of so many, and that you might once and for all choose out for yourself some solitude wherein to lead the life of an anchorite or hermit, or seek even the austerity of a Carthusian prison. But seeing that you were called to the Church (which, as all acknowledge, you govern with such auspicious guidance after its long affliction at the hands of tyrants) ... that it might breathe again and rejoice in the freedom that is its due, if you should now thus suddenly desert it and once more expose your English flock to the teeth of wolves, would not that be a clear sign of sloth or even of detestable cowardice rather than of sound prudence or laudable vigour, since the Most High hath not ceased to stretch out his right hand over you? ... For your wise and pious discretion knows right well which are dearer to Christ; most excellent prelates or hermits wandering alone and anchorites shut up within their cells? The former rule, the latter are ruled; the former feed their flock, the latter

[1] See Lloyd, p. 641.   [2] *R.S.* I, 402.

COMPLAINT AGAINST A MONK

are fed, so that the recluse is to the prelate as the flock to its shepherd. Prelates restore to God with great increase the talents that have been committed to their charge and cease not to win souls, for which Christ laid down his life; but the recluse, intent only on their own salvation, hide the talent committed to them. The prelates bring rich harvest to the granaries of God, true grains of wheat, not husks of chaff; but those others live solitary and alone and do nought to multiply God's harvest ... But in addition to this there is something that I would say at the close of this letter, by leave of the monks and above all with your permission. For a monk, who is your personal chaplain and shares your board (black-dyed without, and would he were not also black-dyed within!) has with depraved judgment, as devoid of truth as it is of charity, declared in the hearing of many that both I and the book which I presented to you (a scandalous work in his opinion) deserve to be consumed with fire. Nay more, he has constantly affirmed, with violent threats, fierce glances, and words as affected as they are confused, that he will shortly put the book into the fire with his own hands. Such is his Pharisaic scorn, such his Dorobernian pride![1] Wherefore I have thought fit to beseech your pious Paternity that this man of commination, who has more of bitterness in him than of humbleness or charity, may neither have access to or custody of the book which is both yours and mine, lest he corrupt it by scraping away what I have written or by wickedly inserting something of his own. For, as you know, nothing has ever been so well said or written that it is beyond the reach of malice to distort it. But let him not be debarred from hearing sentences read aloud from the book by another (if he should desire to listen), that so by hearing just rebukes of men such as himself, rebukes which have been uttered for the correction of error by the zeal of true righteousness ... he may him-

[1] Dorobernia = Canterbury.

THE END

self be corrected or, if he be past correction, may wither away with filthy jealousy.

With this letter the curtain falls. Giraldus lived on into the reign of Henry III and seems to have died in 1223, since in that year his death was notified to the Bishop of Lincoln and his living at Chesterton in Oxfordshire was filled.[1] Tradition has it that he was buried at St. David's and a tomb has been shown as his. But it is a fourteenth-century tomb and there is no evidence to show where he lies.[2] It is fit that his story should be ended by his own words.

And so Giraldus ran the course that was ordained for him, while he could and while the time permitted, nor in his day was he a sluggard or a coward. But now that others run and follow the court and pile up vain vexations, let him take his rest and in his humble habitation indulge his love of books and in the corners of churches weep for his sins and wail for his offences and for the welfare of his soul with penance wash them away and wipe them out.'[3]

Such was his prayer and such we may hope was its fulfilment.

---

[1] See Lloyd, p. 631, n.93.
[2] Ibid.   [3] *Invect.* v, 23.

APPENDIX

(I)

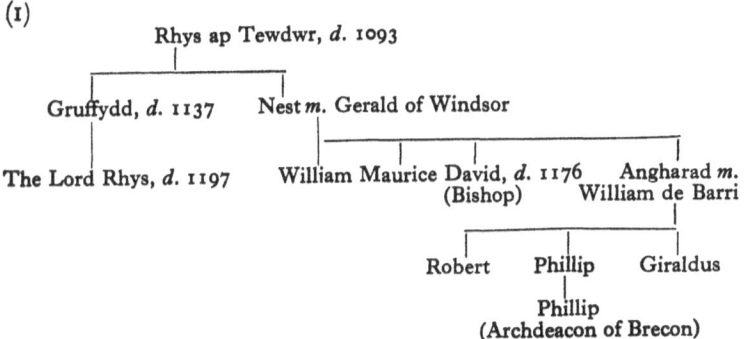

Nest, a lady of many lovers, had other children born out of wedlock (see pp. 44, 83.)

(II) That Giraldus disliked Bishop Peter is clear; but their relations are somewhat obscure. Besides the quarrels here mentioned, we have two letters from Giraldus to the Bishop, in which he defends himself and the Canons of St. David's (*Symbolum Electorum* 7 and 8), which have been omitted here because they throw little real light on the circumstances which gave rise to them and are exceptionally verbose. He also (ibid. 31) denounces the Chapter for taking the Bishop's part in depriving him of certain of his possessions: this letter is long, abusive, and too allusive to be worth insertion here. Finally in the *De iure et Statu* (R.S. III, 159-61) he deals faithfully with the alleged frailties of the Bishop. Whatever truth may underlie his statements, we may suspect considerable exaggeration on the part of Giraldus, to use no stronger term. It is moreover noticeable that we have never even a bare mention of the Bishop's great work in rebuilding the Cathedral.

(III) The 'pyramids' were apparently square stone crosses, presumably identical with the two 'pyramids in the monks' cemetery' mentioned by William of Malmesbury (R.S. I, 25) as bearing the names of a Saxon King and Bishop and two Saxon Abbots. Giraldus is alone in recording the words *cum Wenneuereia uxore sua secunda*, perhaps a

APPENDIX

deliberate interpolation. The rest of the inscription agrees with the transcript given by Camden and claiming to reproduce the 'ancient Gothic letters' of the original. In the edition of 1607 (Brit. p. 166) the cross is actually figured with the same script. The cross had been detached from the stone when Giraldus saw it (*Spec. Eccl.*, l.c.). Leland (*Assertio Arturii*, fol. 22) states that it was about a foot long, and that he examined it carefully and had it in his hands. In his *Itinerary* (III, 63) he gives a description of the new tomb in the Church; it stood in the middle of the presbytery between the tombs of Edward the Elder (to the North) and Edmund Ironside (to the South). The description ends *Crux super tumulum*. This has been held to be the leaden cross.

(IV) The Archbishop had however ceased to be Justiciar on July 11th, five days before the death of Bishop Peter. He had been succeeded by Geoffrey FitzPeter, who according to Hoveden commanded at the battle of Pains Castle. Gervase of Canterbury on the other hand, like Giraldus in his letter to the Archbishop (p. 131), attributes the victory to him. The Archbishop refuses the Archdeacon's compliments in general terms which would perhaps be consistent with either view (see p. 136). Giraldus in his next letter says not without sarcasm that the Bishop won the victory by praying for it, many miles away in the Church of Bridgenorth (see p. 138).

(V) The Archbishop had been compelled (1198) by Innocent III to give up the Justiciarship as a result of the scandal caused by the suppression of Longbeard, 1196 (see p. 271). But he was made Chancellor by John on the occasion of his coronation in 1199 (see p. 155). The statement made by Giraldus as to his temporary loss of the Chancellorship cannot be substantiated and may be regarded as a mere invention or as an embroidery of some rumour that had reached Giraldus at Rome or as a later insertion made when he was revising the *Invectiones* for publication. The same story is told in greater detail in *Invect.* I, 10 — a speech delivered in 1203, and Giraldus asserts that the incident occurred in 1202, a year after the speech with which we are now dealing. See pp. 215, 270. The inconsistency may be due to a lapse of memory, or to the fact that the

APPENDIX

speech delivered at Rome in 1203 was largely composed for future use in 1202 or even earlier, or to an ill-considered *remaniement* of his speeches, as suggested above.

(VI) These two incidents may have taken place during the visit of Giraldus to the Princes of Gwynedd and Powys a little earlier (see p. 221). They are recorded in *Invect.* v, 4 and were perhaps also in the lost portion of *De rebus*, II, 89, where the Table of Contents has *De honore Giraldo in Venedocia facto*. But it is possible that they took place after his departure and were recorded, like the interview with the Justiciar, in *De rebus* III, 106, where the Table of Contents ends *De aliis ad laudem ipsius pertinentibus*.

(VII) This is an obscure incident. There is a reference to it in *De rebus* (Table of Contents III, 166, *quam modicam in socio et quam magnam in extraneo Faentiae liberalitatem inuenit*). Clearly the Elect of Bangor, gave him little assistance when he was in financial straits, while a stranger extricated him. But whether he merely lost the money which he had got from Bolognese money-changers at Troyes, and only recovered it with difficulty; or whether it refers to difficulty found in cashing a bill of exchange, it is impossible to say. The gold mark was worth about ten silver marks (£6 13s. 6d.) at this period. The mark is not an actual coin, but a sum of money, like our guinea to-day.

(VIII) This is an interesting, but curiously inapposite quotation. It comes from a story (the medieval original of Merimée's *Vénus d'Ille*) which is told by William of Malmesbury (*Gesta Regum Anglorum*, II, 205). The ring so rashly placed on the finger of the statue of Venus is recovered by the magic arts of Palambus, a priest of Rome, who sends a letter to Demon — a Pagan god, perhaps Jupiter, rather than the Devil — bidding him get the ring from Venus. On reading the letter the Demon exclaims, '*Deus omnipotens, quam diu patieris nequitias Palumbi presbyteri?*' After which he sends his servants to fetch the ring, which Venus reluctantly restores. But Palumbus dies soon after in horrible torment.

(IX) *Diuionenses* is a certain correction of the MS. reading *duniones*, through the contraction *diuiones*. This is rendered

APPENDIX

certain by the fact that Giraldus was in Burgundy at the time and that the *deniers* of Eudes III, Duke of Burgundy (1193-1211), which were struck at Dijon (*Diuio*) carry, on the reverse, the legend DIVIONENSIS, by which name they were known. These coins were inferior in weight and value to the English penny, despite the fact that the penny itself, under Richard and John, had also decreased in value. I am indebted to Monsieur Adrien Blanchet for this information.

INDEX

ABBEVILLE, 114
Aberconwy, 208, 251
Aberhonddu (Brecon), 247, 329
Aberteifi (*See* Cardigan)
Aberyskir, 224
Adrian IV, 87
Alexander III, 67, 186
—— of Ford, 139, 147
Anacletus, Pope, 254
Andelys, 150, 207, 298
Andrew, 203-4, 206 ff
Angharad, 35, 83
Angle, 44
Arden, 163-4
Arras, 70
Arthur, 119ff
Avalon, 119ff

BALKINGLASS, ABBOT OF, 91
Bangor, 117; Elect of, 173, 208, 211, 213, 220, 225, 251, 265-7, 271, 277, 308-9; Robert, Bishop of, 208, 211, 213, 225; Gwion, Bishop of, 213
Bards, 233
Bardsey, Lawrence, Prior of, 222
Barri, Giraldus de (nephew of Giraldus Cambrensis), 348-9, 354; Philip de, 42, 76, 161, 201, 315; William de, 35
Bath, 254
Bedford, 245
Bernard, St., 101
Biddlesden, 139, 140
Blockley, 77
Blois, Peter de, 283
Bohun, Henry de, 345
Bologna, 65, 67, 265, 308, 311
Bordeaux, 254
Bourges, 254
Brackley, 240, 242
Brecon, 224-5, 227, 240, 247, 329
Bridgnorth, 138, 181
Bromefield, Adam de, 237, 330
Buckingham, Archdeacon of, 228, 240, 262, 307
Buongiovanni, 188-191, 287
Burgundy, Duke of, 312

CADWALLON AB IFOR, 325; Ap Madog, 48, 50, 54-6
Caereu, 40, 42, 44-5
Caerleon, 186-7
Cambriae, Itinerarium, 10, 24, 99, 114; *Descriptio*, 11, 24, 357

Canterbury, Archbishop of, Augustine, 187; Theobald, 19, 185, 193; Thomas, St., 69, 73, 215, 217, 272; Richard, 39, 43, 51, 58, 62; Baldwin, 77, 82, 98ff, 106, 110, 349; Hubert, 129-48, 155, 158, 165-82, 189-92, 195-200, 205, 207-8, 211-9, 220-224, 228, 232, 237, 243, 248, 252-8, 260-2, 270-3, 281-92, 299, 320-1, 326-8, 333, 337, 341-9; Stephen Langton, 352, 357-9
——, Monasteries of: Christchurch, 71, 231-2; Prior of, 228, 230; St. Augustine's, 261, 272
Cantref Bychan, 85, 224
Caradog, St., 200
Cemais, 83, 102, 237
Challi, 264
Chaluz, 153
Châtillon, 313-8
Chester, 254
Chesterton, 262, 360
Chinon, 107, 153
Cîteaux, 140, 265-6, 271, 335
Clairvaux, 265
Clare, St., 83
Clarendon, 87
Clun, 252
Cluniacs, 63, 78
Coventry, Bishops of: Hugh, 283; Gerard, 68; See of, 254
Crickhowell, 330
Crusades, 86, 98ff, 109, 116-7
Cwmhir, 163
Cydewain, 50, 249
Cyfeiliog, 234

De iure et statu Menevensis Ecclesiae, 20, 23, 157, 182-96, 199-209, 219-69, 273-81, 285-357
De Principis Instructione, 25, 37, 87-8, 105-11, 118-20, 351
De rebus a se gestis, 33-76, 81-104, 111-8, 121-37, 146-69
Deugleddyf, 44
Dieppe, 112ff
Dol, 184, 188, 254
Dore, Adam of, 148
Dorobernia, 186, 359
Douai, 264
Dover, 264
Dublin, Council at, 91ff; John, Archbishop of, 89, 91, 283, 318
Dunstable, 253

INDEX

Durham, Bishop of, 306
Duvianus, 180, 186

Einion Clut, 50
Elboeuf, 319, 323
Eleanor, Queen, 141
Elenydd, 163
Elfael, 46, 47, 49, 52, 249
Ely, Bishop of, 195, 227, 240, 246, 256-7, 307, 318-24, 327, 346-7
Emlyn, 83
English, vices of, 209-10
Eu, 113; Philip of, 343
Eugenius III, 185, 192-4, 200-1, 203
Evesham, 79
Exchequer, 215
Exeter, See of, 254

FAENZA, 265
Fagan, 180, 186
Faversham, 263, 272
Ferns, 90
FitzAlan, William, 252
FitzHay, William, 44, 83
FitzPeter, Geoffrey, 150, 222-7, 230-1, 238ff, 319, 342ff
FitzRichard, Robert, 335ff, 341
FitzRobert, Henry, 339; Walter, 82
FitzTancred, Richard, 42
Flanders, Counts of: Philip, 70; Baldwin, 163
Flemings, 39-43
Foliot, Reginald, 129, 148, 203-4, 206-7, 216, 221, 227, 236, 237, 242-5, 248, 274, 284-5, 319-24, 330, 333
Ford, 77, 139, 147

GEDDINGTON, 98
Gemma Ecclesiastica, 24, 165, 281
Gisors, 98, 313
Glanville, Ranulph de, 82, 98, 112
Glastonbury, 119 ff
Gloucester, 37, 79, 217, 318; Archdeacon of, 228
Golwen, 274, 276-9
Gravelines, 264
Guenevere, 119
Gwenwynwyn, 234, 249, 250
Gwynedd, 17, 103, 233, 249, 251

HAIMON, 79
Hainault, 163
Harold, 131
Haverford, 99ff, 331
Hay, 46, 125
Henry I, 13, 18, 187, 254
—— II, 10ff, 39, 56ff, 72, 81, 84, 86-8, 98, 105ff, 120

Heraclius, 86-7
Hereford, 98, 227, 254, 262; William, Bishop of, 82ff, 148; Hugh, Dean of, 344; William Foliot, Precentor of, 344
Hiberniae, Expugnatio, 23, 107; *Topographia*, 23, 92, 97

INNOCENT II, 185, 201
—— III, 164-6, 182-6, 188-94, 203-4, 219, 220, 266-9, 279-81, 284-6, 293-303, 351-2
Inuectiones, 26, 169-82, 189, 196, 201-2, 209-19, 269-73, 281-5, 351-2
Ireland, 86ff

JOHN BELLEMAIN, 215
John, King, 86-90, 101, 118, 153-6, 189, 202-3, 207, 232, 243, 288, 297, 321-4, 352
Jordan, Archdeacon of Brecon, 42, 349
Joseph, 104

KERRY, 49ff, 249

LAMBETH, 289, 342
Lateran, 67-8, 186, 267, 279
Laugharne, 42
L'Aumône, 77, 140
Lawhaden, 41, 76
Leighlin, 90, 157
Le Mans, 105-6
Lincoln, 127, 139; William, Bishop of, 326; Dean of, 344
Llanbadarn, 47
Llanbedr, 83
Llanbister, 50
Llandaff, 121, 265
Llandduw, 49, 76, 224, 232, 330-1
Llandovery, 85
Llanelwy, Bishops of: Adam, 49ff; Reiner, 326
Llanstephan, 83
Llantony (*See* St. Davids, Bishop Geoffrey)
Llanwnda, 76, 252
Llewelyn, 222, 225, 233, 249, 252, 269
Llowes, 123
Llywel, 224
London, 73, 115, 150, 152, 186, 342; William, Bishop of, 326, 347; Dean of, 226, 240, 262, 307
Longbeard (Fitzosbert), 176, 271
Longchamp, William, 116
Lucca, 185
Lucius, King, 180,
—— II, 185, 203

INDEX

MAELGWN AP CADWALLON, 48; ap Rhys, 221, 269
Maelienydd, 46, 47, 49, 52, 249
Madog, 269
Mangonel, Philip, 100
Manorbier, 35, 201-2
Map, Walter, 145, 344
Maredudd, 269
Martin, Canon, 160, 243
Mathry, 76, 247, 252, 260, 349
Meaux, 194
Meilyr, Fitzgerald, 156, 196
Merlin, 187, 210
Modena, 265
Monte, William de, 127
Montmorency, 67
Morganis, 120
Morgannwg, 17

NARBERTH, 83
Nest, 35; children of, 83
Nevelon, 265
Newport, 240
Nicholas maior, 291
Northampton, 57, 98, 319

OSBERT, 216, 220-2, 236, 237, 243-5, 248, 274, 284-5, 288-9, 291, 307, 330-1, 333
Ossory, 157: Bishop of, 96
Oswestry, 103
Otford, 275-6
Otho, King of the Germans, 297
Owain, 14, 15
Oxford, 97, 139, 225, 238, 253

PAINS CASTLE, 125, 131, 136, 138, 181
Palumbes, 271
Paris, 37, 51, 64ff, 265, 318
Parma, 265
Patrick, St., 93
Pavia, 185, 313
Pebidiog, 83, 332
Pembroke, 40, 41, 83; Bailiffs of; Ralph, de Bendevill, 237-41, 243, 252; Nicholas Avenel, 252, 260; Sheriff of: William Carquit, 41
Peter's pence, 87, 187
Philip Augustus, 37, 98, 163
—— a false deacon, 274
—— the Sub-deacon, 191
Pontius, 76, 307
Powys, 17, 50, 103, 225, 234

REDVERS, RICHARD DE, 106
Registers, Papal, 183, 192-4.
Rheims, Archbishop of, 69
Rhos, 39, 40, 42-4, 83, 332

Rhys ap Tewdwr, 35
—— ap Gruffydd, 15, 81, 85, 98, 102
—— ap Rhys, 221, 269
Richard, King, 98, 105, 107, 111-2, 116, 149, 153, 282-3, 291-2
Rochester, Gilbert, Bishop of, 98
Rouen, 113, 319ff; Walter, Archbishop of, 283, 325; Richard, Dean of 343; Roger, Dean of, 65

ST. ALBANS, 247, 253, 269, 318
St. Andrews, 186
St. Asaph (*See* Llanelwy)
St. David's: Bishops of, Sampson, 184, 187, 254; Wilfrid 18; Bernard, 18, 185, 192-4, 254; David, 19, 36, 41, 43, 45, 57, 83; Peter, 63, 74-6, 99, 100, 127, 203, 207, 290, 297; Geoffrey, 145, 147, 158, 160, 189, 196, 288, 329, 330, 343-7, 353-5; Iorwerth, 356-7
St. Dogmael: Walter, Abbot of, 129, 189, 195-200, 204-8, 214, 237, 240, 259, 286ff, 297, 319-21, 328, 330
St. Mary le Bow, 271
St. Omer, 163, 264
St. Osyth, 263
Salisbury, 178
Sandwich, 163, 262, 264
Serlo, 77ff
Shrewsbury, 103-4, 225, 252
Southwell, Simon of, 228, 241, 242
Speculum Ecclesiae, 25, 77-81, 85-6, 250-1, 351
Strathflur, 162, 226, 250
Suffredo, Cardinal of Pisa, 206-7
Symbolum Electorum, 26, 107, 137-46

TALLY, 356
Tenby, 355
Tilbury, 263
Trallan, 224
Treville, 149
Troyes, 265, 308, 311-2, 318
Tynemouth, John, 242, 284, 295, 303-6, 314-19, 329, 346

UGUCCIONE, CARDINAL, 58, 62, 186

VALENCIENNES, 265
Valéry, St., 113
Velfrey, 83
Verdun, Bertram of, 90
Vimeu, 113

WALTHAM, 78, 341
Waterford, 86, 157
Wechelen, 123

INDEX

Wenlock, John, Prior of, 237-8, 330; Peter, Prior of (*See* St. Davids, Bishop Peter)
Westminster, 342
Wexford, 90, 157
Whitchurch, 103, 252
Whitland, Peter, Abbot of, 129, 195-200, 214, 223, 226, 249, 319-21, 328, 335
Wibert, William, 139ff
Wigmore, Abbot of, 237, 330

Winchester, 63; Monks of, 72; Richard, Bishop of, 73; market of, 163
Worcester, 227, 252, 254; Bishops of: Roger, 62; Mauger, 256, 307, 324, 327, 347; Archdeacon of, Peter de Leche, 145

YORK, 178; Roger, Archbishop of, 58; Dean of, 306
Ystradtywi, 224

A GUIDE TO FURTHER READING

John Gillingham

The most stimulating general study of Gerald's life and writings is Robert Bartlett, *Gerald of Wales 1146–1223*, Oxford, 1982. This includes a valuable appendix listing and dating all Gerald's works and the manuscripts in which they survive. Bartlett also wrote the entry on Gerald in the *Oxford Dictionary of National Biography* (2004).

The fullest narrative of Gerald's life remains J. Conway Davies, 'Giraldus Cambrensis 1146–1946', *Archaeologia Cambrensis* 99 (1946–7), 85–108, 256–80.

There is a fine, brief sketch in a booklet in the Writers of Wales series: Brynley F. Roberts, *Gerald of Wales*, Cardiff, 1982. See also Michael Richter, 'Gerald of Wales: a Reassessment on the 750th Anniversary of His Death', *Traditio* 29 (1973), 379–90.

As H. E. Butler observed in his preface, he drew the bulk of the original Latin text from which he produced this remarkably coherent narrative from several of Gerald's works, in particular two that were composed late in life: *De rebus a se gestis* between 1208 and 1216, and *De iure et statu Menevensis ecclesie*, written in about 1218.

In fact both in his own day and in subsequent centuries Gerald was much better known for his earlier books. His first – and also his most popular – were the two books on Ireland. There are English translations of both in paperback: *The History and Topography of Ireland*, trans. J. O'Meara, Harmondsworth, 1982; and *Expugnatio Hibernica, The Conquest of Ireland*, ed. and trans. F. X. Martin and A. B. Scott, Dublin, 1978. The latter contains an essay on 'Giraldus as Historian' by F. X. Martin. His two books on Wales are translated in a Penguin Classic volume, *The Journey through Wales: Description of Wales*, trans. L. Thorpe, Harmondsworth, 1978. All four were brought together in nineteenth-century

A GUIDE TO FURTHER READING

English translation as *The Historical Works of Giraldus Cambrensis*, trans. T. Wright, Bohn's Library, London, 1887.

The brilliance of his two books on Ireland (both written in the late 1180s and from the standpoint of a hostile outsider) elaborated and established an idea that was already beginning to take root in intellectual circles in Europe and especially in England, that the Irish were an inferior and barbarous people. So influential did his expression of this idea become that in the seventeenth century John Lynch was moved to write (in a book intended as a full-scale refutation of Gerald, *Giraldus Eversus*, 1662):

> The wild dreams of Giraldus have been taken up by a herd of scribblers. . . . I find the calumnies of which he is the author published in the language and writings of every nation, no new geography, no history of the world, no work on the manners and customs of different nations appearing in which his calumnious charges against the Irish are not chronicled as undoubted facts . . . and all these repeated again and again until the heart sickens at the sight.

For a measured assessment of both the society of twelfth-century Ireland and of the political context in which Gerald wrote see Marie Therese Flanagan, *Irish Society, Anglo-Norman Settlers, Angevin Kingship: Interactions in Ireland in the late twelfth century*, Oxford, 1989. There is an illuminating appraisal of the intellectual context of Gerald's 'wild dreams' in chapters six and seven of Bartlett's *Gerald of Wales*. See also John Gillingham, 'The Beginnings of English Imperialism', *Journal of Historical Sociology* 5 (1992), 392–409, reprinted in John Gillingham, *The English in the Twelfth Century*, Woodbridge, 2000, and chapter two in Andrew Murphy, *But the Irish Sea Betwixt Us. Ireland, Colonialism & Renaissance Literature*, Lexington, Kentucky, 1999. On the topography of Ireland see Jeanne-Marie Boivin, *L'Irlande au Moyen Âge: Giraud de Barri et la Topograpia Hibernica*, Paris, 1993; David Rollo, 'Gerald of Wales' *Topographia Hibernica*: Sex and the Irish Nation', *Romanic Review* 86 (1995), 169–90.

A GUIDE TO FURTHER READING

By the time he set about writing the story of his life, Gerald sympathised with Welsh aspirations for a church independent of Canterbury, and it is this which led to him becoming known as 'Cambrensis'. On this subject see Michael Richter, *Giraldus Cambrensis. The Growth of the Welsh Nation*, Aberystwyth, 1972; J. C. Crick, 'The British Past and the Welsh Future: Gerald of Wales, Geoffrey of Monmouth and Arthur of Britain', *Celtica* 23 (1999), 60–75; Huw Pryce, 'British or Welsh? National Identity in Twelfth-Century Wales', *English Historical Review* 116 (2001), 775–801. But in the early 1190s when he wrote his two books specifically about Wales, he still hoped that his English court contacts would win him promotion to a bishopric in England, and he revealed very mixed feelings about the Welsh, perhaps not surprisingly given his own Anglo-Welsh background. Seventy years ago, when C. H. Williams and H. E. Butler composed their introductions to this translation, it was taken for granted that Gerald was of Norman and Welsh blood. For discussion of his shifting sense of his own identity, see John Gillingham, 'The English Invasion of Ireland' in eds. Brendan Bradshaw, Andrew Hadfield and Willy Maley, *Representing Ireland: Literature and the Origins of Conflict*, Cambridge, 1993, reprinted in *The English in the Twelfth Century*; Yoko Wada, 'Gerald on Gerald: Self-Presentation by Giraldus Cambrensis', *Anglo-Norman Studies* 20 (1997/8), 223–46; John Gillingham, ' "Slaves of the English": Gerald de Barri and Regnal Solidarity in early thirteenth-century England' in eds. Pauline Stafford, Janet Nelson and Jane Martindale, *Law, laity and solidarities*, Manchester, 2001.

The schematic picture he gives of Welsh society in the *Description of Wales* – characterised by Robert Bartlett (Gerald of Wales, 175), as 'the high point of twelfth-century ethnography' – has been analysed and qualified by Huw Pryce, 'In search of a medieval society: Deheubarth in the writings of Gerald of Wales', *Welsh History Review* 13 (1986–7), 265–81. R. R. Davies, *The Age of Conquest. Wales 1063–1415*, Oxford, 1991, is the indispensable modern guide to medieval Welsh society.

A GUIDE TO FURTHER READING

The context of Gerald's journey through Wales in 1188 is set out in Huw Pryce, 'Gerald's Journey through Wales' *Journal of Welsh Ecclesiastical History* 6 (1989), 17–34; and in Peter W. Edbury, 'Preaching the Crusade in Wales', in eds. Alfred Haverkamp and Hanna Vollrath, *England and Germany in the High Middle Ages*, Oxford, 1996, 221–33.

Just a few of his other works have been translated into English, including one, the *Speculum Duorum*, that at the time of writing H. E. Butler believed had been lost (see above p. 00). This is Giraldus Cambrensis, *A Mirror of Two Men*, ed. Y. Lefèvre, R. Huygens and M. Richter, trans. B. Dawson, Cardiff, 1974. The others are: Gerald of Wales, *The Jewel of the Church. A Translation of Gemma Ecclesiastica*, trans. John J. Hagen, Leiden, 1979; and Gerald of Wales, *The Life of St Hugh of Avalon, Bishop of Lincoln*, ed. and trans. Richard M. Loomis, New York, 1985.

In addition a translation of Parts 2 and 3 of the three-part work *De Principis Instructione* in which Gerald gave most vehement expression to his jaundiced views of the family of Henry II was published in 1858, and has been reprinted as *On the Instruction of Princes*, trans. J. Stevenson, Felinfach, Dyfed, 1991. On this see K. Schnith, 'Betrachtungen zum Spätwerk des Giraldus Cambrensis: De Principis Instructione', in ed. K. Schnith, *Festiva Lanx*, Munich, 1966.

Gerald's disappointments in his career as a courtier and his role in shaping conventional criticism of the court are analysed in Part 3 of Egbert Türk, *Nugae Curialium. Le règne d'Henri II Plantegenêt (1154–1189) et l'éthique politique*, Geneva, 1977. On his links with another litterateur associated with the court of Henry II, see A. K. Bate, 'Walter Map and Giraldus Cambrensis', *Latomus* 31 (1972), 860–75.

For significant revision of earlier views of Gerald's 'width of classical reading' see A. A. Goddu and R. H. Rouse, 'Gerald of Wales and the *Florilegium Angelicum*', *Speculum* 52 (1977), 488–521. On his theological conservatism towards the end of his life, see R. W. Hunt, 'The Preface to the *Speculum Ecclesiae* of Giraldus Cambrensis', *Viator* 8 (1977), 189–213.

Two other aspects of Gerald's literary output have been considered in articles with self-explanatory titles: Robert Bartlett, 'Rewriting Saints' Lives: The Case of Gerald of Wales', *Speculum* 58 (1983), 598–613; and U. T. Holmes, 'Gerald the Naturalist', *Speculum* 11 (1936), 110–21 and cf. Antonia Gransden, 'Realistic Observation in Twelfth-Century England', *Speculum* 47 (1972), 29–51.

www.ingramcontent.com/pod-product-compliance
Lightning Source LLC
Chambersburg PA
CBHW022008300426
44117CB00005B/79